The Rhetoric of Religion

The Rhetoric of Religion

Studies in Logology

Kenneth Burke

University of California Press
Berkeley · *Los Angeles* · *London*

University of California Press
Berkeley and Los Angeles, California
University of California Press, Ltd.
London, England

Acknowledgments
The author wishes to acknowledge with thanks
permission to quote from "The Language of the Old
Testament" by Norman H. Snaith and "The Book of
Genesis. Exegesis" by Cuthbert A. Simpson,
both of which appear in *The Interpreter's Bible,*
Vol. I, published by Abingdon Press; and *Myth and
Guilt* by Theodor Reik, published by George
Braziller, Inc.; also for permission to reprint those parts of
the essay "On the First Three Chapters of Genesis"
which first appeared in *Daedalus* and subsequently
in *Symbolism in Religion and Literature,* edited
by Rollo May and published by George Braziller, Inc.

The paper used in this publication meets the minimum
requirements of ANSI/NISO Z39.48-1992(R
1997)(Permanence of Paper)

Foreword

Religion has often been looked upon as a center from which all other forms of human motivation gradually diverged. It is seen as a unifying principle, the vision of an original Edenic one-ness, with endless varieties of action and passion deriving from it somewhat as the many languages that came to beset the building of the Tower of Babel eventually followed expulsion from the Garden.

Whatever the unifying nature of religion in this technical sense (with theology as a central science, to terms of which all else might be "reduced"), the history of religions has also been the history of great discord. It would seem that nothing can more effectively set people at odds than the demand that they think alike. For, given our many disparate ways of life, we couldn't really think alike, even if we wanted to. Though we repeated exactly the same articles of faith, we'd understand them differently to the extent that our relations to them differed. The rich man's prayer is not the poor man's prayer. Youth's God is not the God of the aged. The God of the wretch condemned to be hanged is not the God of the lucky chap who just won at bingo under ecclesiastical auspices.

The subject of religion falls under the head of *rhetoric* in the sense that rhetoric is the art of *persuasion*, and religious cosmogonies are designed, in the last analysis, as exceptionally thoroughgoing modes of persuasion. To persuade men towards certain acts, religions would form the kinds of attitude which prepare men for such acts. And in order to plead for such attitudes as persuasively as possible, the religious always ground their exhortations (to themselves and others) in statements of the widest and deepest possible scope, concerning the authorship of men's motives.

In this sense, the subject of religious exhortation involves the nature of religion as a rhetoric, as persuasiveness.

Furthermore, in this book we are to be concerned not directly with religion, but rather with the *terminology* of religion; not directly with man's relationship to God, but rather with his relationship to the *word* "God." Thus the book is about something so essentially rhetorical as religious nomenclature—hence the subtitle, "Studies in Logology," which is to say, "studies in words-about-words."

Theological doctrine is a body of spoken or written *words*. Whatever else it may be, and wholly regardless of whether it be true or false, theology is preeminently *verbal*. It is *"words* about 'God.' "

In being words about so "ultimate" or "radical" a subject, it almost necessarily becomes an example of words used with thoroughness. Since words-about-God would be as far-reaching as words can be, the "rhetoric of religion" furnishes a good instance of terministic enterprise in general. Thus it is our "logological" thesis that, since the theological use of language is thorough, the close study of theology and its forms will provide us with good insight into the nature of language itself as a motive. Such an approach also involves the tentative belief that, even when men use language trivially, the motives inherent in its possible thorough use are acting somewhat as goads, however vague.

The essays are the substance of three talks originally given at Drew University in December 1956 and the spring of 1957, but all were later developed at greater length. In particular, I am grateful for the opportunity to complete work on them under the most felicitous of circumstances, as a fellow of the Center for Advanced Study in the Behavioral Sciences at Stanford University, 1957–1958. And I should certainly mention my gratitude for the opportunity to develop much of this material with the help of my classes at Bennington College.

Contents

Introduction: On *Theology* and *Logology*

If we defined "theology" as "words about God," then by "logology" we should mean "words about words." Whereupon, thoughts on the necessarily verbal nature of religious doctrines suggest a further possibility: that there might be fruitful analogies between the two realms. Thus statements that great theologians have made about the nature of "God" might be adapted *mutatis mutandis* for use as purely secular observations on the nature of *words*.

Insofar as man is the "typically symbol-using animal," it should not be surprising that men's thoughts on the nature of the Divine embody the principles of verbalization. And insofar as "God" is a *formal* principle, any thorough statements about "God" should be expected to reveal the formality underlying their genius as statements. The Biblical avowal that *man* is made in *God's image* has made us wary of the reversed anthropomorphic tendency to conceive of *God* in *man's image*. But the present inquiry stands midway between those two positions, contending merely that, insofar as religious doctrine is verbal, it will necessarily exemplify its nature as verbalization; and insofar as religious doctrine is thorough, its ways of exemplifying verbal principles should be correspondingly thorough.

Hence, it should be possible to analyze remarks about the "nature of 'God,'" like remarks about the "nature of 'Reason,'" in their sheer formality as observations about the nature

1

of language. And such a correspondence between the theological and "logological" realms should be there, whether or not "God" actually *exists*. For regardless of whether the entity named "God" exists outside his nature sheerly as key term in a system of terms, words "about him" must reveal their nature as words.

It is not within the competence of our project to decide the question either theistically or atheistically, or even agnostically. This investigation does not require us to make any decisions about the validity of theology *qua* theology. Our purpose is simply to ask how theological principles can be shown to have usable secular analogues that throw light upon the nature of language.

St. Augustine, having arrived at his Trinitarian idea of God, saw manifestations of this supernatural principle in all sorts of sheerly natural phenomena. Every triad, however secular, was for him another sign of the Trinity. For our purposes, we can be content with the analogy alone. We need not decide either with or against Augustine. For our purposes, it doesn't matter whether the supernatural Trinity is or is not made manifest in everything that Roget would list under such a variety of terms as: triad, triplet, trefoil, triangle, trident, tierce, terza, trio, trey, trinomial, triumvirate, etc., etc. We need but note that all members of the lot are analogically classifiable together by reason of their three-ness. However, as we shall try to show when we come to our study of Augustine, regardless of whether or not there is a Holy Trinity such as he postulates, the trinitarian pattern in his idea of God must be considered as a radical aspect of his psychology, though we conceived of that psychology in a purely secular sense.

As for a unitary concept of God, its linguistic analogue is to be found in the nature of any name or title, which sums up a manifold of particulars under a single head (as with the title of a book, or the name of some person or political movement). Any such summarizing word is functionally a "god-term." What, then, might be the relation between such a term and the countless details classifiable under its "unifying" head? Is there not a sense in which the summarizing term, the over-all name or title, could be said to "transcend" the many details subsumed under that head, somewhat as "spirit" is said to "transcend matter"? The question indicates the ways in which the study of theology might be applied "logologically."

The short introductory essay, "On Words and The Word," considers the subject in general. The second essay, "On Verbal Action in St. Augustine's *Confessions*," analyzes Augustine's development from a teacher of pagan rhetoric (what he calls a "word merchant," *venditor verborum*) to a preacher of The Word. Here the approach is the other way round, by close textual analysis. And quite as the *Confessions* ends on the subject of Genesis, so our third essay makes this same turn. However, in keeping with our pattern, the Augustinian distinction between "time" and "eternity" is treated in its *linguistically* analogous form, as the distinction between the unfolding of a sentence through the materiality of its parts and the unitary non-material essence or meaning of the sentence (an analogy, incidentally, which Augustine himself points out).

The concluding essay, "On the First Three Chapters of Genesis," combines both generalized approach and textual analysis. Whatever may be the embarrassments as regards theological attempts to square this wonderful story literally with modern theories of evolution, it is just about *perfect* for the purposes of the "logologer." So we used every resource at our command, including a "Tautological Cycle of Terms Implicit in the Idea of 'Order,'" a summarizing look at Hobbes's *Leviathan* for the insight it gives into the important subject of "Covenants," and a series of last-minute addenda attempting to clinch one or another aspect of our case.

Formally, the investigation heads in an attempt to study the point at which narrative forms and logical forms merge (or begin to diverge!), the exquisite point of differentiation between purely temporal and purely logical principles of "priority," an overlap that comes to a theological focus in the shifts between God as *logical* ground of all *moral* sanctions and God as originator of the *natural, temporal* order. The cyclical chart of terms for "Order" sums up the "directionless" way in which such a cluster of terms imply one another. The Creation Myth at the opening of Genesis is analyzed as the paradigm of ways whereby such interlocking motivational principles are translated into terms of an irreversible narrative sequence.

And finally, though the logologer cannot hope to offer the reader something even remotely approaching either the vast ultimate promises or the equally vast ultimate threats which the theologian holds forth, there is at least an important "moral" to be drawn from this study. It derives from the great stress we have laid upon the sacrificial principle which, we try to show, is intrinsic to the idea of Order. If we are right in what we take the Creation Myth in Genesis to be saying, then the contemporary world must doubly fear the cyclical compulsions of Empire, as two mighty world orders, each homicidally armed to the point of suicide, confront each other. As with dominion always, each is much beset with anxiety. And in keeping with the "curative" role of victimage, each is apparently in acute need of blaming all its many troubles on the other, wanting to feel certain that, if the other and its tendencies were but eliminated, all governmental discord (all the Disorder that goes with Order) would be eliminated.

In sum:

> Here are the steps
> In the Iron Law of History
> That welds Order and Sacrifice:
>
> Order leads to Guilt
> (for who can keep commandments!)
> Guilt needs Redemption

(for who would not be cleansed!)
Redemption needs Redeemer
(which is to say, a Victim!).

Order
Through Guilt
To Victimage
(hence: Cult of the Kill). . . .

Along these lines, the author would propose to replace the present political stress upon men in rival international situations by a "logological" reaffirmation of the foibles and quandaries that all men (in their role as "symbol-using animals") have in common.

As for the Appendix, the "Prologue in Heaven": It is offered somewhat after the analogy of the "satyr-play" which, in the ancient Greek theater, traditionally followed a trilogy of solemn tragedies. This "purely imaginary" dialogue between The Lord and Satan was originally intended merely as a "light" way of recapitulating the case for "logology" as developed in the three foregoing essays.

Let us hope that its "lightness" does not seem like "levity." The fact is that, once things got going, the conceit tended to take over, by developing unexpected quirks of its own. Perhaps a Satan with even as mild a character as the figure in this dialogue is likely to make a writer break loose somewhat, particularly since the dialogue form so readily permits one to say things with which one might personally disagree.

The reader should bear in mind that this dialogue is intended to illustrate the principles not of *theology* but of *logology*, a purely secular subject. Basically, it is designed to uphold the position that, in the study of human motives, we should begin with complex theories of transcendence (as in theology and metaphysics) rather than with the terminologies of simplified laboratory experiment.

1   On Words and The Word

We are to be concerned with the analogy between "words" (lower case) and The Word (*Logos, Verbum*) as it were in caps. "Words" in the first sense have wholly naturalistic, empirical reference. But they may be used analogically, to designate a further dimension, the "supernatural." Whether or not there is a realm of the "supernatural," there are *words* for it. And in this state of linguistic affairs there is a paradox. For whereas the words for the "supernatural" realm are necessarily borrowed from the realm of our everyday experiences, out of which our familiarity with language arises, once a terminology has been developed for special theological purposes the order can become reversed. We can borrow back the terms from the borrower, again secularizing to varying degrees the originally secular terms that had been given "supernatural" connotations.

Consider the word "grace," for instance. Originally, in its Latin form, it had such purely secular meanings as: favor, esteem, friendship, partiality, service, obligation, thanks, recompense, purpose. Thus *gratiis*, or *gratis* meant: "for nothing, without pay, through sheer kindness," etc. The pagan Roman could also say "thank God" (*dis gratia*)—and doubtless such early usage contributed to the term's later availability for specifically theological doctrine. But in any case, once the word was translated from the realm of social relationships into the supernaturally tinged realm of relationships between "God" and man, the etymological conditions were set for a reverse process whereby the *theological* term could in effect be *aes-*

7

theticized, as we came to look for "grace" in a literary style, or in the purely secular behavior of a hostess.

To cite other obvious instances:

"Create" apparently comes from an Indo-European root meaning simply "to make" and having such Greek derivatives as the words for "strength" and "accomplish" (*krátos, kraínō*). In theology, it comes to have the meaning of production *ex nihilo*—and this in turn gives rise to the semisecularized view of poetic production as (in Coleridge's words) a "dim analogue of Creation."

"Spirit" is a similar word. Having moved analogically from its natural meaning, as "breath," to connotations that flowered in its usage as a term for the supernatural, it could then be analogically borrowed back as a secular term for temper, temperament and the like.

The course of such words provides us with tiny models of the Platonic dialectic, with its Upward Way and Downward Way (a form that we shall consider more fully later in this essay).

So, if we would "analogize" by the logological transforming of terms from their "supernatural" reference into their possible use in a realm so wholly "natural" as that of *language* considered as a purely empirical phenomenon, such "analogizing" in this sense would really be a kind of "de-analogizing." Or it would be, except that a new dimension really has been added. And there is a sheerly *logological* justification for this new dimension that the theological analogies have added to words thus taken over for religious doctrine. There is a sense in which language is *not* just "natural," but really *does* add a "new dimension" to the things of nature (an observation that would be the logological equivalent of the theological statement that grace perfects nature).

The quickest and simplest way to realize that words "transcend" non-verbal nature is to think of the notable difference between the kind of operations we might perform with a *tree* and the kind of operations we might perform with the *word* "tree." Verbally, we can make "one tree" into "five thousand trees" by merely revising our text, whereas a wholly different set of procedures would be required to get the corresponding result in nature. Verbally, we can say, "To keep warm, cut down the tree and burn it" and we can say this even if there is no tree. Or whether we call the tree generically a tree or refer to it as some particular species of tree, the fact remains that our term for it has "transcended" its unique individuality. And if we put an apostrophe after the word "tree," thereby getting the possessive form, "tree's," we'd have something quite different from the way in which a tree "owns" its bark, branches, etc. Finally, since the word "tree" rhymes with the words "knee," "be," and "see," we here have an order of associations wholly different from entities with which a tree is physically connected.*

* Once when I was analyzing the symbolism of sun and moon in Coleridge's poem, "The Ancient Mariner," a student raised this objection: "I'm tired of hearing about the symbolic sun in poems, I want a poem that has the *real* sun in it."

Answer: If anybody ever turns up with a poem that has the *real* sun in it, you'd better be about ninety-three million miles away. We were having a hot summer as it was, and I certainly didn't want anyone bringing the real sun into the classroom.

True, a distinction could be made here corresponding to the difference between "concept" and "idea" in the Kantian terminology. The notion of sun *qua* sun, as the sheerly physical object that we grow our crops by, would be a "concept." And the notion of the sun as "avenger" or as the "glorious" sight that, when it "uprist," was "like God's own head," would carry us into the realm of "ideas." The student was correct in feeling that a stress upon "symbolism" can blunt our concern with the sheerly literal meaning of a term (as when critics become so involved with the "symbolism" of a story that they ignore its nature simply as a story).

But our present considerations are answering a different kind of question. A distinction between the thing tree (nonsymbolic) and the word for tree (a symbol) makes the cut at a different place. By the "symbolic" we have in mind that kind of distinction first of all. As regards "symbolic" in the other sense (the sense in which an object possesses motivational ingredients not intrinsic to it in its sheer materiality), even the things of nature can become "symbolic" (insofar as they "stand for" ideas over and above their description as concepts— as some particular house might be *conceptually* described in terms of the architect's drawings, but it might "stand for" an *idea* of parental security, or of confinement, or of a human body, etc.).

Thus, even logologically, there are good grounds for paying close attention to this complicated process whereby, instead of merely staying always within the narrower terminology (as a sheerly naturalistic terminology is "narrower" than the kind you get when natural terms are borrowed and applied analogically to "supernatural" referents), we propose to go the full circuit. And so, even logologically, we'd agree that there are good grounds for the borrowing, since it adds a new dimension needed for analyzing man even in the sheerly secular sense as the "symbol-using animal." And next we'd "discount" such borrowing. But once again, for caution's sake, I should point out: This double process, as viewed in the perspective of logology, has nothing essential to do with theology. My claim is merely that, if we thus participate in the double process, we'll arrive at a truer understanding of language, even in its sheerly secular nature, than if we made a shortcut that avoided such circuitousness.

Overly "naturalistic" views conceal from us the full scope of language as motive, even in the sheerly empirical sense. But such oversimplification of linguistic complexities can be avoided if we approach the subject roundabout, through a systematic concern with linguistic principles exemplified with thoroughness in the dialectics of theology. They warn us of a dimension which we should not omit from our study of language, even if that dimension is to be treated not literally, but as a sheerly *technical* kind of "transcendence." There is a sense in which the *word* for tree "transcends" the thing as thoroughly as does the Platonic idea of the tree's perfect "archetype" in heaven. It is the sense in which the name for a class of objects "transcends" any particular member of that class.

First Analogy

For the first analogy, that between "words" (lower case) and "The Word" (in capitals), some primary texts would be: The opening sentence of the Gospel of John: "In the beginning was the Word, and the Word was with God, and the Word was God"; John 1:14: "The Word was made flesh, and dwelt among us"; Revelation 19:12-13: "And he had a name written, that no man knew, but he himself. . . . And his name is called the Word of God"; First Epistle of John 5:7: "For there are three that bear record in heaven, the Father, the Word, and the Holy Ghost: and these three are one."

In his dictionary of heresies, sects and schisms, Blunt tells of a faction (the Alogians, or *Alogi*) who denied the Johannine doctrine concerning the Logos, hence rejected John's writings entirely. The same dictionary also quotes from Augustine, in his book on Heresies: "*Alogi sic vocantur—quia Deum Verbum recipere noluerunt, Johannis Evangelium respuentes.*" From the standpoint of our present concerns, let these Alogi be anathema—for obviously, our logological enterprise would be stopped at the start if there were no theological doctrine of The Word, as with those who would "spit back the Gospel of John."

However, even without these texts we have equally relevant passages from the Old Testament, such as the creative fiat of Genesis 1:3 ("And God said, Let there be light"); or Psalms 33:9: "He spake, and it was done; he commanded, and it stood fast." Similarly, however differently interpreted, "The representation that the divine word was the agent of creation is found in the Babylonian, Egyptian, and Indian cosmogonies." *

* "The Book of Genesis. Exegesis" by Cuthbert A. Simpson, in *The Interpreter's Bible* (Nashville: Abingdon Press, 1900), I, 468.

Apparently, the primary name of the deity in Genesis has explicitly verbal connotations, as the word "Elohim" is said to be formed from *El* (meaning strength, or the strong one), and *alah* (to swear, to bind oneself by an oath), while the *im* is grammatically a plural, as with "cherubim" and "seraphim."

Even our English word "God" seems to have developed from analogy with the verbal. Apparently it is related to the Sanskrit *hūta*, the past participle of a verb meaning to beseech, to implore.

On its face, Martin Buber's "I-Thou relation" is similarly marked by a strongly verbal element, involving a grammatical distinction to do with the personality implicit in certain forms of address.

The verbal principle is clearly recognized in St. Anselm's theological dialectic concerning the three stages of faith, understanding and vision (*fides, intellectus, contemplatio*). One learns the faith, he says, through being told (*ex auditu*). Indeed, whatever one may think of the theological notion that the saints can perceive the truth about God intuitively (by sheer "vision," *contemplatio*), Saint Anselm is here dealing with the obvious fact that a doctrine, a creed, is formulated and taught by verbal precept (as indicated in the very word "gospel"). Also, Anselm doubtless had in mind Romans 10:17: "So then faith cometh by hearing [*ex auditu*], and hearing by the word of God."

Having such examples in mind, one might feel justified in resisting a tendency to equate "Logos" too strictly with "Reason." Of some 270 instances where the word *logos* appears in the New Testament, by far the majority use it in the sense of the uttered word, ranging from sheer locution (as in Matthew 15:23: "He answered her not a word") to "the word of God" (as in Mark 7:13). Might not "Reason" too greatly restrict the range of connotations, even when the word is applied to godhead?

Anyhow, an early patristic writer, Irenaeus (in the latter part of the second century), gives us authority for such a reservation. I cite from the eleventh edition of the *Encyclopaedia Britannica*:

> Before him the Fourth Gospel did not seem to exist for the Church: Irenaeus made it a living force. His conception of the Logos is not that of the philosophers and apologists; he looks upon the Logos not as the "reason" of God, but as the "voice" with which the Father speaks in the revelation to mankind, as did the writer of the Fourth Gospel.

The Arians apparently carried out this principle of "voice" so literally that, according to Blunt, "they wished to establish that the Son was only the *logos prophorikos*, by which they assigned to Him a beginning; inasmuch as the thought must precede the sound which gives it utterance."

That is, the first and second persons of the Trinity would be related to each other as the *thought* that leads to utterance is to the *uttered word* that expresses the thought. And insofar as a thought can be said to precede its utterance, such a strict following of the verbal analogy would imply that the second person would follow the first person *in time*. A usage by St. Anselm, "in the Word by which thou sayest thy very self (*in Verbo quo te ipsum dicis*)," indicates something of this same concern with the relation between thought and utterance, though of course without the Arian conclusion.

All these considerations should indicate why, in a kind of "linguistic fundamentalism," we should keep ourselves reminded of this strongly verbal connotation in the word Logos, quite as the translation of the Bible does (in translating it as "Word"), even while commentators often stress the more philosophic meaning.

So much, then, for our master analogy, the architectonic element from which all the other analogies could be deduced. In sum:

What we say about *words*, in the empirical realm, will

bear a notable likeness to what is said about *God*, in theology.*

There are four realms to which words may refer:

First, there are words for the natural. This order of
terms would comprise the words for things, for material operations, physiological conditions, animality, and the like. Words
like "tree," "sun," "dog," "hunger," "change," "growth." These
words name the sorts of things and conditions and motions
there would be in the universe even if all ability to use words
(or symbols generally) were eliminated from existence.

Second, there are words for the socio-political realm.
Here are all the words for social relations, laws, right, wrong,
rule and the like. Here belong such terms as "good," "justice,"
"American," "monarchy," "out of bounds," "property rights,"
"moral obligations," "matrimony," "patrimony."

Third, there are words about words. Here is the realm
of dictionaries, grammar, etymology, philology, literary criticism, rhetoric, poetics, dialectics—all that I like to think of as
coming to a head in the discipline I would want to call "Logology."

These three orders of terms should be broad enough to
cover the world of everyday experience, the empirical realm

---

* In Homer, the word for "word" is *mythos*. In later Greek, it
gave way to *logos*. The current stress upon *mythology* particularly
needs the corrective of *logology* because mythology has come to place
too great stress upon the sheer *imagery* of thought. The strongly
terministic concern of logology is designed to correct this deficiency
without leading on the other side to an overly scientistic view of
language as motive. Surely, the mere fact that the symbol-systems of
chemistry, bacteriology, and nuclear physics now make it possible for
persons in authority, if they will, to poison the entire planet is not of
itself evidence that such terminologies are "accurate," and that they
should be taken as models which even the terminologies of the social
sciences and the humanities should imitate. Rather, are they not on
their face evidence that we must still keep searching? It is necessary
to consider *all* the symbolic dimensions involved in the motives of the
symbol-using animal. And this text is intended to show why any secular
theory of language that ignores the hints provided by theology is
bound to be inadequate, whether or not theology is "true."

for which words are preeminently suited. But to say as much is to realize that we must also have a fourth order: words for the "supernatural." For even a person who does not believe in the supernatural will recognize that, so far as the purely empirical facts of language are concerned, languages do have *words* for the supernatural.

However, even if one assumed it as beyond question that there really *is* a realm of the supernatural, nevertheless our *words* for the discussion of this realm are necessarily borrowed by analogy from our words for the other three orders: the natural, the socio-political and the verbal (or the symbolical in general, as with the symbol-systems of music, the dance, painting, architecture, the various specialized scientific nomenclatures, etc.).

The supernatural is by definition the realm of the "ineffable." And language by definition is not suited to the expression of the "ineffable." So our words for the fourth realm, the supernatural or "ineffable," are necessarily borrowed from our words for the sorts of things we can talk about literally, our words for the three empirical orders (the world of everyday experience).

To quote from my article on "The Poetic Motive" that appeared in *The Hudson Review* (Spring 1958):

Since "God" by definition transcends all symbol-systems, we must begin, like theology, by noting that language is intrinsically unfitted to discuss the "supernatural" literally. For language is empirically confined to terms referring to physical nature, terms referring to socio-political relationships and terms describing language itself. Hence, all the words for "God" must be used analogically—as were we to speak of God's "powerful arm" (a physical analogy), or of God as "lord" or "father" (a socio-political analogy) or of God as the "Word" (a linguistic analogy). The idea of God as a "person" would be derived by analogy from the sheerly physical insofar as persons have bodies, from the socio-political insofar as persons have status and from the linguistic insofar as the idea of personality implies such kinds of "reason" as flower in man's symbol-using prowess (linguistic, artistic, philosophic, scientific, moralistic, pragmatic).

By now we should have enough coordinates established to make more speed with our survey of the other analogies.

Second Analogy

Words are to the non-verbal things they name as Spirit is to Matter.

That is, if we equate the non-verbal with "Nature" (using "Nature" in the sense of the less-than-verbal, the sort of sheerly electro-chemical motion there'd be if all entities capable of using language ceased to exist), then verbal or symbolic action is analogous to the "grace" that is said to "perfect" nature.

There is a sense in which the word "transcends" the thing it names. True, there is also a sense in which the word itself is material, a "body," a meaning "incarnate." For there is the dimension of sheer physicality (sheer "motion") by which a word is uttered, transmitted, heard, read, etc. Or there is the sheer physicality of the motions of the brain when the brain is in any way using words, "thinking."

But the word's "meaning" is not identical with its sheer materiality. There is a qualitative difference between the symbol and the symbolized.

A duality of realm is implicit in our definition of man as the symbol-using animal. Man's animality is in the realm of sheer matter, sheer motion. But his "symbolicity" adds a dimension of action not reducible to the non-symbolic—for by its very nature as symbolic it cannot be identical with the non-symbolic.

However, there is also a notable sense in which these two realms cannot be kept rigidly apart. The most obvious example is in the case of "psychogenic illnesses." Or think of cases where a food, though physically wholesome, can cause revulsion in persons who approach it through a tradition, or

context of "ideas," in accordance with which it is repellent.
When I was preparing this article, there was a story in the
press concerning a savage on some island, of the South Pacific,
I believe, who had been hexed by members of his tribe and
was dying, despite the efforts of modern medicine to save him.
No actual material harm had been done to him. He had
merely returned to his tent and found the magic signs that
pronounced upon him the tribal sentence of death, and he
forthwith began to sicken.

I am sorry to say that, at that point, the newsmen apparently turned to other matters. At least, if there was a later
story on the outcome of the battle between modern material
medicine and the rhetoric of primitive magic in the case of a
tribesman most highly susceptible to its persuasions, I missed
it. But regardless of the outcome, the physical ravages already
done the poor devil by his terror on reading the "fatal" signs
are enough to illustrate the point about the way in which the
realm of symbolism can effect the sheer motions of a physical
body, as manifested by a turn from health to grave illness on
the part of a body swayed by symbolism. Similarly, ideas can
buoy us up, hence the market for tracts on "the power of positive thinking."

In all such cases, where symbolic operations can influence bodily processes, the realm of the natural (in the sense of
the less-than-verbal) is seen to be pervaded, or *inspirited*, by
the realm of the verbal, or symbolic. And in this sense the
realm of the symbolic corresponds (in our analogy) to the
realm of the "supernatural."

Third Analogy

The third analogy concerns the negative, which plays a
major role in both language and theology.

We should begin with the point that the Korzybski

school of linguistics stresses so insistently (and with justice—
for though the formula is obvious in principle, it is repeatedly
ignored in practice).

Language, to be used properly, must be "discounted."
We must remind ourselves that, whatever *correspondence*
there is between a *word* and the *thing* it names, the word is
not the thing. The *word* "tree" is *not* a tree. And just as effects
that can be got with the thing can't be got with the word, so
effects that can be got with the word can't be got with the
thing. But because these two realms coincide so usefully at
certain points, we tend to overlook the areas where they radically diverge. We gravitate spontaneously towards naive
verbal realism.

It is somewhat as though a mathematician were to say:
"We can solve certain problems in mathematics by using the
square root of minus one. Our solutions of such problems can
be applied to the needs of engineering and the like. So students of nature should undertake a search for the square root
of minus one in nature itself." However, as useful as the
square root of minus one may be in solving certain kinds of
problems, it is purely and simply an expression internal to a
specific symbol-system, and not a "thing" discoverable in nature, insofar as we use "nature" in the sense of the less-than-
symbolic, or other-than-symbolic, the sort of things there
would be if all symbol-using animals and their symbol-systems
were obliterated.

The paradox of the negative, then, is simply this: Quite
as the *word* "tree" is verbal and the *thing* tree is non-verbal,
so all words for the non-verbal must, by the very nature of
the case, discuss the realm of the non-verbal in terms of *what
it is not*. Hence, to use words properly, we must spontaneously have a feeling for the *principle of the negative*.

The most obvious formal instance of this feeling for the
negative discount is in irony, a figure which, at its simplest,
states A in terms of non-A (as when, on a day of bad weather,

we might say, "What a beautiful day it is!"). And all metaphor involves a similar feeling for the discount. Thus, the expression "to sail the ship of State" is interpreted properly only insofar as we know that statesmen are not sailors and the State is not a ship.

A big eye-opener to me was a chapter in Bergson's *Creative Evolution*, on "The Idea of Nothing." Surely this chapter is a major moment in the theory of language, for it helps one realize that the negative is a peculiarly linguistic marvel, and that there are no negatives in nature, every natural condition being positively what it is.

For a fully adequate statement of Bergson's thesis, I can but refer you to his chapter. Also, I have tried to point out its value in some articles of mine on "A 'Dramatistic' Approach to the Origins of Language." * Bergson begins by observing that, if you try to conceive of "Nothing," you can do so only by conceiving of *something*. For instance, you may close your eyes and think of a black spot, or you may think of something and then think of it as being obliterated, or you may think of an abyss, etc. Insofar as an *idea* of "Nothing" involves an *image*, it must be an image of "something," since there can be no other kinds of image.

Or you can get the point by stopping to realize that you can go on forever saying what a thing is *not*. This thing I pick up *positively is* a book. It is not an apple, not an elephant, not a railway train, etc. It *positively is* here. It is not in China, not in the Middle Ages, not on the moon, etc.

Bergson points out the important role of the negative as regards matters of *expectancy*. For instance, if I am asked whether the thermometer reads 37°, I may find that the thermometer actually, positively reads 35°, or 38°, or 42°, etc. Whatever the thermometer positively reads other than 37°, I

*Reprinted in my *Language As Symbolic Action* (University of Californina Press, 1966). pp. 419–479. The fourth of these pieces is entitled "Postscripts on the Negative."

can say "It is *not* 37°." Such considerations cause us to realize that the negative is a peculiarly linguistic invention, not
a "fact" of nature, but a function of a symbol-system, as intrinsically symbolic as the square root of minus one.

From the Dramatistic point of view, however, Bergson's
observations might be modified at one point. His statement of
the case inclines towards the "Scientistic" slope. For he begins with the *propositional* negative, as with a sentence like
"It is not. . . ." But Dramatistically (that is, viewing the matter in terms of "action"), one should begin with the *hortatory*
negative, the negative of command, as with the "Thou shalt
not's" of the Decalogue.

This slight modification would shift our problem from
the "Idea of Nothing" to the "Idea of No." And perhaps, since
"No" is a *principle* rather than a paradoxical kind of "place"
or "thing" (such as "Nothing"), we are not so pressed to conceive of it in terms of an image. One can "get the idea" of
the negative by merely knowing how to use it. One doesn't
have to "see" some positive No, like a tree or a rock, in nature.
Its reality as a principle is symbolic, though there is of course
the kind of "body" that goes with the sound of the word, or
the sight of it on a page, or the sense of how it might be used
in varying contexts, or with the neural activity required of us
to "get the idea" of it.

(Incidentally, in consulting the records to do with the
training of Laura Bridgman and Helen Keller, whose sensory
privations caused them to learn language much later than
normal infants, I found that in both cases their teachers, without thinking specifically of this problem, had spontaneously
begun with the negative of command and had later introduced
the propositional negative.)

Existentialists such as Heidegger and Sartre should certainly be examined quizzically for their tendency to "reify"
the negative, by starting from the quasi-substantive "nothing"
rather than from the moralistic "no." Consider, for instance,

Heidegger's "meonic" notion that, if "Being" can "be," then *Nichts* can *nichten,* the symbolic negativity here being given quasi-positive substantiality by the suggestion that *Angst* is the evidence of non-being's validity as the metaphysical ground of being.

The negative being what it is, when you have arrived at a term as highly generalized as "Being," there is one notable dialectical "advance" still available. You can add the negative, and thereby arrive at "Non-Being" (*Nichts*), which can be treated as the *contextual ground* of your highly generalized term, "Being." For such an absolute opposite is all that's left. Whether or not it actually refers to anything, it is a "reasonable" operation linguistically.

An uncompromisingly naturalistic view of such linguistic maneuvers would simply dismiss them as sheer nonsense. But Logology would admonish us to take Heidegger's comedy seriously. For there is always the possibility that, if language does lead ultimately to this generalized use of the negative, the *implications* of such an end are present in even our *ordinary* thoughts, though in themselves these thoughts possess no such thoroughness. That is, though they are far from taking us "to the end of the line," they may *imply* this end, if we were but minded to follow them through persistently enough. So such an end may be lurking in them, an implied end that we cannot avoid by merely being trivial. For if man is the symbol-using animal, and if the ultimate test of symbolicity is an intuitive feeling for the principle of the negative, then such "transcendental" operations as the Heideggerian idea of "Nothing" may reveal in their purity a kind of *Weltanschauung* that is imperfectly but inescapably operating in all of us.

Thus, where positivism would simply dismiss such operations as sheer nonsense, Logology must watch them as carefully as a Freudian psychologist watches the nonsense of a patient's dreams. If the symbol-using animal approaches nature in terms of symbol-systems (as he inevitably does), then he will inevitably "transcend" nature to the extent that symbol-systems are essentially different from the realms they symbolize. And these realms will be *necessarily* different, inasmuch as the translation of the *extra-symbolic* into *symbols* is a translation of something into terms of what it is not.

For the moment, the main thing is to stress the fact that the whole problem of negativity in language, and the similar dialectic of Heidegger's metaphysics, has its analogue in "negative theology," the defining of God in terms of what he is not, as when God is described in words like "immortal," "immutable," "infinite," "unbounded," "impassive" and the like.

When words such as "Love" or "Father" are applied to God, these must be understood not as positives, but rather as *quasi-positives*. For they must be understood analogically— and analogy, like metaphor, makes sense only insofar as we discount it for the negative. That is, we must add: "By 'love' we don't mean such love as people have for one another, for that would be merely human. And by 'father' we don't mean father in the literal, legal or naturalistic sense of the term."

In this sense, quite as language involves a principle of negativity in its very essence, so theology comes to an ultimate in "negative theology," since God, by being "supernatural," is *not* describable by the positives of nature. To be sure, there are stylistic or dialectical devices whereby the "supernatural" can be called the "truly" positive, and the positives of the empirical realm can be called negative. (Recall, for instance, Spinoza's formula: *omnis determinatio est negatio*.) It is not our point here to argue for or against any particular style of dialectic. All we should do is to point out the critical role of the negative principle in all such thinking. (And as regards Spinoza, his theory was explicitly in the spirit of negative theology, since he made much of the point that the idea of "order," for instance, could not mean the same to us as to

God—indeed, God's idea of order might even resemble our idea of disorder.)

The positives of nature become "quasi-positives" insofar as they become infused with the principle of negativity (the "Thou shalt not") that is so basic to the sense of the ethical. It is thus with sexual functions, for instance, insofar as these are brought under the control of moralistic proscriptions. Or forms of monastic discipline, penance and the like, while thoroughly positive in the sheer "motions" they involve, are guided by the negatives of the ethical. In the longer and earlier of Emerson's essays on *Nature,* there is a passage that serves perfectly to illustrate how thoroughly the positives of the natural order can become infused with the principle of negativity, particularly when this principle is extended to include the thought of ultimate theologic sanctions:

> Sensible objects conform to the premonitions of Reason and reflect the conscience. All things are moral; and in their boundless changes have an unceasing reference to spiritual nature. Therefore is nature glorious with form, color, and motion; that every globe in the remotest heaven, every chemical change from the rudest crystal up to the laws of life, every change of vegetation from the first principle of growth in the eye of a leaf, to the tropical forest and antediluvian coal-mine, every animal function from the sponge up to Hercules, shall hint or thunder to man the laws of right and wrong, and echo the Ten Commandments. Therefore is Nature ever the ally of Religion: lends all her pomp and riches to the religious sentiment.*

* Though we have contended that one must have the "idea" of the negative in order to use *any* language properly, Emerson's reference to "right and wrong" suggests considerations whereby we could settle for less, in case the reader resists so radical a claim. It involves the obvious empirical distinction between "positive" terms and "polar" terms. By "positive" terms would be meant terms that imply no direct "logical opposite," as distinct from "polar" terms, that do imply logical opposites. Thus, a word like "table" is "positive" in the sense that it implies no contradictory term such as "anti-table," or "non-table." But "polar" terms such as "right," "true," "order," "yes" imply respectively: "wrong," "false," "disorder," "no." The moralistic ("Dramatistic") vocabulary (the vocabulary of "action") centers in such "polar" terms (with their strong sense of *choice*). The quotation from Emerson sug-

Fourth Analogy

The dialectic of the fourth analogy is so interwoven with that of the third, they are hard to treat of separately. So I shall make a transition from the third to the fourth by using an example that clearly implicates the two:

Imagine that you began with a world of positives, in the strictest sense of the term, a world of material things and operations. Gradually you made wider and wider categories. For instance, you went from this tree to all trees, from all trees to all growing things, from all growing things to all objects, etc. And finally, to embrace the entire realm of positives, you might, in noting how they all impinged upon one another, sum up the situation by calling this natural realm the realm of "The Conditioned." Once you get to a term so highly generalized, then from the standpoint of the negative, what do you have left? Obviously, by the sheer dialectics of the case, "The Conditioned" would have as its partner a term of equally high generalization, "The Unconditioned." Similarly, if The Conditioned is the realm of Necessity, then The Unconditioned would be the realm of Freedom. If The Conditioned is the realm of Means, The Unconditioned would be the realm of Ends. If The Conditioned is the realm of the "sensible" (Phenomena), The Unconditioned would be the realm of the "intelligible" (Noumena). If The Conditioned is the realm of things in their relation to one another, then The

gests how even the sheerly "positive" world (of "sensory objects") can become infused with the negativity of the "polar," a vocabulary that makes sense only insofar as a corresponding "negative" is necessary for the placement of each "positive." Whereas "isms" *look* positive, they are all negatively infused, taking their form antithetically to other "isms" (some elements of which, paradoxically, they often end by incorporating).

Incidentally, Logology would treat Metaphysics as a coy species of Theology.

Unconditioned would be the realm of things-in-themselves (a quasi-positive which was used by Kant, and which Fichte disclosed for the negative it was by calling Kant's *Ding-an-sich* a *seiendes Unding,* a being non-thing).

The fourth analogy involves the linguistic drive towards a Title of Titles, a logic of entitlement that is completed by thus rising to ever and ever higher orders of generalization. In the Platonic dialectic, such a movement towards the abstract was equated with a movement towards the Divine, since it was away from the realm of merely naturalistic positives, the objects of sheerly sensory experience.

Imagine the ideal title of a book. An ideal title would "sum up" all the particulars of the book. It would in a way "imply" these particulars. Yet the particulars would have all the material reality. Similarly with a movement towards a title of titles (the unifying principle that is to be found in a sentence, considered as a "title" for the situation it refers to): such a movement is towards a kind of *emptying,* it is a *via negativa.* (Thus, recall Hegel's observation that, when you go from this being to that being and the other being, and so on, until you have a term for "Pure Being," such "Pure Being" is indistinguishable from "Nothing," for there is not a single thing you can point to as an example of "Pure Being." And recall here Heidegger's use of Nothing as the contextual counterpart, or "ground," of Being.)

The stress in the fourth analogy is not upon this negative element, but upon the search for a title of titles, an over-all term (which turns out to have this negative principle as an essential part of its character). Insofar as the third and fourth analogies can be treated separately, the third concerns the correspondence between negativity in language and its place in negative theology, while the fourth concerns the nature of language as a process of entitlement, leading in the secular realm towards an over-all title of titles. Such a secular summarizing term would be technically a "god-term," in the sense that its role was analogous to the over-all entitling role played by the theologian's word for the godhead.*

Note that we could also view this fourth analogy in reverse direction. That is, instead of looking upon "God" as the title of titles in which all is summed up, one could look at all subclasses as materially "emanating" or "radiating" from this "spiritual source." And thus, just as religion could be viewed as central, with all specialized fields such as law, politics, ethics, poetry, art, etc. "breaking off" from it and gradually becoming "autonomous" disciplines, so there is a technical sense in which all specialization can be treated as radiating from a Logological center. Logology could properly be called central, and all other studies could be said to "radiate" from it, in the sense that all -ologies and -ographies are guided by the verbal. They are all special idioms (in the special fields of the physical sciences, the social sciences and the humanities).

However, to conceive of this ideally perfect subject as placed at the center of a university's curriculum is by no means the same as viewing such "derivation" literally. Actually, the courses of a curriculum developed through time; their accumulation is historical, not logological. If we put the university in place of the universe, with Logology as center

* Often in earlier times the opening words of a work were used as its title. One should keep such "firsts" in mind when we later consider the ways in which "essences" can be stated in terms of *temporal* priority.

There is a related puzzle of this sort: In my *Grammar of Motives* (University of California Press, 1969) I made much of a terministic pentad: *act, scene, agent, agency, purpose.* At first glance they all might look like quite "positive" terms—and without thinking explicitly about the problem, I took them to be so. For they are not terms that readily imply logical opposites. But later I came to realize that, though they are not thus "polar," neither are they simply "positive." They are really *questions.* By *act* was meant: "What was done?" By *scene:* "In what sort of situation was it done?" And so on. Thus, they are really but a set of *blanks to be filled out.* They are an algebra, not an arithmetic. The *functions* of these terms could be analyzed in relation to one another, without concern for any specific answers with which some particular terminology of motives might fill in the blanks.

and circumference of the university (as "God" has been called the center and circumference of the universe), the "derivation" of the curriculum from this source would be purely schematic, purely theoretical, an "ideal" derivation that could be important to the forming of academic attitudes and educational policies, but that would be "beyond the imagination" literally. Logology is also analogous to theology in the sense that, though ideally central, in practice it would be but one particular specialized study, like any other division of the curriculum.

Fifth Analogy

Our fifth analogy concerns the relation between "time" and "eternity," and we can use as our text a quotation from St. Augustine's *Confessions* (Book IV, chapter X). When discussing transient things, Augustine says:

> Thus much hast Thou given them, because they are parts of things, which exist not all at the same time, but by departing and succeeding they together make up the universe, of which they are parts. And even thus is our speech accomplished by signs emitting a sound; but this, again, is not perfected unless one word pass away when it has sounded its parts, in order that another may succeed it.

Here the succession of words in a sentence would be analogous to the "temporal." But the *meaning* of the sentence is an *essence*, a kind of fixed significance or definition that is not confined to any of the sentence's parts, but rather pervades or inspirits the sentence as a whole. Such meaning, I would say, is analogous to "eternity." In contrast with the flux of the sentence, where each syllable arises, exists for a moment, and then "dies" to make room for the next stage of the continuing process, the meaning is "non-temporal," though embodied (made incarnate) in a temporal series. The meaning in its unity or simplicity "just *is*."

Alice's Wonderland nearly always has moments that
illustrate dialectical subtleties of this sort. Recall, for instance,
the episode of the Cheshire Cat. It smiles. That is, so far
as sheer *appearances* are concerned, certain motions, postures
and the like take place, and these are interpreted as the signs
of a smile. The smile is the *essence* of these material conditions, the *form* or *act* of the sheer motions. It is what the
motions "mean." Then the cat disappears, all but its smile.
The smile's "temporal" aspects vanish, leaving but their *essence,* their *meaning.* Strictly speaking, the transformation
could not be illustrated. The drawing can at best eliminate
all of the cat but the portion of its face that can depict a
smile. But the sheer essence or smiliness of smile would not
permit of even such parsimonious picturization. "Smiliness"
is not picturable; the closest we can come is to picture one
particular smile, by the use of elements that in themselves are
not smile. These would correspond to the merely "temporal"
aspect of the smile's "eternal essence" or meaning that "transcends" any of the visible details.

This same analogy (involving verbal counterparts to
"time" and "eternity" respectively) could be approached by
another route. Consider our definition of man as the symbol-
using animal. Two quite different ideas of "eternity" can be
conceived, depending upon which of the terms we start from.
The *generic* designation, "animal," suggests the kind of "eternity" we get when we think of eternity as *time extended forever,* though eternity is said to be "beyond time." Or the
specific designation, the differentia, "symbol-using," suggests
by analogy another kind of eternity, the idea of the "fixed"
or "immutable," as with principles, universals, definitions of
essence. An analogy of this sort (the sort that Santayana
treats so brilliantly in his writings on the "realm of essence")
would fail to suggest the thought of endless *living* that is
suggested by the comparing of eternity to animality indefi-
nitely prolonged.

This distinction between two ideas of "eternity," or between terms for "temporal" orders and terms for "fixed" orders, also involves an ambiguous relation between terms for "logical priority" and terms for "temporal priority"—but perhaps that point can best be considered in the light of our sixth analogy.

Sixth Analogy

This analogy concerns a notable likeness between the design of the Trinity and the form underlying the "linguistic situation." And it is built about the consideration that, as regards the persons of the Trinity, the Father is equated with Power, the Son with Wisdom, and the Holy Spirit with Love.

Think first of the relation between the thing and its name (between a tree and the word "tree"). The power is primarily in the thing, in the tree rather than in the word for tree. But the word is related to this power, this thing, as "knowledge" about that thing. Hence, derivatively, it has a kind of power, too (the power that is in knowledge, in accurate naming). But primarily power is in the materials, the things, that we can build with, or heat with, or strike with and so on.

To carry the analogy a step further: Quite as the first person of the Trinity is said to "generate" the second, so the thing can be said to "generate" the word that names it, to call the word into being (in response to the thing's primary reality, which calls for a name).

Next note that there is a kind of *correspondence* between the thing and the name for the thing. There is a state of *conformity*, or *communion*, between the symbolized and the symbol. Insofar as we are considering merely the relation between a name and the thing it names, some such technical term as "correspondence" or "conformity" will serve our pur-

poses. But insofar as the Trinity is said to be composed of
"persons," we must translate our idea of perfect correspondence into correspondingly *personal* terms. And the word for
perfect communion between *persons* is "Love."

Note also that whereas the first moment (the thing)
provided the ground for the second moment (the appropriate
name), both of these moments, taken together, form the "correspondence" between them. Here again the analogy with
the Trinity holds, since the First Person is said to "generate"
the Second, whereas the Third proceeds from the First and
Second in their togetherness. That is: The technical *correspondence* between thing and name would have as its theologic analogue the "Love" between the First and Second
Persons.

Since Hegelian metaphysics is so close to theology,
much the same sort of structure can be discerned in the
Hegelian dialectic. Given the genius of the negative, the term
"thesis" of itself implies "antithesis"—and both together imply
"synthesis," the element of communication between them. At
this point, one might object: "But the Hegelian 'antithesis'
is *antagonistic* to 'thesis,' whereas the Son, as the Word, is
rather in a 'like-father-like-son relationship.'"

And such could, indeed, be the case, since so much
nineteenth-century thinking was under the sign of Antithesis.
(See its role, for instance, in Kierkegaard, despite his avowed
resistance to Hegel). But we should point out that the idea
of *opposition* can yield to the idea of *counterpart*. For instance, in Greek:

antistrophos (a word used by Aristotle to define rhetoric
as the counterpart of dialectic)

antimorphos (which means: formed after, or corresponding to, something)

antitimao (which means: to honor in return)

Or, in case you feel that we are going far afield here, note that in Coleridge's dialectical pentad, at one point where he puts "The Scripture" as thesis, he puts "The Church" as antithesis. (Coleridge complicates the triadic system by adding "prothesis" and "mesothesis" to the Hegelian three.)*

But the mention of Hegel serves as a reminder of the point previously mentioned, concerning the relation between temporal and logical notions of priority. (By temporal or "narrative" priority is meant such a sequence as yesterday, today and tomorrow; logical priority involves a kind of "simultaneity," as in a sequence such as prevails among the parts of a syllogism, where the argument proceeds *from* the first premiss, *through* the second premiss, *to* the conclusion, but not in a

* See the Shedd edition of Coleridge, "Notes on the Pilgrim's Progress," (New York: Harper & Brothers, 1853), V, 256:
All things in which the temporal is concerned may be reduced to a pentad, namely, prothesis, thesis, antithesis, mesothesis and synthesis. So here:

Prothesis
The Word—Christ.

Thesis	Mesothesis	Antithesis
The Scripture.	The Spirit.	The Church.

Synthesis
The Preacher.

In *Aids to Reflection* (Shedd, I, 218-219) he writes:
For the purposes of the universal Noetic, in which we require terms of most comprehension and least specific import, the Noetic Pentad might, perhaps, be:

Prothesis.
Sum.

Thesis.	*Mesothesis.*	*Antithesis.*
Res.	*Agere.*	*Ago, Patior.*

Synthesis.
Agens.

Here he discusses this Dramatistic grammar at considerable length.

temporal sense.) Much more on this subject will be said in
the later chapters of this book. But in the meantime, we can
get a relevant preview by dwelling on the interrelationships
among the three terms of the Trinity.

The ambiguous relation between the two styles of placement (the narrative and the logical) can be seen if we stop
to consider again the way in which the Second Person of
the Trinity is said to "proceed" from the First, and the Third
from the First and Second. Though we think of a Father
as *preceding* a Son in time, and though we conceive of
"generation" in temporal terms, orthodox theologians admonish
that the process whereby the Father is said to "generate" the
Son must *not* be conceived temporally, that Father and Son
are one eternally. We might say that the First Person is "prior"
to the Second rather in the *logical* sense (as the first premiss
could be called prior to the second premiss of a syllogism).

Note that the idea of personal relations involving two
"generations" contains this ambiguity. Though there is a
sense in which a Father precedes a Son, there is also a sense
in which the two states are "simultaneous"—for parents can
be parents only insofar as they have offspring, and in this
sense the offspring "makes" the parent. That is, logically,
Father and Son are *reciprocal* terms, each of which implies
the other.

Many ancient theological quarrels hinge about this possibility of shifting between the two kinds of sequence,
temporal sequence and logical sequence. And Joachim of
Floris (1145-1202) offered a theory of history which well
illustrates how the shift can occur. He divided history into
three stages:

First: age of the Father, of Law, of the Letter;
Second: age of the Son, of the Gospel (intermediary
            between Letter and Spirit);
Third: age of the Spirit.

The age of the Father called for obedience; the age of the Son, a period of study and wisdom, involved a striving after mystical insight and a stress upon reading; the age of the Spirit, the monastic age then prevailing, was to be devoted to prayer and song.

Here, clearly, the relations among coeternal persons of the Trinity are translated into a temporal series, as regards the unfolding of history. And Hegel, of course, built his theory of history about an ambiguity of the same sort. From the strictly logical point of view, Hegel's history was over before it ever began; the "Idea" contained all its possibilities from the very start. But the manifesting of this "Idea" in terms of nature and history was like the gradual revealing of these logical implications one by one.

It is my notion that, following such cues, we can finally develop a considerable body of conceptual instruments for shifting back and forth between "philosophic" and "narrative" terminologies of motives, between temporal and logical kinds of sequence, thereby finding it easy to translate discussions of "principles" or "beginnings" back and forth into either of these styles, and thereby greatly cutting down the distance there seems to be between poetic and philosophic styles of statement.

Our six analogies, then, have been:

(1) The likeness between words about words and words about The Word.

(2) Words are to non-verbal nature as Spirit is to Matter.

(3) Language theory, in coming to a head in a theory of the negative, corresponds to "negative theology."

(4) Linguistic entitlement leads to a search for the title of titles, which is technically a "god-term."

(5) "Time" is to "eternity" as the particulars in the unfolding of a sentence are to the sentence's unitary meaning.

34 The Rhetoric of Religion

(6) The relation between the name and the thing named is like the relations of the persons in the Trinity.

In offering this list, we are but schematizing a mode of thought that is now quite prevalent. But as a rule such thinking is fragmentary, and uncertain in its aim (beyond the clear resistance to overly positivistic canons of meaning). In particular, such thinking is apparent among critics who like to approach secular literature in terms of "myth," a word that ambiguously embraces both "religion" and "poetry" (along with certain discarded bits of "science" now usually called "magic"). In the case of my earlier writings,* there has been my concern with the "creative" nature of the word, in connection with my speculations on orientation, transformation, "perspective by incongruity," "exorcism by misnomer" and re-simplification (in *Permanence and Change*); on "secular prayer" (in *Attitudes Toward History*); on "rebirth" (in both these books and *The Philosophy of Literary Form*); on "god-terms" (in *A Grammar of Motives*); on "glamor," "romance" and "beauty" as purely secular, social analogues of "divinity" (in *A Rhetoric of Motives*); on "pure persuasion" † (also in

---

* See K. Burke: *Permanence and Change*, 2d. ed. rev. (Los Altos, Calif.: Hermes Publications, 1954); *A Grammar of Motives* (University of California Press, 1969); *A Rhetoric of Motives* (University of California Press, 1969); *The Philosophy of Literary Form* (New York: Alfred A. Knopf, 1957); *Attitudes Toward History*, 2 vols., rev. ed. (Los Altos, Calif.: Hermes Publications, 1959).

† "Pure persuasion" involves a linguistic marvel of this sort: Insofar as language is formed through its use for communicative purposes, a communicative motive is implicit in its sheer form (with its three "moments": speaker, speech and spoken-to). This design gets its fulfilment in such modes of expression as praise, invective and exhortation. The use of these resources for practical purposes would be examples of "persuasion" in the ordinary sense of the term (as understood, for instance, in Aristotle's *Rhetoric*, which lists the many "topics" available to the speaker for such operations). By "pure persuasion" is meant the sheerly formal use of such expressiveness, as were one to write a piece of invective not for the specific purpose of affecting people's attitude towards some policy or person, but through sheer "love of the art" (as, for instance, the voluble word-play that delights us in the case of a character like Falstaff). "Pure persuasion" would take delight in the sheer *forms* of courtship for their own sakes. Hence

the *Rhetoric*) and on catharsis (in current attempts to decide how poetry "purges" the edified customer).

But many of these efforts lacked the particular "logological" reservation which I would now plead for. And even the later ones lacked the specific formulation of this essay. In general, there was a tendency to assume a simple historical development from the "sacred" to the "profane," from the "spiritual" to the "secular." But Logology systematically admonishes us against so simple a dialectic.

To get the point, we need but consider the development of ecclesiastic vestments in connection with religious ceremonies in the Christian churches. It seems that such vestments were not borrowed from the ritual garments of other faiths (were not adaptations, for instance, of the vestments worn by pagan or Jewish priests). Rather, they were originally *secular* garments, styles worn by people outside the Church (the primary ritualistic requirement being that they be neat and clean). However, these garments came to take on a *purely ritualistic* meaning. For as the secular styles of clothing gradually changed, the traditional vestments worn by the priests were still retained for use in the liturgy. Thus gradually the ecclesiastical vestments came to be piously "set apart" * from the common secular styles. The habitual habits, the customary costumes, of priests and laymen thus in time diverged (a development to be noted in the very word "vest-

it could *remain* "pure" only insofar as a practically "successful" outcome were precluded. Protestations of love addressed to some ideal "unattainable" mistress such as Dante's Beatrice would represent a personalized variant of such formality. Viewed from this sheerly formal point of view, "God" represents the principle of an ideal audience. Insofar as the human animal forms its character by the use of a medium intrinsically persuasive, there is a purely formal incentive towards the idea of a "perfect" audience, with an ultimate tendency to attempt conceiving of address to this "audience" in wholly non-utilitarian terms, a recipient of praise and thanksgiving without "ulterior purpose." Such would be the motive of "pure persuasion" when stated in theological terms viewed in logological terms.
    * The full significance of this expression will become apparent when we discuss the "Cycle of Terms Implicit in the Idea of 'Order.'"

ment" itself, which is now usually applied to specifically ecclesiastical forms of dress, but originally referred to "clothing" in general).

Thus, along with historical trends whereby religious
modes become secularized (as when James Joyce, for instance
transforms his Jesuit religious education into a jesuitry of art,
estheticizing religion in terms of a secular character who would
become a "priest of the imagination"), there is also the contrary trend whereby symbols that begin secularly can gradually *become* "set apart" through the development of a religious
tradition.

Accordingly, the relation between theology and logology
should not be conceived simply as proceeding in one direction.
It is a consideration on which we have already touched
several times, and on which we shall end.

From the standpoint of a theological dialectic, the idea
of a supernatural person is especially interesting in this respect. We have previously noted that personality, as an
empirical concept, is composed of ingredients distributed
among the three empirical orders (words about nature, words
about the socio-political, words about words). And personality as a term for deity is extended by analogy from these
empirical usages.

Note however that at this stage a theological dialectic
strategically reverses its direction. That is, it conceives of
personality here and now as infused by the genius of the
analogical extension. Thus, when the three-term empirical
system is expanded into a four-term system (with the fourth
term analogically referring to a realm that transcends the
empirical), dialectical conditions are then present whereby
the first three terms can be viewed as modified by the nature
of the fourth term. In brief, *empirical* personality can be
looked upon as sharing in the spirit of the *supernatural* personality. The fourth term is thus treated as in essence "prior"
to the other three, and as their "ground."

This is, of course, an instance of the two movements in a Platonist dialectic. First, there is the "Upward Way" from "lower terms" to a unitary transcendent term conceived "mythically" (analogically); and then there is a reversal of direction, a "Downward Way," back to the "lower" terms with which the dialectician began his climb; but now the "lower" terms are viewed as having become modified by the unitary principle encountered en route. The secular, empirical terms are "infused by the spirit" of the "transcendent" term.

Even empirically, one further refinement is now possible. The terms for the supernatural, themselves derived by analogy from the empirical realm, can now be borrowed back, and reapplied—in analogy atop analogy—to the empirical realm, as when human personality here and now is conceived *in terms of* "derivation" from a transcendent super-personality.

But though there is this area wherein analogies may fold back upon themselves, reilluminating the place they started from, the fundamental materials out of which our terms for the supernatural can be analogically constructed are:

First, the sweep and power of the natural (of storms, of seas, of mountains), also the structural consistencies, as with crystals and with the symmetries of biologic organisms. Second, in the socio-political order, the dignities and solemnities of office—and the intimacies of the familial. And third (and here I thought I found myself compelled to make up a word), the "symbolicity" of the symbolic.

From the standpoint of the present investigation, the third of these sources for analogy is to be rated "foremost among the equals."

All told, then, there are three sources of analogy, plus analogies reborrowed from the fourth realm, itself analogical. As regards thoughts of ultimate purpose, it is in such terms that poets imagine, that philosophers conceive and that prophets threaten or promise. The important thing, for our purposes, is to study theological texts for hints as to how this "fourth realm" of language might figure as motive, even in situations not thus explicitly rationalized. The "transcendence" of man's symbol-systems operates in many ways, even when the terminology is supposedly designed for quite different purposes. Texts explicitly concerned with transcendence, as theological doctrines are, provide us with "perfectly thorough" instances of such processes. And Logology studies them with such considerations primarily in mind.

So much for the Analogies, the six here featured and the several others lying about their edges. They might be summed up as: the "words-Word" analogy; the "Matter-Spirit" analogy; the "Negative" analogy; the "Titular" analogy; the "Time-Eternity" analogy; the "Formal" analogy; the "Creativity" analogy; the "Courtship" analogy; and the "Reversible" analogy. A few more comments might be in order, with regard to the "philosophy of language" that is here being presented roundabout, through the analysis of two texts particularly suited to our purposes. Often I have sloganized my position under the name of "Dramatism," because action is so important an aspect of drama, and I define language as a species of action: "symbolic action."

This perspective might be most quickly indicated by two contrasts.

First, I would set "Dramatism" against "Scientism." In so doing, I do not necessarily imply a distrust of science as such. I mean simply that language in particular and human relations in general can be most directly approached in terms of *action* rather than in terms of *knowledge* (or in terms of "form" rather than in terms of "perception"). The "Scientistic" approach is via some such essentially epistemological question

as "What do I see when I look at this object?" or "How do I
see it?" But typical "Dramatistic" questions would be: "From
what, through what, to what, does this particular form proceed?" or "What goes with what in this structure of terms?"
or "How am I 'cleansed' by a tragedy (if I am cleansed)?"
Either approach ends by encroaching upon the territories
claimed by the other. But the *way in* is different, Dramatism
beginning with problems of act, or form, and Scientism beginning with problems of knowledge, or perception. (One
stresses the "ontological," the other the "epistemological"—
though to say as much is to be reminded that each ends by
implicating the other.)

The second rough-and-ready opposition is: A stress upon
"action," as against a stress upon "motion." "Motion" is a
necessary category, but if we treat all problems of motivation
in terms of "motion," we get reduction *praeter necessitatem*.
Behavioristic terminologies of motives would reduce "action"
to "motion," whereas Dramatism holds that "action" is a more
inclusive realm, not capable of adequate description in terms
of "motion" only. "Action" is to "motion" as "mind" is to
"brain."

However, though there can be "motion" without "action"
(as when balls roll down an inclined plane), there cannot
be "action" without "motion." *Empirically*, that is, though
there can be brain without mind, there cannot be mind without brain. Thus, Dramatism assumes that, though "action"
cannot be properly described in terms that reduce this realm
solely to the dimensions of "motion," there will always be an
order of "motion" implied in the realm of action. For instance,
the rules of a game define the nature of the players' "action"
in that game; but the players can act ("competitively co-
operating" to enact the game as a whole) only insofar as they
can move their bodies about the field in accordance with the

game's purposes and limitations (its "form") as defined by the rules.

In this view, "meaning" is not ideally reducible to "information theory," mechanical "interpretation" of "signals," and the like. In no system at present is meaning actually, empirically, so reduced. But apparently in such systems as Cybernetics it is "ideally" so reducible, "if we could but make a machine complex enough." *Dramatism assumes a qualitative empirical difference between mental action and mechanical motion.* If men ever invent a "machine complex enough" to obliterate the present empirical distinction we make between our dealings with people and our dealings with machines, the Dramatistic position will have to be abandoned, or at least greatly modified. But as things now stand, Dramatism is based on the obvious *empirical* distinction all men make between their approach to "people" and their approach to "things." "People" are entities capable of "symbolic action"; to varying degrees they can be addressed, "reasoned with," petitioned, persuaded. "Things" can but move, or be moved.

In this connection, our empirical definition of man would be:

Man is

(1) The symbol-using animal
(2) Inventor of the negative
(3) Separated from his natural condition by instruments of his own making
(4) And goaded by the spirit of hierarchy.

And now a few brief comments on the four clauses of this definition might be in order:

(1) As regards the classic definition of man (the "rational animal"), note that we substitute for "rational" the neutral, less honorific differentia, "symbol-using."

(2) In this first essay we have already indicated why we consider the negative as the special mark of man's linguistic genius. A sheerly "Dramatistic" shortcut to the same position would be as follows: *Action* involves *character*, which involves *choice;* and the *form* of choice attains its perfection in the distinction between Yes and No (between *thou shalt* and *thou shalt not*). Though the concept of sheer "motion" is non-ethical, "action" implies the ethical (the human personality). Hence, the obvious close relation between the ethical and the negatives of the Decalogue.

(3) Man's "separation" from the state of nature through his many kinds of mechanical invention provides a kind of secular analogue to the "fall" from the state of Eden. Man as inventor is traditionally called *homo faber;* his inventions are guided by his prowess as *homo sapiens,* which is another synonym for his nature as "symbol-using animal."

(4) By "hierarchy" we refer to the motive of the socio-political order, made possible and necessary by social differentiations and stratifications due to the division of labor and to corresponding distinctions in the possession of property (distinctions that are made possible by the "symbolicity," or terminology, of deeds and contracts, and by the negativity of the law). Here is the motive of the social ladder, or social pyramid, involving a concern with the "higher" as an organizing element, in men's modes of placement. (Also, included in such a notion of the "higher" would be the ways whereby the terms for social superiority, coupled with terms for moral strivings and with the "Platonic" forms of a sheerly *dialectical* "ascent," can provide analogies for ideas of "God.") Clause 4 is under the sign of a Latin formula used by Coleridge: *a Jove principium,* which might be "roughly" translated: "from the top down" (or, Logologically, "begin with an over-all 'god-term,' a title-of-titles, and view everything else *in terms of* that summarizing Word, considered as 'source' of the lot").

In brief, as regards clause (4):

> If, to seek its level,
> Water can all the time
> Descend,
> What God or Devil
> Makes men climb
> No end?*

* The fourth clause has been given a rhetorical flourish related to current exigencies. It could be protectively neutralized thus: "moved by a sense of order."

Also, as regards the first clause, many persons have argued that "symbol-using" should be changed to "symbol-making." To meet such objections without sacrificing my emphasis, this clause might be: "The animal that makes, uses and misuses symbols."

2 Verbal Action in St. Augustine's Confessions

Plus loquitur inquisitio quam inventio.

Confessions, xɪɪ, i

Outline of the Inquiry

VI. *En Route* (*b*). Personal attachments. During aesthetic period, close attachment to male friend who died. Alypius; his "curiosity"; material for high comedy. The discussion group. Mistresses (anonymous). Adeodatus, Augustine's natural son. His mother, Monica; her piety; possible influence upon imagery Augustine applies to God; her concern with portents; nature of her prayers. Possible relation between Monica's simple religious beliefs and Augustine's complicated theological doctrines. Contrast between Augustine's response to the effects of style and Stephen's in *Portrait of the Artist as a Young Man.* Dialectic of part and whole, applied to theology. Relation to "rest," "search" and "turn" contexts. Monotheism vs. polytheistic tolerance. Corporeality (metaphysical, and with regard to Augustine's mistresses). Possible names in text, "enigmatically." Before conversion, he has already abandoned the idea of God as corporeal and the Manichaean doctrine of evil, while to Platonist doctrines of Logos he has added the scapegoat principle. . . . Aside, explaining shift in author's views on the nature of Augustine's conversion.   73-86

VII. *Whence Evil?* Problem of accounting for evil in world created by all-powerful good God. Imagery: evil as "eclipse." Stage when good was treated as monad, evil as dyad. Associations of evil with fecal. Logological equivalent of Augustine's views on unreality of evil: "will" and the negative. Talk of evil leads to talk of dominion. Reference to growing faith in Christ. Later battles against Pelagians, whose doctrines would have weakened the symmetry built around idea of Christ's sacrifice. Review of Augustine's experiments prior to conversion. Platonism fares least badly. In sum: Augustine as "seeker."   86-93

VIII. *Adolescent Perversity.* In the form of a *Quaestio* in the *Summa Theologica,* this chapter asks why Augustine placed so much stress upon a prank of his adolescence, when he joined with other youths in stealing pears which they threw to the pigs. The act is analyzed as a complete parody ("perverse imitation") of his religious motives. The band of adolescent conspirators corresponds perversely to brotherhood within the Church. Gratuitous nature of the crime. Insight into its nature gained by comparison with works by such writers as André Gide. Next, the Book is analyzed in detail, to show more fully the grounds for our view of the offence. Finally, the connections are affirmed, though in a reverse direction, by citing Biblical reference to "day of the Lord" as "thief."   93-101

IX. *The Middle* (*Conversion, Turn, Peripety*) *in Detail.* "Decision-making," in voting, buying, questionnaires and drama. Distinction between "decision-making" and "conversion," illustrated by reference to drama. *Othello,* as perversely analogous to Augustine's conversion. Two meanings of "conversion." Relation between conversion and perversity. Chapter i: Its nature as introduction; "Trinitarian" critique of a difference in two codices. Chapter ii: Personal example of Victorinus, who was converted. Chapter iii: Most general observations on form of repentance. Chapter iv: Further thoughts connected with conversion of Victorinus. Chapter v: Introduces theme of two conflicting wills. Chapter vi: Contrasts between poor jobs in pagan society and the lives of devout Christians. Chapter vii: Mounting sense of internal conflict. Chapter viii: Augustine retires to garden; flurry of words to do with conflicts of volition; reasons for taking these as corroborative of our theses. Chapter ix: Quoted entire, for its agitated style and its flare-up of words for "command," interwoven with references to "will." Chapter x: Augustine turns aside to refute Manichaeans by reduction to absurdity; tentative explanation how this logical device may serve a psychological purpose. Chapter xi: Augustine's state of "suspense" between thought of his mistresses and an idealized madonna-like figure, *Continentia.* Chapter xii: The critical moment. The mistresses replaced by Continentia. Inner irresolution could now be replaced by controversy. (Footnote on three main directions: against Manichaeans, Pelagians and Donatists.) Further details of the conversion. Alypius's conversion follows. News announced to Monica. Conversion done "by God."   101-117

X. *The Book of Monica.* Ninth book might be said to complete Augustine's conceiving of the Holy Spirit. Though the son died before the mother, Augustine so arranges the narrative that the book ends on the theme of the mother's death. A chapter detailing a mystical conversation with her is said to have occurred "when the day of her death was impending." Comments on terms describing the situation in which the conversation took place (our analysis being designed to indicate how the maternal motive figures as an important strand in his views on the Holy Spirit). Translation of passage describing silence of eternity. Possible significance of the passage (in combining simple and sophisticated motives). Sentence that contrives bridges from idea of parents to idea of churchly family.   117-123

XI. *What All Is Memory?* Autobiography ends, and different kind of terministic development takes over. Simplified summary of developments in the last four books. His turn from *narrative of memories to principles of Memory* is "logological" equivalent of turn from "time" to "eternity." Announcing now the stress on problem of knowledge. To whom the Confessions are addressed. . . . Images associated with Augustine's idea of Memory. Technical operations of the Memory. How Memory can suggest figure of oxymoron. Memory not just of sense impressions. Kinds of recognition that must come from still remoter area. Mathematical knowledge would belong here. Reflexive stage (as with remembering remembering). Augustine does not mention effect of his memorizing of Biblical texts; sense in which "God" is in his Memory, since "God" is explicitly or implicitly in all Biblical terminology. "Transcendence" by tautology or *nonsequitur*. How the applying of the same images to two different terms in effect makes one of the terms implicit in the other (whereby genius of highest term can be felt to infuse the lot). Augustine will "transcend" Memory.   123-129

XII. *To Cling* (Inhaerere). John Bowlby's "five instinctual responses" of infants. Augustine mentions three: crying, smiling, sucking. Does not mention clinging and following. Following as adult response implied in Augustine's attitude toward authority of Bible. (Logical sequence in Spinoza.) Augustine adds response that Bowlby omits: rest. Resting and clinging seem to imply each other in Augustine's idea of afterlife. List of relevant contexts. Relation between such *verbal behavior* and the infantile *act* of clinging.   129-133

XIII. *Trinitarian Considerations That Complicate the Ascent.* Equating of search for God with search for happy life. Passing reference to stylistic felicity as an analogy. Each man has "memory" of God insofar as he remembers search for happiness. "Mind" as part of "memory." Shift to subject of Temptation. Psychological difference between relations to second person of Trinity and relations to third (*knowing* more intellectual, *rest* more purgative). Love (or appetition generally) relates most directly to Holy Spirit; but insofar as appetites become unruly, purgative element figures in idea of Christ as sacrifice. Christ a Mediator in two senses: mediation as intercession; mediation as bridge between realms of time and eternity. (Poetic analogy: Keats's Urn.) Need of "double plot" to treat of Logos and Spirit (Wisdom and Love), in their relation to Authority (*Potestas*). How concern with Imagery leads to concern with Temptation.   133-138

XIV. *Imagery, Sensation, Temptation and Mediator.* How talk of images in sleep leads into subject of Temptation. Paragraph on mortification, cited from Joyce's *Portrait of the Artist as a Young Man*. Notable details in Augustine's assessment of his Temptations. His summing up, with resonant sentence again referring to his beginnings on subject of Memory. Next steps: Temptation leads to talk of Mediator; dual nature of Mediator leads to subject of relation between time and eternity; this problem in turn is reducible to the problem of a *beginning*.   138-141

XV. *In the Beginning* . . . This chapter, on *principium*, relates more directly to Word than to Holy Spirit, though all three motives of Trinity involve one another. Traits with which the vigor of Augustine's rhetoric, as guided by terminology of Bible, endows "Eternity." Stress now upon technical problem of relating "Time" and "Eternity." Analogues of "time" and "eternity" in nature of sentence. Logological counterpart of "eternity" is to be found in way terms can imply one another; logological counterpart of time is in the rectilinear nature of narrative. List of main contexts in which Augustine relates terms for time and terms for eternity by reference to terms for beginnings. Eternal silent Word and divine words in time. Same words understandable in terms of either time or eternity. (Dialectically, the problem is reducible to this: If you have but two essentially different orders of terms, where locate a term that represents the point at which the second order of terms emerges out of the first?) Words as beginning in sense that Scriptures teach what to do (an end). Words also equatable with God's Will (thereby bringing Holy Spirit into the design). Pantheistic possibilities here, as indicated by Spinoza. Eternity as pure present (distinction between such idea of eternity as Living and the kind of formal eternity suggested in Yeats's Byzantium poems). Respect in which one cannot speak of eternity as before or after time. Heaven of heavens, as "participant" in eternity, though not co-eternal with it. Principle of divisiveness in idea of participation (ambiguity of Latin *abs* in this regard; how Hegel's triad reveals inchoate divisiveness in design of Trinity). Etymology of *exordium, initium, and principium*. Logological equivalent of statement that heaven of heavens partakes of eternity. "Day" as eternally present. How past and future can only be thought of as present (analogy of motion pictures in this regard). Augustine's inquiry is placed outside the realm of "curiosity," though he is aware of this possible objection to his speculations. Use of grammatical distinction between active and passive to distinguish between a term used with connotations of the eternal and same term used with connotations of the temporal. "Free" creation out of nothing (that is, *innovation*) as the essence of an act. (How Spinoza's view of rationally necessary act treats the same problem.) "God" as word for idea of wholly free act, translated into terms of agent. Since to create is to form, and prime matter is formless, there enters also the problem of God's creating formlessness (the "creatable" and "formable"). Four ways of understanding *principium* as *primo* ("first"): (1) by eternity, as God precedes all things; (2) by time, as flower precedes fruit; (3) by choice (*electione*) as fruit may be preferred to flower; (4) by origin, as the sound precedes the song. (Logological comments on these distinctions.) A "breakthrough,"

where Augustine sees "in an enigma" how all three persons of the
Trinity are mentioned in the opening verses of Genesis. (How
this in effect makes Creation not "Elohist" or "Jehovist," but "Christian.") Sense in which Son is more of a beginning than Father.
Principium in *De Trinitate:* Father as *principium* of Son; Father
and Son as *principium* of Holy Spirit; entire Trinity as *principium*
of created things. "Father" and "Son" are reciprocal terms. Logological interpretation of statement that Holy Spirit exists as "Gift"
even before being given. Imagery of stretching, used in Augustine's
terms for time. "Spaces of times." God viewed essentially after
analogy of time rather than space, yet "in" is essentially a spatial
concept.   141-155

XVI. *Multitudes and Abundances* (Ubertates) *and Increases.* In
sum, on form of last four books. Analogy with four-act play. How
problem of the *principium* reduces everything to oneness which
(in its nature as ordinal rather than cardinal) suggests radiation
from this center. Hence, "time" viewed in terms of "eternity."
Relation to Upward Way and Downward Way of Platonist dialectic: turn from infoliation to exfoliation. Specifically episcopal
slant, in relation to problems of ecclesiastical administration
(though the subject is not stressed). Last book could be called
"Book of the Holy Spirit." The role of "Spirit" with regard to
Scriptures and Church. Hence, another kind of "first": those who
"spiritually precede" those "spiritually subject" to them. "Spirit"
and "Gift." Giving "in the name of." No "natural history" here.
Proneness to allegorical interpretation, as with "logology," which
would particularly note how Augustine's observations on the "firmament of authority" link ideas of sky, Scriptures and ecclesiastical
leadership. Methodological point, possibly reducible for logological
purposes to relation between ideas and images. Relation between
ideas of *genus* and *generation.*   155-160

XVII. *Conversion of a Word.* Citation of passage embodying Aristotle's hierarchical notion that each thing in nature seeks its proper
level. Equating of "love" and "weight." List of contexts in which
references to "weight" appear. Notable passages where verb-forms
of the same root figure. How Augustine's "weight" finally comes
to levitate.   160-163

XVIII. *In Conclusion.* Author's position when beginning this analysis. Major change of plans concerns the discovery that the *Trinitarian* nature of Augustine's thinking should be stressed in connection with the *form* of his conversion. The basic pattern: Being,
knowing, willing; or memory, intellect, will. Without either affirming or denying Augustine's Trinitarianism considered as theology,
we would treat it as relevant to his own psychology as an empirical

person. His psychic economy, as so viewed: "Power" as motive ("Father"); Word as motive ("Son"), and respects in which it could be considered both as derivative and as a beginning in its own right; cathartic aspect of Logos as Mediatory still missing; "Holy Spirit" would be term for correspondence between the thing ("Father") and its name ("Son"); "Love" would be word for "perfect" correspondence expressed in terms of personality; how a synonym, "will," presents problems, as doctrine causes our wishes to be at odds with one another; how Word takes over the resulting problem of guilt; how Word also becomes infused with principle of Spirit; three strategic spots at which, by Augustine's doctrine, the world is "Christianized"; role played by mistresses and enemies in the process of victimage. Problem of analysis: In one sense, we watch the emergence of the Trinitarian pattern, yet in another sense it is there before the book is begun. Another kind of "predestination" possible: Augustine's way of responding to early experiences may already implicitly contain the attitudes he would develop later. Documentary and experimental nature of our search for key terms. The maternal strand of motives associated primarily with Augustine's idea of Holy Spirit. While theology begins in religion, it also reflects high development of social order as such. Theology, technology and money. Logological calculus favors tendency to stress continuities between theology and technology, since such a position helps keep us on the lookout for *symbolic* motives in technology.   163-171

I Of Words Here Generally

Regarding his turn from teacher of pagan rhetoric to Christian theologian and bishop, Augustine twice refers to the role of word merchant (*venditor verborum*). In a way, the fourth part of his *De Doctrina Christiana* marks the same crossing, or conversion, as the *Confessions*. It, too, concerns the development from the selling of words to the preaching of The Word. But in the work on Christian rhetoric, he is partly asking how to adapt for ecclesiastical purposes the verbal skill of the pagans, and partly attempting to show that Christianity already had an eloquent body of letters, whereas the autobiography places the emphasis upon the break rather than the bridge between the two realms.

Augustine is to be studied here, first of all, because he so clearly points up the relation (or disrelation!) between secular words and the theological Word.

Also at the very start, let us recall, for what it might be worth, that in his treatise "On the Teacher" (*De Magistro*), a discussion with his son on the subject of what would now popularly be called "semantics," he holds that the word *verbum* is derived from a verb meaning "to strike" (*a verberando*)—and the notion fits in well with his references to the lash of God's discipline. See, for instance, *Confessions* (x, vi), where he says that he loves God because God had struck (*percussisti*) him with His Word. Augustine's praise is for a God who is both a fountain of mercies and an avenger (*deus ultionum et fons misericordiarum simul*, iv, iv).

The dialogue "On the Teacher" derives "name" or "noun" (*nomen*) from the verb "to know" (*a noscendo*). But though this derivation is more likely than the other to be accepted by modern etymologists, both are equally Augustinian.

Perhaps Augustine's most condensed treatment of the meanings assignable to *verbum* is in Book xv, chapter xi of his treatise *On the Trinity*. There he systematically discusses the "dark" or "enigmatic" analogies between human words and Word in the theologic sense. Typically, he says that the word we conceive "within" has more right than its spoken replica to be called a word. And he makes a further distinction between a spoken word imagined in silence and a kind of word that is but "spoken in the heart." It arises from knowledge (which seems here equatable with memory). Augustine quotes Ecclesiasticus: "A word is the beginning of every work," and apparently has in mind something that might be a mixture of "idea," "purpose," "plan" and "attitude." So, all told, he here offers this range of meanings: the spoken word; the spoken word silently conceived as spoken (presumably words silently read or written would also fall under this

head); the preparatory attitude, guided by experience, that
precedes human action; the word of God in the sense of religious doctrine transmitted by Scriptures and preachers; the
Word of God as Wisdom, second person of the Trinity; the
Word of God made flesh.

A major aspect of Augustine's views on words is his
stress upon the relation between language and volition. Thus,
in *Confessions* (ɪ, viii), where he is discussing how an infant
learns to interpret words and signs, he says that the infant
is prodded to learn language by its keen desire to make its
wants known. Here the words "will" and "to will" (*voluntas,
velle*) appear eight times in seventeen lines. The brief chapter
as a whole concerns that evanescent state of infancy when
verbal action is first emerging out of sheer bodily motion.
Thus, here also, along with talk of words, signs, wishes, willing
and will, there is his typical stress upon the role of the
memory, along with his equally typical word "whence"
(*unde*). His word for "observe" here (*adverti*) happens
characteristically to be a compound of the word for "turn,"
which constantly recurs throughout the *Confessions* in many
notable forms, as one might expect of a book that is the account of a man who significantly "turned" ("was converted").

II   The Beginning

The first thing to note about the beginning is the theme
of *innerness*. The work opens with an invocation, using various grammatical forms of the verb *invoco* eight times in
twelve lines. For present purposes, the prefix is the thing to
be stressed.

The same word appears three times in the next chapter,
which also happens to be the next paragraph, or we might

even say the next "stanza." (The book begins with brief,
one-paragraph chapters, strongly incantatory, and ends similarly, with occasional aria-like interludes of similar quality
scattered throughout, though generally the intermediate chapters are much longer.) Note also quite a number of prep-
ositional *in's:* "in me . . . in Thee . . . in which . . . in
hell. . . ."; also the adverb "thence" (*inde*)—and the passage ends on a word which, while literally meaning "fill,"
introduces another variant of the *in* theme: *impleo.* This
word, having closed the second "stanza," is taken up as the
musical theme of the next, where forms of *impleo* appear
seven times in fifteen lines. (Augustine is setting forth a
rhapsodic accountancy that balances between talk of himself
and the world in God, and talk of God in him and the world.)

In the fourth paragraph, another kind of *in* gets strong
development. Besides the directional *in* (consonant with the
Augustinian stress upon the "inner man"), there is now a
pronounced stress upon the *in* of negation. There has been
a scattering of these already, as with the words *inquietum* and
nesciens, and quite a sprinkling of *not's* and *without's* (*non,
sine*), along with the Latin word for "discover" (*inveniunt*)
that literally means "come into." Also, there were instances of
"unless" and "nor" (*nisi, nec*).

But now, after first addressing God in ten superlatives
("highest, best, most powerful, most omnipotent, most merciful, most just, most secret, most present, most beautiful, most
strong"), he moves into epithets typical of negative theology:
"incomprehensible, immutable." These quickly shift into oxy-
morons: "changeless, ever changing; never new, never old."
Then comes "making all things new" (*innovans omnia*—a
shift back to the *in* of direction, though used figuratively).
We should also note that when he says "always acting, always
quiet," the duplicating of "always" has the same effect as
with the duplicating of "never" in "never new, never old."

(Perhaps this is in accordance with the mathematical paradox whereby infinity equals zero. In any case, it indicates how well the negatives of negative theology fit with ideas of "all-ness" as applied to God.) Several more of such paradoxical oppositions follow, mostly by negatives, one even double: "never without resources" (*numquam inops*). And for a close, there is a new twist along the same lines: Woe to those that keep silent about God; for where he is concerned, even the talkative are as though speechless.

The oxymoron-like treatment of IV attains its completion in v, the transition from the introduction (or the "prelude") into the narrative proper. Here, praying to see God's face, he ends on a quite incantatory formula: "Let me die, lest I die, that I may see it" (*moriar, ne moriar, ut eam videam*). Repetition of "die," along with the negative that causes the same word to be understood in two contrasting senses, gives a sibylline quality to the first part of the formula; and this quality is re-enforced in the second part by the rhyme of *eam-videam* (partially subtilized perhaps by there being more of a stress on the *e* of *eam* than on the *e* of *videam*).

All told, by thus harping on both the *in* of in-turning and the *in* of negation, these introductory paragraphs symphonically attain a merger of these two principles. We are stressing first of all the sheer musicality of such underlying repetitiveness. But there is a logic of sense here as well as of sound. For the negative is in its very heart moralistic; it is the act of dissuasion reduced to one syllable—and Augustine invariably equates ethical improvement with innerness. Thus, it is hard to think of any other way whereby his most characteristic motives could have been so accurately symbolized, somewhat enigmatically perhaps, but there nonetheless, and quite revealingly, too, when one goes back and looks at them in the light of the developments that they had thus implicitly foretold.

Incidentally, through the four paragraphs, the proportions change as follows:

Paragraph	In of direction	In of negation
I	14	6
II	23	10
III	7	8
IV	4	18

Thus, the fourth considerably reverses the distribution of the first.

But though these first five brief chapters clearly have the formal function of a beginning (in the sixth he starts speculating on his infancy, and the narrative proper is under way), with a writer as skilled in composition as Augustine we can get good results even by thinking only of his first sentence as the beginning. It is built of quotations from Psalms 145:3; 147:5. "Great art Thou, O Lord, and greatly to be praised; great is Thy power, and of Thy wisdom there is no end." The Latin word for "power" here (*virtus*) has connotations ranging primarily from manliness to moral nobility, so far as its application to humans is concerned. Like all such abstractions, it had also been personified by the pagans as a goddess, Virtue. As we shall see later, there are reasons for noting that the Latin word for "wisdom" (*sapientia*) comes from a verb *sapio*, the primary meaning of which was "to taste of, smack of, savor of, have the flavor of," with such derivative meanings as "to have taste, discernment." Thus, for him, the word could readily belong in the same category with his talk of heavenly "food," a kind of expression which he uses at strategic moments, in this regard also having the Bible itself as his stylistic authority.

As for the epithets "great" and "greatly to be praised" (*laudabilis valde*): they mark the essence of the verbal fountain which Augustine had at his command, when memorizing so much from the Psalms. Ambrose had suggested that he especially study Isaiah (a part of the Old Testament that could most readily be interpreted as foreshadowing the New Testament and Paul's doctrine of salvation for the Gentiles). But Augustine says that he had trouble understanding Isaiah —and as we read the laudatory exclamations with which the *Confessions* are studded, we can well understand his stylistic motive for such reliance upon the Psalms (about one-third of the book's thousand or so Biblical quotations being from this source). For doctrinal reasons, quotations from the Epistles are numerous. But the Psalms as model contribute most to the rhetorical ejaculations that keep the work vibrant.

In praise there is the feel of freedom. In total admiration, one is wholly free. Praise "wells up." Augustine thought of it as a power that, coming from God, enabled him to praise God. While the pagan world about him was falling into decay, he nonetheless could praise vigorously, by praising as it were the very Principle of Laudability. Where he could not praise the world of contingencies, he could praise the Absolute. A clear indication that praise was for him the verbal equivalent of love is in his ejaculation (v, i): "But let my soul praise Thee, that it may love Thee" (*sed te laudet anima mea, ut amet te*); and the rest of the sentence rounds out the motivation by deriving the power to praise God from his "confessing" to God's mercies. (Behind that stage, in turn, would lie his theory of election according to which he would derive from God the power to confess to God.)

Eagerness to praise may also imply fear of not praising. "Woe to those that keep silent," Augustine admonishes. Thus, there is a lesser form of praise that serves as a device for mollifying the angry. The source of mercies was also, by the same token, the God of vengeance (*Deus ultionum*). Furthermore, insofar as praise is a form of thanksgiving, in its nature as the acknowledgement of past favors it can also be secondarily a plea for future favors (an ingredient of motivation that is burlesqued in the style of business correspondence: "Thanking you in advance, we remain," etc.). Yet even praise

that is sheer hypocritical flattery for an ulterior purpose retains something of the "lift" that informs the act of praising
at its best.

But praise can serve as a kind of dispraise. For praise
of A can imply a refusal to praise B. In comparison with an
object of great praise, other things seem despicable—and it
has often been observed that critics can praise dead authors
as a way of detracting from contemporary rivals. Augustine's
praise of God was a way of *not* praising the emperor. In one
sense, all of Creation can be treated as despicable, in comparison with the Creator. Thus, Augustine strongly distrusted
any tendency to love or admire or even study the things of
this world, in and for themselves, without reference to an
origin in God. Accordingly, "curiosity" was for him decidedly
a bad word (in contrast with Veblen's views, for instance,
on "idle curiosity" as an admirable scientific motive). Yet
there is also the sense in which all things become "good"
when thought of as infused with the principle of laudability
from which he would derive them, through the *Sapientia* of
the creative Word.*

Looking again at those introductory paragraphs, we see
how many notable notes were struck at the very first, before
the reader could know how they were to be built upon. Here
would belong such words as: know, believe, seek (*quaero*, a
word shifting between connotations of quest and question,
while his use of *inquisitio* and *inquisitor* removed them from
the morbid meanings they were to take on later in Church
history), preach, man, will, creature, testimony, ministry, sin,
mortality—and those two ubiquitous pronouns, *tu* and *ego*, for
this is the "I-Thou" book to perfection (the "Thou" set having
about thirty-two instances in the first paragraph, or forty if

* In the *De Dono Perseverantiae* (11.25) Augustine quotes Psalms
8:3: "Out of the mouth of babes and of sucklings Thou hast perfected
praise." This would suggest another motivational dimension, somewhat surprisingly relating praise to infancy.

we include "Lord" when in the vocative, while in the second paragraph the "I" set has a count of about thirty-three*).

We should mention one other word: the characteristic "Whence" (*unde*), that is to figure later in his sloganlike cry, "Whence evil?" . . . "Whence this monster?" (*unde malum?* . . . *unde hoc monstrum?*) The typical Augustinian pattern is the direction inward, in search of a "whence," *unde* also having a semi-partner, *inde*, "thence." In the last book, the principle of the "whence" will allow for a reversal of direction, ending on exfoliation.

Meanwhile, here is an impressionistic imitation of the Augustinian I-Thou fountain:

In Thyself, Lord, (am) I myself. Once I was a seller of words, beaten by my vices. Now I am beaten by the blows of Thy Word. Behold! I, and my memory, and the memory of Thee, Lord, (dwell) in Thee eternally.

(*In te ipso, domine, ego ipse. olim eram venditor verborum, flagellatus flagitiis meis. nunc ego flagellor verberibus Verbi tui. tu es in memoria mea; ecce autem ego, et memoria mea, et memoria mea tui, domine, in aeternum in te.* To which we might add, still more impressionistically: *in* . . . *intus* . . . *inter* . . . *intra* . . . *intrare* . . . *internus* . . . *interior* . . . *intimus* . . . *inde* . . . UNDE . . .)

Out of what secret depths, he asks himself, was his free will summoned forth, to accept God's yoke, God being (IX, i) "more inward than all secrecy" (*omni secreto interior*). And in I, xviii, he explicitly classes the writing of his book under this same motivational head when saying: "Surely there is no science of letters more inward (*interior*) than conscience put into writing" (*conscientia scripta*). In X, vi the proportion is

---

* Where verb and pronoun appear together, the combination is counted as but a single instance. Thus, *ego* alone, or *ego sum*, or *sum* alone would each be considered as but a single incidence. Sometimes "God" or "Lord" is grammatically in the third person when having rhetorically the force of a second person.

purely and simply: Body is to soul as outer (*exterius*) is to inner (*interius*).

He will not, until Book x, discuss at length the important role played by the internalities of memory; but near the end of Book i, he refers to the vigor of his memory (*memoria vigebam*). More later on the turbulent cluster of terms that surround his idea of the memory. At this point we need but note how, to his store of autobiographic recollection, he added an avid memorizing of sacred texts—and this storehouse clearly provided rich material for the fountain of his ejaculations. It was a lore under the sign of seeking (as he indicates by that naggingly recurrent word, *quaero*).

He policed his senses in general, he says, by an inner sense (*custodiebam interiore sensu integritatem sensuum meorum*). The principle of governance is thus located within. Whatever its source for him in the ground of all being, it came by a route *ab intra,* though part of its internality was obviously the work of memory. The great store of Biblical texts, learned verbatim and spouted forth at appropriate moments, were like attitudinally slanted names for situations. Each time a situation arose, it presented itself to him in terms of some Scriptural formula that in effect "adopted a policy" with regard to it. Thus by confronting a current situation in terms of a Biblical response, such citations had the effect of making the situation itself essentially Biblical, to be classed with conditions not literally present at all. Thus there is a sense in which his Biblical terminology of motives enabled him to "transcend" the sheerly empirical events of his times.

III The End

The last word of the *Confessions* is a verb meaning "it shall be opened." (The middle will be considered in the light of both beginning and end, and of the development as a

whole.) As Augustine had begun with a quotation from the
Psalms, he ends by adapting a quotation from Matthew (7:7):
"Ask, and it shall be given you; seek, and you shall find; knock,
and it shall be opened unto you." Whereupon, going back to
take another look at the beginning, we discover that this final
note had also been struck there. To lead into the oxymoron
about dying whereby he would live to see God's face, he had
said, "Behold, Lord, the ears of my heart are before Thee;
open thou them (*aperi eas*), and say unto my soul, I am thy
salvation." So the final word is there at the start, along with
two other notables, "soul" and "salvation."

Unfortunately, Augustine's sentence does not lend itself
readily to a translation even remotely as pliant as the original.
But that isn't so important in this case, since our main concern
at the moment is with the sound rather than the sense. To
this end, the problem is to compare the structure of Augustine's sentence with the corresponding sentence in Matthew.

The English version used in the Random House edition,
Basic Writings of Saint Augustine, is: "Let it be asked of Thee,
sought in Thee, knocked for at Thee; so, even so shall it be
received, so shall it be found, so shall it be opened."

The corresponding Latin is: "*A te petātūr, in te quaerā-
tūr, ad te pulsētūr: sic, sic accipiētūr, sic inveniētūr, sic ape-
riētūr.*"

The corresponding passage in the Vulgate is: "*Pétite, et
débitur vobis; quaérite, et inveniétis; pulsáte, et aperiétur
vobis.*" *

Whereas in both the Vulgate version and the English
translation the word "and" (*et*) appears three times, there is
no conjunctive in Augustine's version. His alteration would
seem to be in keeping with the rhetorical rule on which Aris-

---

* In the opening paragraph of Book XII, Augustine quotes the
Biblical version of this sentence. There his transformations would be
inappropriate, as the sentence is not there used as an ending. Also, by
including that earlier reference, in the Vulgate version, he allows the
final transformation to function like a variation on a theme.

totle ends his treatise on Rhetoric: "In order that the end of
a speech may be a peroration and not an oration, the most
fitting style is that which has no connecting particles." Aristotle gives as an example this asyndeton: "I spoke, you heard,
you know, decide."

But the main difference between Augustine's version and
the Vulgate is due to Augustine's treatment of the verbs. By
his arrangement, all six verbs have the same ending: *tur*.
Further, such homoioteleuton becomes downright rhyme with
petatur-quaeratur and *pulsetur-accipietur-invenietur-aperietur*.

Perhaps something along psychological lines might be
made of the fact that the Vulgate version (like the Greek)
has four of the verbs in the active voice, whereas in Augustine's version all six are passive. The possibility is worth thinking about; but in any case, as regards the sheer *musicality* of
the sentence, such transformation of the verbs into pas-
sives is the device whereby the uniform sound pattern is ob-
tained. Many other internal adjustments could be noted, as
regards both similarities and counter-movements; but the main
arrangements still unmentioned are the imperfect repetition
got by the *a te, in te, ad te* set, and the fourfold occurrence of
sic, which is wholly absent from the passage in Matthew.
(Incidentally, is it not also true that *sic* is stronger than our
word "so," here having incipiently the effect of "yes" thus
four times repeated in one sentence?) Finally, there is the
fact that Augustine's version ends on a verb whereas the Vulgate version ends on a pronoun, the pronoun being perhaps
better for a direct conversational appeal made en route, but
the verb being better for the formality of a close.

Later, the book's ending will be treated in a much
broader sense, after we have surveyed the steps leading up
to it. At present, confining ourselves to the thought of the last
word as a key word, let us list some other places in the book
where it figures notably:

vi, iv: Augustine tells how Ambrose helped him by explaining figuratively certain passages of the Bible which, if

explained literally, seemed to teach "perversity" (a word that is an important member of the "turn" clan). His word for such laying open of the true meaning is *aperiret*—and the process is done "by removing the mystic veil" (*remoto mystico velamento*).

VI, V: The Bible is said to express itself in "words most open" (*verbis apertissimis*) while at the same time preserving the "dignity of its secret."

VI, VII: Augustine tells how his friend Alypius was started on his way towards conversion by a simile that Augustine had borrowed from the circus, in order to explain a point in rhetoric. Alypius, whose regrettable "curiosity" made him an addict of the gladiatorial games, was jolted; for he took Augustine's remark to be a jibe at him, whereas Augustine had not been thinking of him at all. Here, Augustine says, was a correction that should clearly (*aperte*) be attributed to the work of God.

VIII, VI: Here the word occurs in a somewhat "conspiratorial" context (or rather, the context would be rated "conspiratorial," had not Augustine's doctrine triumphed over the pagan culture by which he had been nurtured and from which he turned). Here Augustine tells how, when he and a friend (the charmingly "me, too" Alypius) were entertaining one Pontitianus, who held a high office in the emperor's court, Pontitianus picked up a book, expecting it to be something used by Augustine in connection with his work as a teacher of pagan rhetoric. He opened it (here is the gong word, *aperuit*), and found to his surprise that it was by the Apostle Paul. Whereupon he in turn surprised them by confiding that he was a baptized Christian. This opening of the book was a major moment in Augustine's development; for Pontitianus proceeded to recite the exploits of the Egyptian monk, Antony, and of Christian monasteries, and of those anchorites who inhabited the "fertile deserts of the wilderness" (*ubera deserta eremi*, the word for "fertile" here being etymologically related to the word for udder, pap, teat, breast). Pontitianus was doing well, but fundamentally despised his job. In the discussion that follows, rewards for service with the Emperor are compared unfavorably with rewards for service under God (the word for "service" in both cases is *militia*). The highest you could climb at court, Pontitianus is reported as saying, was to become one of the Emperor's ministers—yet by the sheer act of wanting to become God's friend one has already become God's friend.

There are several other major variants of the word "open" (*aperire*) in Book viii. And, significantly, that is the book in which the conversion comes to a head. But before considering Book viii in detail (and in the light of other major strands leading up to it) we might go back and take one more look at the passage in vi, iv, where Augustine was telling how Ambrose "laid open" the Bible for him by interpreting some things figuratively. He says he was still hesitant, since he could not conceive of anything "spiritual" except in terms of the body. But the point to be emphasized now is that he goes on to speak of himself as being "killed by suspense" (*suspendio . . . necabar*). For his ideas of such suspense, and its resolution, will finally come to a head in what is perhaps the firmest of his formulae for summing up his motives.

We are saying, in sum: The final term of the *Confessions* might be called a "sesame" word. So we watch for it in other contexts as well (only a few of which are here listed). We particularly note where it impinges upon a term for suspense because, as later analysis will make clear, this is a strategic usage.

IV   The Middle, in Sum

Augustine's conversion passes its critical point almost at the mathematical center of the *Confessions* as a whole. In the preceding chapter (viii, xi) he was still "suspended" (*pende-*

bam, and a few lines previously, *suspendebar*) between the thought of the women who had been his "toys" and the "chaste dignity of Continence" which now "was revealed" to him (*aperiebatur*), calling upon him to "mortify" his unclean members (as Paul advises, in Col. 3:5). Then, in the next chapter, where the ultimate motivational change takes place, the strategic word "open" is used three times: first, when he has heard the child's voice saying somewhere in the distance, "Take up and read" (*tolle, lege*), and he interprets it as a call from Heaven to open (*aperirem*) the Bible; next, when he opens it (*aperui*); and finally, when loyal "me, too" Alypius, immediately after Augustine's conversion, himself promptly tries the same experiment, with a similar result, though through the medium of a different passage, which he disclosed (*aperuit*) to Augustine and which he interprets as Heaven's particular admonition to him.

In the next book (IX, vii) the word is used twice in connection with the account of a miracle, as God is said to have made known (*aperuisti*) to Ambrose by a vision the secret burial place of two martyrs—and there were attendant marvels, as with the case of the blind man whose eyes were opened (*aperti*) after he had touched the bier with his handkerchief.

Since the work hinges about a conversion, as might well be expected, the whole *vert*-series is particularly active (adverse, diverse, reverse, perverse, eversion, avert, revert, advert, animadvert, universe, etc.). The chapter in which the conversion comes to a crisis sums up by speaking of God as having "converted" Augustine (*conversisti enim me ad te*), and his mother's mourning as having been "converted" into gladness, which he calls more fertile or "breastful" (*uberius*), though also dearer and more chaste, than if her son had presented her with grandchildren by the flesh.

Surprisingly, and perhaps significantly, the first time the word "convert" appears (it is in the form of the past participle, *conversus*), it is applied not to himself but to God. The usage gives a slight hint of Augustine's views on predestination, the notion that man can be "turned" to God only insofar as God is "turned" to man (that man's conversion must start rather with God than with man, though man can of his own free will turn *away from* God, if God turns away from him). Part of Augustine's conviction on this point came from the fact that he had experienced the difference between a moment when he couldn't believe and the next moment when he could (without, so far as he could see, any new intervening act of will on his part). Some new thing had come from somewhere—and if someone were to say that the change was due simply to Augustine's own perseverance, he would have replied that even such perseverance is possible only if God has already granted the grace to so persevere.

In any event, Augustine has been saying (i, vi) that his confessions are addressed to God's mercy, not to a human who might deride him (*non homo, inrisor meus*). But even if God does deride him, he says, when God is turned (*conversus*) to him God will have compassion on him.

This reference to derision could send us in another direction. Augustine is not a humorous man. Though he does speak of an infant learning to laugh, at first when asleep and later when awake (*dormiens primo, deinde vigilans*), except for two other places in the *Confessions* (unless some instance has been overlooked) laughter has for him the connotations of derision. The *in* (of *inrideo*, or its modified form, *irrideo*) is not that of innerness, but of antagonism. And as we proceed, many of such usages will be encountered.

But our central concern involves a contrast between "conversion" and "perversity." In this respect Book viii, where the "watershed moment" of conversion occurs, should be treated as antithetical to Book ii, on the stealing of pears (an act which he considers the essence of the perverse because it was not merely corrupt, but corrupt *in principle*). Thus we might best point up the chapter on his final conversion by

juxtaposing it with the chapter on perversity, though in the
Confessions they are separated by a stretch of about sixteen
years.

But first we should try classifying the major motivational
elements that led up to the moment of crisis, the accumulating
load that was unloosed in the avalanche of Book VIII, chapter
xii.

V En Route (a)

Augustine was born in North Africa, in 354. Tradition
was later to round out the symmetry of things by holding that
Pelagius, against whom he was to inveigh so strongly, was
born the same year. He was converted to Christianity in 386,
and wrote the *Confessions* in 397, soon after becoming a
bishop. His *City of God* was written between 413 and 426,
following the sack of Rome by the Goths in 410. He died in
430.

His father, Patricius, was a pagan, who became converted not long before death, when Augustine was about
sixteen. His mother, Monica, now sainted, was a devout Christian, and apparently a woman of strong will, though she seems
to have got her way by petition rather than command, being
in no way imperious, but much given to devout practices and
prayer. Though Augustine says that she was an obedient wife,
he also says that she wanted him to grow up having God as
his father. Despite her earnest desires that Augustine become
a Christian, he had not been baptized when young, his
mother's notion being that, if his baptism was delayed, it might
wipe away sins committed before baptism, whereas if these
sins were committed after baptism they would count against
him to the maximum. Even though, during a grave illness and
fearing that he might die, he begged her to have him baptized,
she delayed, in accordance with her pious scheming.

And now, the steps:

At first, he says, all he "knew" (*noram*) was how to suck (*sugere*), to rest (*adquiescere*) and to cry (*flere*). The term "fill," that in the opening invocation had been applied to God (in His plenitude filling all Creation) is here applied literally to the milk that filled the breasts (*ubera implebant*) of the women who had nursed him. (I, VI) The connection is simultaneously established and put at one remove by his statement that God's abundance was thus channeled to the infant through such overflowing. A similar bridge between infancy and adult motivation is also explicitly supplied by a parallel he draws between the "consolations" of God's mercies (*consolationes miserationum tuarum*) and the "consolations" of human milk (*consolationes lactis humani*); also a reference to the "fountain of milk flowing and richly abounding" (*in fonte lactis ubertim manante atque abundante*) could remind us of his earlier reference to God as the "fountain of mercies" (*fons misericordiarum*), while it in turn suggests a reference (IX, iii) to God as not a fount but a mount, fertile and flowing with milk (*in monte incaseato, monte tuo, monte uberi*). In the opening invocation of Book IV, when deriding Manichaean views on food and holiness, he speaks of himself as sucking God's milk and eating of Him as a food that does not perish. Characteristically, when speaking of the Word made flesh (VII, xviii), he calls it a food whereby God's Wisdom (*sapientia*) might give milk (*lactesceret*) to our infancy. And when nearing conversion he likens the memory of God to the odor of an appetizing food that he smells but cannot eat.

Whether one ascribes such imagery to a strict identification in his own mind between ideas of God and ideas of nourishment, or treats it merely as the artful use of a Biblical tradition (see, for instance, I Peter 2:2, or John 6:27), the motive fits well with the strongly *oral* nature of his specialty as a rhetorician, ranging from his feel for words as such ("select as precious vessels") to thoughts of Christ the Word as "the goblet of our ransom." Augustine also indicates roundabout the strongly oral associations which words have for him when he finds it a matter of comment that Ambrose, besides his great gifts as a preacher, made it a habit to read solely with his eyes, "while voice and tongue were quiet" (*quiescebant*). Secondarily, we might recall here that it was Ambrose who most directly induced Augustine to abandon his earlier tendency to conceive of everything, perhaps after the fashion of the Stoics, as varying attenuations of the corporeal.

When he speaks of himself as having survived his infancy, which is said to have died though he lived on (a mode of expression he later also applies to his adolescence), perhaps we should examine this trope for traces of more than a mere literary conceit. In any case, he here uses it as transition into a somewhat Platonist speculation on the possibility that he may have had a life even prior to the period of memory-less, intra-uterine gestation—(*intra viscera matris meae*) that preceded his birth into infancy.

Infancy itself he considers essentially sinful, on the grounds that infants manifest rage, and even jealousy. He says that their so-called "innocence" derives not from their wills, but from their sheer physical weakness. They are "innocent" only in the literal sense that they cannot do the harm they would do if they could. Though the observation would go well with ideas of "infant depravity" and "original sin," Augustine does not discuss such matters here. Judged from the purely formal point of view, his remarks contribute to the consistency of the *Confessions,* by endowing even his infancy with its measure of sinfulness, as he concludes that in infancy he deserved to be rebuked, though he could not have understood a rebuke. But in adult years, he says, he would justly be derided and rebuked if he cried, not exactly for the breast (*non quidem uberibus*), but for food befitting his years (*escae congruenti annis meis*). Surprisingly, the Latin here uses not the conditional ("I should be derided and rebuked") but the simple future indicative ("I shall be . . .": *deridebor atque reprehendar*), though the second of these verbs could be interpreted as either future or conditional.

The major sin of his next phase was disobedience, due to curiosity and love of play. He says that such "curiosity" is also characteristic of the very adults who punish their children for it. While children were punished for being interested only in play, adults also merely trifled, though their toys were called "business." The word for "toys" or "trifles" here (*nugae*) he would later apply to his mistresses.

A notable feature of this stage is his stress upon the beatings he received in school, as a standard part of the educational process. The habit of flogging was currently "praised" (*laudabatur*), and though he prayed to God that he be spared such beatings, his parents laughed at him, as adults are laughed at for praying to God in times of great torment. The connection between "praise" and "God" is still visible here, but complicated by the wrangle of such derision. In any case, we can see how this experience helped make the association between chastening and flogging strong in him—and such a cluster of imagery seems to lie, in principle, behind his challenge, in the opening invocation of Book IV, inviting the derision of the arrogant who have not been "savingly cast down" by God "and stricken."

When discussing his early training in the standard pagan education of the times, on one occasion he even uses his characteristically bad word, "curiosity," in a good sense. He has been saying that he probably preferred Latin to Greek because he learned it without any "crucifying" (*cruciatu*), by merely taking notice (*advertendo*, a member of the "turn" family). He says that had Greek been his native language and had he been compelled to learn Latin by study, he doubtless would have preferred Greek literature. For a "free curiosity" seems to him a better help to learning than does "fear-laden compulsion" (*meticulosam necessitatem*)—but characteristically, he next observes that such restraints are good inasmuch as God's laws, from the rod of the schoolmaster to the trials of the martyrs, introduce a wholesome bitterness, to drive back whoever has strayed.

As regards Augustine's transgressions during adolescence (though in those days the age of sixteen would probably still be classed under *pueritia*): This was the stage of perfect "perversity," which he likens to a place of destitution (*regio egestatis*), doubtless in contrast with his idea of God as plenitude. Perversity (II, ix) is also associated with the idea of fellow-conspirators who take derisive delight in deception. Primarily it is a cult of evil for its own sake, and is thus the most extreme case of what Augustine always associates with evil, namely: anything sought for itself, whereas things should be sought only in terms of the search for God. "Perversity," as so defined is in effect the perfection of the idea of autonomy, if we may use the word "perfection" ironically.

"Perversity" was about the same thing as "subversion," the "subverters" (*eversores*) presumably being a band of rowdy students with whom he associated at Carthage and who took great delight in derision and deception, and in finding ways to "attack the modesty of strangers." He so intermingles his references to this intellectual gang with references to his "arrogance" at becoming head of the School of Rhetoric at Carthage, one might be justified in concluding that he equated his job itself with "subversion."

In calling Carthage a stew or frying pan of indecent amours, he may have intended a kind of pun (*Karthago-sartago*). In any case, the principle of autonomy in the bad sense now took the form of "being in love with love" (*amabam amare . . . amans amare*), "polluting the stream of friendship with the filth of concupiscence," while craving to be thought *elegans et urbanus*. It was clearly a time when his greatest ambition was to be smart. An admirer of Cicero, he derided (*inridebam*) the Christians.

Yet by jealousy, suspicion, fear, anger, and quarrels he
was beaten as with burning iron rods; and already he was
beginning to reveal his more serious tendencies by his growing interest in Manichaeanism. Augustine's long association
with the Manichaeans might conceivably be treated from the
dialectical point of view as a notable and necessary step along
his road to Christianity, but he characteristically saw it in the
light of his later fierce theological disputes with the Manichaeans. (Manichaeanism was to him what communism is to
an ardent ex-Communist.)

Looking back upon the motive of metropolitan smart-
ness, he writes (in rhetorical parallelism) of those who would
weep at the death of Dido for love of Aeneas, yet do not weep
at their own abandonment in failing to love God. Though
ashamed of the slightest barbarism or solecism in their speech,
he says, they were completely unconcerned with the rules for
salvation, and took pride in the praise they got for their
stylish ways of describing their own indecencies. He resents
it that the promise of praise and the threat of punishment were
used for training in secular verse, or that he had been praised
for declaiming in mock passion whereas praises of God might
have served as "supports for the vine-sprouts" of his heart
(*suspenderent palmitem cordis mei*—and incidentally note
that here again is another member of the "weight" or *pondus*
family, a terministic clan especially worth watching because
later, in a notable formula, he will equate his "weight" with
his "love").

His search for rhetorical elegance, which he explicitly
equates with the merchandising of words and grammar, leads
directly into the economic motive—and we should get a quite
false idea of Augustine (as of early theological controversy in
general) if we viewed his concern with salvation in terms too
exclusively "soulful." When a higher authority pronounced a
doctrine anathema, this usually meant the unseating of one
faction and the incumbency of another, unless the proponents

of the anathematized doctrine recanted or were strong enough
to establish a schism. Behind the battles of theology lie battles over jobs (though this is by no means the same as saying
that the battles of theology are reducible to battles over jobs).
Similarly, though Augustine's search is not even remotely reducible to sheerly economic terms, his motivation as a whole
clearly had a strong economic strand. For nearly fifteen
years, he worked at detestable jobs, and he says so.

Thus (in v, viii) he says that his "greatest and almost
only reason" for giving up his job at Carthage and going to
Rome was that the students were so unruly. His description
of the poor discipline in the classroom would be a solace to
any modern teacher who found it hard to keep order. Turbulence that should have been prohibited by law, he says, was
sanctioned by custom—and when he found himself suffering
as a teacher from the very unruliness that he had indulged in
when he was a student, he left for Rome where, he was assured, things were done differently.

Similarly, (v, xii) he later gave up his job at Rome for
one at Milan because of the "eversions" practised by the students, particularly a way they had of working in gangs to cheat
the schoolmaster of his fees. He hated them, he says, though
not with a "perfect hatred." (That is, he resented their conduct not on principle but for the inconvenience it caused him
personally.)

Again, there is a nauseated account (vi, vi) of the day
when he was preparing, in his role as rhetorician, to give a
speech in dishonest praise of the Emperor (a pagan task that,
nonetheless, helped fit him for the laudatory style he was soon
to develop so vibrantly in the I-Thou structure of his *Confessions*). It was a time, he says, when God derided (*inridebam*)
his desires for worldly honors, wealth, and marriage. And he
bitterly contrasts his care-laden ambitions with the real though
temporary delights of a drunken beggar whose antics that
same day he had watched with envy.

Also (vi, xiv), near the end of the experimenting that
preceded his conversion, he considered plans for a somewhat
communistic colony in which about ten of his group were to
live in retirement and at ease (*remoti a turbis otiose vivere*).
The colony was to include some persons of wealth, particularly a relative of his close friend, Alypius, one Romanianus,
whose recommendations carried special weight because his
funds were so much greater than the others'. But when the
men began to ask how their present or prospective women (the
somewhat dubious word *mulierculae* is used here) would take
to such a scheme, the plan fell through; and thus did God
deride (*deridebas*) their counsel.

However, he continues, in due course God was to open
his hand (*aperturus manum*) and to fill (*impleturus*) their
souls with blessings.

But the turn here to the thought of divine intercession
was characteristic of all the references to economic cause.
Thus, though he consciously left Carthage to get a better position at Rome, he says that God was making things miserable
for him at Carthage so that he might decide to clear out. Similarly, though he consciously left Rome for a better job in
Milan, after his conversion he assumed that God had planned
things thus in behalf of his spiritual betterment; for in Milan
he came to know the renowned Christian bishop Ambrose,
who received him *paterne* and *episcopaliter*. As Augustine
summed it up epigrammatically (v, xiii): He was unknowingly led *to* Ambrose *by* God that he might be knowingly led
by Ambrose *to* God (*ad eum autem ducebar abs te nesciens,
ut per eum ad te sciens ducerer*—any pagan orator would
have admired that structure). Likewise, recalling the period
of the laudatory oration, when he sought (*quaerebam*) to
please men not for purposes of instruction but merely to please,
he ends on a reference to Proverbs 20:15, on being beaten by
the rod of God's correction. The pattern was indicated in i,
xviii where, when on the subject of purely secular ambitions,

he has three "seeks" in one sentence (*quaerentem, quaesivi, requiram*), in line with a double motivation whereby God "plucks forth" (*erues*) from the immensest depth (*de hoc inmanissimo profundo*) the God-seeking soul. (He did not here consider the doctrine which he would later stress in his controversies with the Pelagians on the subject of grace and free will and according to which man cannot be turned towards God unless God was already turned towards man.)

VI   En Route (b)

As regards personal attachments: Under this head we should probably list the perverse theft described in Book II; for he makes clear that companionship was an important aspect of its motivation. We shall consider this matter further when we return to that chapter after analyzing the account of his conversion. In Book IV he writes poignantly of a male friend whose death, when Augustine was in his twenties, caused him intense grief. Incongruously, applying his idea of the ultimate religious goal, he says that he *came to rest* in bitterness (*requiescebam in amaritudine*), as he got comfort from weeping at his loss. This friend had been baptized when unconscious during illness. When he recovered, Augustine had expected to join him in deriding (*inridere*) the baptism, but his friend found it no laughing matter—and a few days later, when Augustine returned after an absence, his friend had had a relapse and died. They had been as one soul in two bodies, he says; and after the friend's death he felt but half alive. Though this is probably a reference to an expression (*animae dimidium meae*) in one of Horace's odes, there is no reason to believe that Augustine was merely being "literary" here. For Augustine often mentions states of internal divisiveness. In fact, his very stress upon the importance of the will was matched by a corresponding stress upon conflicts within the

will, a tension that increased as he approached the moment
of crisis in his conversion.

Yet in one sense there is a good "literary" reason why at
this point Augustine's account of the motives behind his conversion incorporated a quotation not from the Bible but from
a purely secular source in pagan poetry. For his close attachment "by the glue of love" to this friend whose death so
greatly unsettled him coincided with what we might call an
attempt at an "aesthetic" solution of his problems. About this
period, Augustine also wrote some books ("two or three, I
think," a revealing lapse of memory on the part of a man with
an exceptionally good memory) on beauty and fitness (*de
pulchro et apto*), identifying *pulchrum* with a kind of wholeness while by *aptum* he meant the relation of parts to the
whole or such accommodations as "when a shoe fits a foot."
However, though this design foreshadows the dialectic to
which he will eventually subscribe regarding the relation of
creatures to God as creator, he expressly notes that he chose
all his examples from the realm of the "corporeal."

Surely Book VI should be entitled "Of Alypius." If the
life of Augustine were to be made into a drama, this solemn,
loyal, deeply earnest fellow, who "clung" to him (*adhaesit*)
from the time they met in Rome, would be material for the
highest kind of comedy, a butt of laughter not "derisive" but
affectionate. Typically, when Augustine became converted,
only a few minutes passed before solemn, loyal, "me, too"
Alypius followed suit. If Augustine had decided to sell his
soul to the devil, doubtless in a flash Alypius would have done
likewise. At one stage, though he took no interest in women,
he even thought that maybe he should try to become involved
along these lines, he was so impressed by Augustine's intense
engrossment with female flesh. (Typically, Augustine attributed Alypius' notion to "curiosity.") When, since he had an
intense aversion to the gladiatorial games (*aversaretur et de-
testaretur talia*), some prankish friends forcibly dragged him

to the amphitheater, despite his high resolves he could not resist opening his eyes at the shout of the spectators witnessing the kill. He was "conquered by curiosity" (*curiositate victus*). He did not turn away (*non se avertit*), but despite himself morbidly fed his gaze on the sight of blood. And thereafter for a long time he could not resist these gruesome entertainments. (Admittedly, the comedy here would become strained, except insofar as one could play up Alypius' plight and play down the plight of the contestants.) But on one occasion, when Augustine happened to use the example of the gladiatorial games as illustration for a point he was making in rhetoric, Alypius (in a "whom the shoe fits" mood) took this as a sly dig at his own weakness, a misunderstanding which Augustine attributes to the workings of God, since it had the effect of leading Alypius to throw off his obsession.

The incident of this ultra-respectable citizen being mistaken for a thief and pursued by an angry mob suggests possibilities of the treatment that Shakespeare designed for Cinna the Poet in *Julius Caesar* (when the mob pursued him because they were enraged against Cinna the Conspirator). It would be funny because the misunderstanding was cleared up before it led to dire results.

Like Augustine, Alypius was much impressed by the Manichaeans' "show of continence." (vi, vii. *Continentia* is a highly important word in Augustine's scheme. Grammatically feminine, at the critical moment it becomes personified.) And when engaged in political activities, he profoundly scorned bribes (*inrisit animo*) though such corrupt practices were the norm. Augustine says explicitly (vi, xii) that Alypius prevented him from marrying, on the grounds that a marriage would have kept him and Alypius from living together, though Augustine did cite to him examples of married men who pursued wisdom, deserved well of God, and yet had been on good terms with friends.

Among other close associates, there was the group of ten

or so, apparently including Alypius, who met to discuss philo-
sophical and theological matters (and many or all of whom
presumably later became Christians). There were his mistresses, his "trifles" or "toys" (*nugae*), so improper that they
do not even rate proper names in the *Confessions*, though one
of them was the mother of his precocious son, Adeodatus.

This boy, who died early, is referred to anonymously in
connection with the statement that, his mother having planned
a marriage for Augustine, his mistress was dismissed forever
—though shortly after, since there would be a delay of two
years before the marriage was consummated, in the interim
Augustine found himself impelled to take on another mistress.
When the earlier mistress was sent away, he says, she left with
him his natural son, who had been born of him carnally, in sin
(*ex me natum carnaliter de peccato meo*). In the ninth book,
the son is mentioned once by name, in connection with his
baptism, his exceptional talent, his remarkable discourse with
Augustine as reported in the *De Magistro*, and his death
(which Augustine recalls with a feeling of security, in contrast
with the anguish he had felt over the death of his pagan friend
before Augustine had adopted the Christian views concerning
the promises of heaven).

Throughout the early chapters there is the important
figure of his mother, Monica, who seems to have prayed constantly for his salvation in the most exactingly spiritual sense
while also assiduously planning for him to make a good marriage in the wholly worldly sense. Somewhere in between,
there was her scheming whereby, for all her concern lest her
son fail to be saved, in his early years she would not consent
to his being baptized, even when he thought himself near
death. For, in accordance with the pious accountancy of those
days, she wanted to make sure that, if he did survive, he would
not have too many transgressions charged against him *after*
the purgative rites of baptism.

As regards the possible extent of her influence upon Augustine, there was first of all her meticulous piety, which included a great readiness to change her habits if told by her spiritual advisor to do so. This was a trait quite relevant to the fact that, just as Augustine was going through a wide range of temperamental and doctrinal experimentation, Christian organization and doctrine were still largely in solution, with many latitudinarian possibilities that were later to be pronounced anathema as the result of such controversies as Augustine himself would engage in with such brilliant fervor, following his conversion and ordination as a bishop. It was a time when even the Christian popes might openly reverse their pronouncements on doctrinal matters, since this was long before the doctrine of papal infallibility had been made law. (See, for instance, John Henry Blunt's *Dictionary of Sects, Heresies, Ecclesiastical Parties, and Schools of Religious Thought*, pp. 416-417 in the article on the Pelagians, where he notes how Zosimus under pressure flatly reversed his stand on the Pelagian doctrine of free will.)

From the standpoint of her possible influence upon Augustine (beyond, of course, her role as the particular mother who might most directly suggest to him an image for the Church as Mother and for God as overflowing breasts conceived in the absolute), her other most notable trait seems to have been her great concern with *portents*. And it is easy to see how such a stress upon the revealing of divine intent (in dreams, visions or natural circumstance) can lead readily to the idea of predestination. Early in his life, she had a dream of her son in connection with a *rule*. (Incidentally, in this dream she saw him laughing at her, *arridentem*, to our knowledge one of only two places in the *Confessions*, besides the previously discussed reference to infancy, where laughter is mentioned in a favorable sense.) She interpreted this dream as a good sign, indicating that he would eventually become a

Christian, and would abide by the only mode of life she considered regular. Judged as imagery which invites one to form oneself in its image, her conviction that she had read the signs correctly can be seen as quite suggestively persuasive, if communicated to a son who himself did much eager inquiring into the possibilities of astrological prophesying.

Later, when Augustine decided that astrology was nonsense, the most obvious remaining choices would be between doctrines of pure chance and such predestination as his mother had in mind, regarding her kind of Christian oneiromancy. And, prophesying *after* the event, we can now say for sure that, if Augustine's only choices were between chance and order, for all his temperamental turbulence he was temperamentally bound to choose order. And the idea of the ordained would attain its ultimate perfection in the idea of the pre-ordained. Also, on the sheerly theoretic level, he could find many Biblical texts to back this temperamental leaning with its theologic counterpart. Sheerly materialistic determinism would be rejected in the course of rejecting the Stoics' doctrine that all things could be reduced to terms of the corporeal, "mind" being conceived by them as but "body" in a diffuse form. And as for Lucretius' type of materialism, the world of his *De Rerum Natura* was not rigidly deterministic at all, "free will" residing in the atomic particles' ability to "lean" or "swerve" a bit from their "natural" line of fall.

His mother, also (to the satisfaction of herself and her son at least) proved her previsions to be accurate when, during a sea-voyage that frightened even the sailors, she calmly assured them that, in accordance with a dream of hers, they would land safely—and they did.

The quality of her prayers, as reported by Augustine, is also noteworthy, from the standpoint of her possible influence upon him. She did not ask, he says, "for gold or silver, or any transient or changing good," but simply for the salvation of her son's soul (*salutem animae filii sui*). Even though based on the notion that God was willingly made a debtor by his own promises (*etiam promissoribus debitor fieri*), such prayer as this was not along the lines of sheerly material benefit. And the fact that he once survived a dangerous illness though he had not asked for baptism is explained by him as indication that God must have spared him in response to the great piety and constant beseechings of his mother. (This incident makes an interesting match with the one previously mentioned, where she herself delayed his baptism though he had begged for it.)

He says that when she prayed, God was present, and was hearing and doing in the order (mark that word) in which he had predestined that these things would be done (*aderas et exaudiebas et faciebas ordine, quo praedestinaveras esse faciendum*). It is a place to remember when we study the idea of Order in the next essay, on "The First Three Chapters of Genesis." Such "predestination" is but the principle of order made absolute (something done, or "perfect," before beginning), while at the same time such order is conceived as unfolding in terms of temporal sequence, like a Chinese paper flower dropped into water. As finally worked out by Augustine, we might say it was by God preordained that God would give Monica the grace to pray of her own free will for Augustine so earnestly that God would respond by granting her prayers in his behalf, thereby, in turn, giving Augustine the grace to pray and persevere of his free will. (The circular nature of such terms for combining ideas of grace, free will and predestination will be considered "logologically" in the next essay on Genesis.)

In any case after first taking astrology seriously and then "deriding" it, Augustine would wholly parallel his mother's views in his conviction that his development, like all development, was divinely guided, an attitude which, looking back in the light of his conversion, he formulated economico-theologically thus (IV, x): All things proceed from their "indebted" beginning to their "indebted" end (*ab initio debito*

usque ad finem debitum)—and in the Word by which God
created them they hear the from-what and the to-what (*hinc
et huc usque*). Looking back, he felt that the locally famous
Faustus' inadequacy as a propounder of Manichaean doctrine
was part of God's design since, in disappointing Augustine's
hopes for cogent explanations, Faustus contributed to Augustine's conversion.*

The divine scheming had gone still further. Recall, in
Joyce's *Portrait of the Artist as a Young Man*, how love of
language figures in Stephen's apostasy from Catholicism to
aestheticism. Though having lost his belief in the Bible as
doctrine, Stephen still savours the words for their style. This is
nearly the reverse of Augustine's course. At first Augustine
listened to Ambrose purely through professional admiration
for him as a speaker, being interested in the manner rather
than the matter of his sermons. Yet imperceptibly, unknowingly (*sensim et nesciens*) he was being drawn closer to belief;
and about three years before his conversion, while still methodically doubting, largely under Ambrose's influence he
decided to become a catechumen in the Catholic Church.

Conjointly with his gradually forming ideas on free will
and predestination (ideas that amounted to something like
the proposition that man is free by his own free will to will in
accordance with the providence and predeterminations of a
God who will have mercy on whom He will have mercy, and

---

* Doctrinally, of course, Augustine built his theory of grace, free
will and predestination around Biblical sources, particularly the Epistles
of Paul, whose teachings did so much to transform Christianity from a
simple evangelical religion into the kind of organization best adapted
to Roman conditions of empire. We can note how Monica's general
attitude on the subject of divine intervention in the affairs of mankind
coincides with Augustine's complicated theological theories, but there is
no indication that she herself was versed in such lore. Though the attitude may be linked with her, the intellectual development of his doctrines seems to have been part of the long "inquisition" which he began,
in connection with speculations largely outside the orbit of Christianity
(except insofar as Christianity, under the influence of thinkers like Augustine, later adapted such thinking to its own purposes).

without Whose grace no one wills rightly though able freely
to will to sin if God abandons him), there were these other
notable motivational strains (doctrinal positions strongly related to the sheer corporeality of the human animal): (1) a
dialectic of part and whole conceived along Platonist lines;
(2) the need to find a substitute for the Manichaean doctrine
of evil (hence the resonant refrain, *Unde malum?*); (3) the
adding of an intensely tragic principle (mediation by divine
scapegoat) to the Platonists' theories of the Word.

As we have seen, in his aesthetic phase there was his
stress (IV, xiii) upon the part's accommodation to the whole
(*universum suum*—nor should we fail to note that the word
for "whole" here is a member of the fate-laden *vert*-family).
Aquinas was later to modify Augustine's Platonist stress, by
pointing in the direction of Aristotle's devices for admitting
such principles of specialization as the ever-increasing division
of labor would make more and more necessary. At the beginning of IV, x, the pattern is explicitly related to the *vert*-
family when, after calling upon God to "convert us," he says
that wherever (*quoquoversum*) the soul turns (*se verterit
anima*) it is affixed to sorrows unless it is turned towards
God (Who is, of course, the unitary principle). Or (IV, xi),
the soul is said to be "perverse" in following its own flesh,
whereas the flesh should be "converted" to follow the soul,
which in turn must look not towards the particularities of the
body but towards the wholeness of God. He also associates
this dialectic with his verbal interests, as he next likens the
flesh to the syllables of a sentence, which must successively
fly past (*transvolare*) in order that the sentence may be
heard as a whole. Presumably God would correspond here to
the *meaning* of the sentence.

A bit earlier, the "lowest universe" (*infima universitas*)
was said to attain its completion by such a constant passing
of its parts. Now the talk of parts and wholes leads into talk
of the search for rest (*requies*), while forms of *quaero* here

appear five times within a space of fourteen words. The
part-whole relation is theologized in the proposition that
whatever is from God is loved unjustly if God is deserted in
the loving of it (*iniuste amatur deserto illo quidquid ab illo
est*). Just before the end of this book, there is another passage where reference to the part-whole relation leads into a
quite emphatic use of the *vert*-family. Insofar as we are
turned away (*aversi*) from God, we are perverted (*perversi*).
We should return (*revertamur*), lest we be overturned (*ut
non evertamur*). A few lines previously, Augustine had been
discussing the *perversitas* of those who are *adversum* God. At
another point he says: At a time when his soul went "crooked
ways," instead of loving God's beauty for its sake (*gratis*) he
loved his friends for their sakes and knew himself to be loved
for his sake.

At another point he says, "By my own swelling I was
separated from Thee" (*tumore meo separabar abs te*), a
variant of the Stoic admonition against the "abscess," the part
that withdraws from the whole. Though, from the standpoint of a Marcus Aurelius, Christianity itself had seemed
like such an "abscess," from the standpoint of emergent
Catholicism paganism stood for the principle of separation.
Christianity provided a new synthesis, in contrast with the
clutter of local deities that marked the dying paganism.
However, that hodgepodge had been liberally tolerant of
religious differences, the usual procedure being simply to
bring the local god of each conquered tribe to Rome, set
up an appropriate temple, thus centrally located, in his honor
and allow for full freedom of worship, if only the devotees
back home paid their taxes on time. It had been a fairly
mellow scheme, even in its decay, but it had been cantanker-
ously challenged by both the Christians and the Jews, who
would not concede the right of any God but theirs.

This part-whole dialectic was related to the motive of
corporeality in accordance with the trend that St. Thomas

Aquinas, many centuries later, would epitomize in his definition of matter as the "principle of individuation." The bodily was the separate, the partitive, analogous to the individual syllables of the words in a sentence, of which the meaning or spirit in its non-temporal wholeness transcended the passing temporal physicality of the syllables' audibility, in their successive rise and fall.

Metaphysical speculations on corporeality had an immediate motivational force, with Augustine, in connection with his attachment to the women who, whatever their contribution to him as steps along his way, don't even rate names. Yet maybe we should not be so exacting along these lines. Perhaps if we knew what to build on, we might find roundabout that the names of his mistresses, those "trifles," those so strenuously hungered-after *nugae*, are ambiguously lurking in odd places throughout the text, like partially overgrown initials carved on trees. But we should have to know the names in the first place, in order to begin guessing which words might be their punning, enigmatic transformation. In the autobiography of a great verbalizer to whom the feel of words meant so vibrantly much, such disguised confessions are almost certain to be present. Intimacy with a woman must always argue special intimacy with some word or words like or nearly like the sound of her name. So probably they are there, shining out like unseen stars, ambiguously split perhaps between terms in the constellation of the divine and terms for the problematic body.*

* The author might here make a "logological" confession: He inclines to the notion that the adjective for "modest" (*modica*) is Augustine's pun-name for "Monica." And the similarly enigmatic name for himself would be the word for "strait" or "narrow": *angustus*. Terms connected with his aesthetic period or with Manichaeanism would be the most relevant hiding place for the names of his "toys"; or the word *nuga* itself is a possibility. We say all this merely to indicate how certain expressions of an author might have "personalities" that are nearly impossible to detect, and even harder to prove. But the likelihood is that such "enigmas" do figure as a strand in a writer's terminology.

The change that was to take place at the moment of
conversion had unquestionably come closer when Augustine
learned how Ambrose applied Paul's distinction between the
letter that killeth and the spirit that giveth life. Here was
the doctrinal principle that enabled him to transform his
earlier theoretical stress upon the corporeality of beauty and
God, a transformation that somehow paralleled a temperamental change whereby he permanently abandoned not only
mistresses but also the thought of marriage. Doctrinally, the
line would be from the formula in St. Paul, to Ambrose's
habit of interpreting Old Testament passages as prophetic of
the New Testament rather than simply as they were on their
face; next would be the stress upon the incorporeal in the
Platonists' doctrine of the Word; and finally there would be the
kind of corporeality-with-a-difference that characterized the
Christian doctrine of the Word made flesh. The Manichaeans,
Augustine observes, had no doctrine of the Word; the Platonists did have, but without the Christian stress upon the
Word as incarnate and sent to perform the sacrificial office
of mediation between two qualitatively different realms, the
natural and the supernatural.

Even before his conversion, he says, he had finally
abandoned his earlier views of God as infinitely corporeal
(though even when conceiving of God as corporeal, he had
not assumed that God had the form of a human body). Also,
he had abandoned the Manichaean doctrine of the reality
of evil (the doctrine that good and evil were rival powers
competing for supremacy, and that nature accordingly was
permeated with an intrinsically evil principle, a teaching
categorically denied in the first chapter of Genesis where all
of nature is explicitly said to be "good"); but he says that
he was being "suffocated" by his attempts to account for evil
otherwise. The writings of the Platonists were leading him
towards Christian doctrine both by their stress upon the in-
corporeality of ideas and by their omitting of the sacrificial

principle (the doctrine of the perfect scapegoat) that would center in the Christian stress upon the Crucifixion.

When originally planning this essay, the author had intended simply to build the analysis of the form around the critical moment in the garden. Everything should be shown as leading up to and away from that moment. But when he began analyzing the development in detail, he came in for a surprise. It finally dawned on him that the development is not analyzable simply as a "conversion" in general, but must be treated as a specifically *Trinitarian* conversion.

This discovery brought up a problem. Since much of the text had been analyzed without reference to this distinction between conversion in general and specifically Trinitarian conversion, should it be revised in the light of the qualification which the author encountered en route? Or might the author's theories be better illustrated if the original confusion were left, along with the report of the point at which the new position suggested itself?

The second method is being followed. Hence, in this study of conversion, the reader is given an opportunity to observe how the author's own thesis "becomes converted." In particular, the change involves the matter of Augustine's relations to his mistresses. We have just been suggesting that the change was somehow implicit in Augustine's altered views on matter and evil. He had ceased to believe that the spiritual is but an attenuated form of the corporeal, and that nature is intrinsically permeated by an evil principle. And we have suggested that his attachment to his mistresses was somehow connected with these doctrines, which stem from the aesthetic and Manichaean stages of his development. Yet, though he says that these changes in doctrine had already taken place, along with the addition of the scapegoat principle to the Platonist doctrine of the Logos, the critical moment in the garden had not yet taken place.

In brief, accepting the usual Trinitarian equations

(Father equals Power, or Authority, *Potestas;* Son equals Wisdom; Holy Spirit equals Love), we might say that a crucial transformation under the sign of the third person still had to happen, before his mistresses could be definitively abandoned. We might say that Augustine had already been converted in the areas of the first and second persons, except for the notable fact that the first two orders of motivation could not have their full Trinitarian reality until rounded out by the third, whereupon all three click into place. (In his *De Trinitate,* v, xi, Augustine gives the theological equivalent of this formula, in saying that we can't properly call the Trinity either the Father or the Son, but the Trinity can be called the Holy Spirit because it is a communion of Father and Son.) This third motive must involve a *transference* of love from one kind of object to another (in this case, from "corporeal" objects to a "spiritual" object).

VII   Whence Evil?

Before our matching of the "perversion" and "conversion" chapters, one topic must be considered further, as regards Augustine's stages. This concerns his agonized wrestling with the problem of evil, a problem that plagued him with new intensity, the nearer he came to the moment of hysterical weeping that would mark the "critical point" of his conversion.

To common sense, the expression "problem of evil" usually suggests the question: How get the evil out of the world? But for Augustinian theology, the question is quite the reverse: How can evil get into the world? For if God is good and His creation is good, "Whence Evil?" (*Unde malum?*)

"And I sought (*quaerebam*) the source of evil (*unde malum*), and I sought it evilly (*male*); and in that very search of mine (*in ipsa inquisitione mea*) I did not see the evil" (vii, v). The Manichaean doctrine that evil was outside himself was an impiety that had divided himself against himself (*adversum me . . . me diviserat*). But in renouncing the Manichaean doctrine of moral evil as a power in nature itself, outside the individual, he flatly confronted the problem of explaining how evil could arise in a Creation that is by definition good. If God fills (*implet*) all, what could be the root, the seed of evil?

In Book v, after the invocation to a God "either pitying or vengeful" (*aut miserans aut vindicans*), when he is describing the tentatives of his twenty-ninth year, we can see his theory of evil (as regards its imagery, at least) emerging out of his concern with the Manichees. They had learned how to predict accurately eclipses of the sun, he says, but could not perceive the lack of light in their own doctrines. The Latin word for "eclipse" being *defectus*, the Manichaeans were described by him as deficient in God's light (*deficientes a lumine tuo*). That is, they were in partial eclipse.

Thus, in contrast with the Manichaean doctrine of two rival powers, Good and Evil (the powers of Light and Darkness), equally substantial and confronting each other in universal combat, Augustine would contend after his conversion that good alone is real, an *e*fficient cause, while evil is but a *de*ficient cause, that is, an *eclipse* of goodness. Thus, the notion of evil as a mere absence of good in a world of goodness could borrow strength from analogy with the notion of darkness as the absence of light in a world grandly shined on by the ever-blazing sun.

At another point (v, vii), when discussing how God orders the steps of a man's life, Augustine rounds out the pattern by the sheer resourcefulness of Latin prefixes, in saying that salvation comes only through God's remaking what he had made already (*reficientem quae fecisti*). This alignment would allow for distinguishing the de-ficient, re-ficient, and (ef)ficient. Our point is, however, that whereas these words in general are forms of a word for "making" (*facio*),

the one of them that he applies to evil (*deficiens*) gives such
"de-making" or "un-making" a kind of imagistic suggestive-
ness borrowed from the notion of darkness as the mere
absence of light (with light being the only one of the pair
that exists as an actual power, and darkness being a kind of
"eclipse" that does not at all impair the power of the source
from which the light is derived). This metaphorical re-enforcement of the idea would be all the stronger owing to the
traditional equating of truth with light.

In his essay on Beauty and Fitness, Augustine seems to
have struck a stage halfway between sheer aesthetics and
Manichaean theology. For he says that he there equated
peace with virtue, love and unity; and he equated discord
with vice, hate and division (IV, xv). He called unity a
monad, and division a dyad. He had thought of such unity
as the rational soul, "without sex," and an unchanging good.
But he had also thought of the divisive dyad as a kind of
substance (and in this respect, obviously, his monad-dyad
distinction had a Manichaean slant). The presumption would
also seem to be that the discordant dyad was not *sine ullo
sexu*, particularly since it was marked by passions and lust
(*libidinem in flagitiis*).

The image of the eclipse gains re-enforcement from
imagery of a quite different order (VII, xvi). For when he
vindicates God by situating evil within the human will, he
speaks of the will as "casting out its bowels and swelling in-
wardly" (*proicientis intima sua et tumescentis foras*). Here
is a puzzling variation on the Augustine theme of inwardness.
The first part of the expression is apparently an oblique
reference to Ecclesiasticus 10:9: "There is not a more wicked
thing than to love money; for such a one setteth even his own
soul to sale: because while he liveth he hath cast away his
bowels" (*proiecit intima sua*). Here the things "innermost"
(*intima*) are equated with the "lowest" (*infima*); and there
seems to be not even an oblique reference to money in Augus-

tine's lines (except, of course, insofar as the figure arises out of such a context in Ecclesiasticus). The usual associations in the case of *tumesco* concern swelling with pride. Thus, any attempt to associate evil here explicitly with connotations of defecation and sexual tumescence must be far-fetched, except along the lines of Freud's "cloacal" theory according to which the sexual, diuretic and excremental functions are readily confused with one another in the realm of imagery. And at another point (VII, ii), Augustine does approvingly cite a friend who had said with regard to the Manichaeans' doctrine that God's creation was so turned (*verteretur*) from goodness to misery as to need purging (*purgari*): It should be abominated, and they themselves should be vomited up. In any case, the passage with the oblique reference to Ecclesiasticus explicitly situates evil in the will's "perversity" (*voluntatis perversitatem*).

Augustine's sense of suffocation came at the stage where, having situated moral evil in free will (*liberum voluntatis arbitrium*), he asked how a good God had made him capable of willing to do evil, or had made an angel that, by some perversion of the will, chose to become a devil eager to tempt him.

Logologically, when (in VII, iii) he reduces the problem to a kind of choice between Yes and No ("willing and not willing"—*velle ac nolle*), we would here salute the emergence of that linguistic marvel, the negative, whereby men can say "thou shalt not" not only to one another, but also scrupulously even to themselves. There is thus a very real sense in which the logological slant on the unreality of evil would parallel Augustine's theological doctrine: Moral evil arises not from the "positives" of natural existence, but from hortatory resources embedded in the negative, which *qua* negative is not "positively real," its only "reality" in the "positive" sense being in the sound or look of the word, or in the neural vibrations needed for thinking of it. Since it is "what man adds to

nature," and since it defines the discriminatory nature of an
act (the yes or no that make the difference between will and
will-not), in this sense it is a function of the "will." Or, more
accurately, as we shall see in the next article, the ideas of
act, will and the negative mutually imply one another.

We also find it of moment that, while worrying over the
problem of evil, Augustine comes flatly upon a paradigm of
dominion (vII, vii) which here lines up as follows: Augustine
is superior to the various things that are in their places in
the world; he is inferior to God; while he is subjected to
God, the things that God created are subjected to him; by
serving God he acquires dominion over the body; if he resists
God, even inferior things become placed above him, to press
upon him, leaving him no room to breathe. As we shall consider at length in the next article when discussing the idea
of Order, the principle of negativity is intrinsic to dominion,
owing to the role of the negative in the forming of laws.

At another point (vII, v), after puzzling on the nature
of evil, he ends with the remark that his faith in Christ was
growing. This statement could be interpreted simply as meaning that he was on the road to the Christian doctrine of evil.
Or it could be taken as a further indication that he would
need the idea of a divine scapegoat as a solution for his
problem (since Christ as perfect victim provides the Mediatory role which, he says, was not present in the Logos of
the Platonists). This matter, too, will be discussed at length
in our next essay. For both of these themes (dominion and
the principle of sacrifice) are logologically implicated in the
idea of the "free will" and its perverse "temptations."

After his conversion, Augustine was to battle as strongly
against the Pelagians on one side as against the Manichaeans
on the other. They were a faction somewhat liberally inclined who apparently wanted to play down the idea of a
Divine Scapegoat, identification with whose passion was
necessary to man's salvation. Hence their denial of the "origi-

nal sin" that, in the Pauline scheme, makes the crucifying of Christ so necessary to human redemption. Shying away from the rigorous doctrine of election and reprobation that Augustine built so powerfully into his teachings on predestination, they stressed instead the somewhat moderate idea that anybody would be allowed into heaven if he but decided of his own free will to live virtuously, and persevered in his decision. Judged even as a doctrine that would contribute purely to the ends of secular governance, the Pelagian scheme lacked the powerful symmetry of the Pauline-Augustinian view whereby all sacrificial motivation came to a head in the stress upon one supernal sacrifice. The difference was like that between a moderately comfortable dwelling and an imposingly mighty architectural pile built for the grandiose ritualizing and commemoration of vindicatory motives, across the sweep of centuries.

Looking over Augustine's long series of quests, questions, and "inquisitions," we see the self-portrait of an inquirer who, though he did not say so in so many words, had experimented tirelessly. Infant spontaneity; childish play; adolescent perversity; imaginative engrossment in the poetry of Rome and Greece; aesthetic liberalism; amours both rowdy and conscience-laden; metropolitan careerism as a rhetorician (a mixture of teaching and salesmanship); astrology; skepticism or systematic doubt (in the style of the Academics); Stoicism (the basic philosophy that went with the Roman cult of governance, and that he would exemplify almost unthinkingly, for though the Stoics as such are not mentioned, he does speak of having been greatly influenced by the moralism of Cicero's *Hortensius,* a work strongly tinged with the Stoic spirit of bureaucracy); "colony-thinking" (if we may so designate the kind of intellectual association that nearly led to the outright setting up of a communal establishment); Manichaeanism; the Platonists; and even a touch of Aristotelianism, as with his thoughts on Aristotle's *Categories,* though he found the discussion of various natural "substances" so irrelevant to the subject of the "simple and unchangeable God" that the four paragraphs of the chapter (IV, xvi) in which this matter is discussed all begin, in derisive rhetorical insistence, with the same refrain: "What did it profit me . . . ?" He was too strenuously Christianizing Plato to find anything but incipient neglect of God in the thought of Christianizing Aristotle (the task that would be undertaken a millennium later by Aquinas).

One might even say that Augustine was spokesman for many varied positions, one after the other; and though all of them had contributed vitally to his development, he represented them with varying reservations or degrees of ill will, in terms of the position he had finally arrived at. Of the others, the Platonists come out best (or least badly). But while conceding that they helped him make the step from his earlier corporeal emphasis to a stress upon the search for incorporeal truth (*quaerere incorpoream veritatem*), he suggests that, had he begun as a Christian, the Platonists might have started him going in the opposite direction, away from Christianity (VII, xx). Thus, he says, God led him to encounter Platonism first, and thereby to have impressed upon his memory the difference between presumption (as a Platonist proud of his knowledge) and confession (as a Christian). He does not say how this observation should be applied to others; he draws no conclusions beyond the thought that the order for him was in accordance with God's designs concerning him.

All told, as we sum up the stages from his infancy to the point where the cluster of incidents immediately surrounding the moment of conversion itself is described, we have (VI, x) "an ardent seeker after the good life" (*beatae vitae inquisitor ardens*) and "a most acute scrutinizer of the most difficult questions" (*quaestionum difficillimarum scrutator acerrimus*). His mind was "intent on questioning and restless for dispute" (*ad quaerendum intentus et ad disserendum inquietus*). Such was his own formula for himself, at the approach of his sudden transformation; and it referred to a kind of inquietude that would be with him to the end, however restful it might be in comparison with the days of fluctuancy prior to that stage which, he says, doctors call a crisis, and which his mother had prophesied he would have to pass through before attaining spiritual health.

We are now ready to consider, in direct contrast, Book II on "perversity" and Book VIII on "conversion." The conversion we shall try to consider from the standpoint of a condensed design. The perversity we shall treat of in the style of a *quaestio* in Aquinas' *Summa*.

VIII   Adolescent Perversity

On the Stealing of the Pears, as recounted in Augustine's *Confessions*, Book II. (Treated after the fashion of a *Quaestio* in the *Summa Theologica* of Thomas Aquinas.)

Question: Whether the Stealing of the Pears was Important.

Objection 1. The stealing of the pears was not important. It was but a childhood prank, not worthy of more than mild regret. There is no evidence that anyone suffered from it, since the pears were not good for eating anyhow. And such inferior pears should have been thrown to the pigs, whereas otherwise they might have been allowed to rot.

Objection 2. The stealing of the pears could not have been important. For despite Augustine's great eloquence and clarity, he himself never succeeds in showing why it was of importance.

Objection 3. The stealing of the pears was important only in the sense that so minor a peccadillo could play a part in so great a reformation, by being treated as grounds for keen repentance.

On the contrary, Augustine says of the theft: "For thus pride imitates high estate, whereas Thou alone art God, high above all." (*Nam et superbia celsitudinem imitatur, cum tu sis unus super omnia deus excelsus.*)

I answer that: St. Augustine being greatly sensitive to symbolism, as attested by his episcopal ministry with its attendant scruples, he could feel that this act (the stealing of the pears) *stood for* motives much profounder than would show on its face.

This was *his* equivalent of *Adam's* first sin. However, the sin was first not in the sheerly *temporal* sense, but in the sense of being a *foremost* or *representative* sin, in the sense in which a *title* might be considered foremost or representative.

It was his foremost sin because it was, in substance, the complete perversion, or perfect parody, of his religious motives.

It was such a parody because, first, it was a "free" or "gratuitous" crime (*gratuitum facinus*). That is, it was an act done not for some sheerly utilitarian gain, but out of pure dedication to crime for its own sake. This would be a perfect parody of acts motivated not by any merely worldly hope of profit, but in terms of the Wide Beyond, as with acts done for the love of God.

Second, the stealing of the pears involves a delight in the fact that the act was sanctioned by a group of like-minded associates, a *consortium peccantium* (whereby it became in effect a conspiracy). This would be a perfect parody of Brotherhood within the Church.

Third, while recognizing a wide range of "lusts," and while being aware that the first offence was not explicitly sexual but an act of disobedience (or "pride") in general, elsewhere in the *Confessions* St. Augustine is at pains to show why, in his opinion, sexual concupiscence is particularly to be stressed.* And insofar as "forbidden fruit" has this same ambiguous meaning, there would be a sexual motive implicit in both of these "first" or "foremost" transgressions. However, insofar as the act, considered sheerly as *imagery*, contained the hint of sexual motives, the inference would be that, since the young thieves were a band of males joined together by some communicative bond, the translation of such a sinister brotherhood into its erotic analogues would stress the narcissistic and the homosexual—and love, as so conceived, would be a perfect parody of the fond mutuality prevailing among the male persons of the Trinity.

Similarly, in the absolute unfruitfulness of such an offence, undertaken for no pragmatic purpose, but for its own sake, (or we might say, enacted "reflexively," as with the grammatical reflexive, that refers to an act directed back upon the agent), here would be the perfect parody of monastic motives generally.

All told, the incident is somewhat analogous to the place in Eliot's *Murder in the Cathedral,* when the Fourth Tempter tempts the Saint in the Saint's own words.

Reply to Objection 1. The stealing of the pears is to be considered in two senses. Considered in itself, it is merely a childhood prank. But in its nature as *representative* of conditions quite beyond itself, it can in its way be as heinous as was the original representative transgression of Adam, which likewise was trivial, if we ignore its *symbolic* nature (since there can be no such thing as a *morally* poisonous tree, except insofar as any naturally good material thing can be used for unethical ends).

Reply to Objection 2. The Philosopher says (*Nichomachaean Ethics,* III, i) that there are six ways in which a

---

* In *City of God* (XIV, xvi), Augustine notes that whereas lust may have many objects, if no object is mentioned we usually assume that the lust is sexual.

man may be ignorant of the circumstances of an act. He may be ignorant of who he is, what he is doing, what or whom he is acting on, what he is doing it with, or to what end and how he is doing it. Thus, though an agent will usually know more about an act than does anyone else, there is a sense in which new light can be thrown upon the act long after its enactment. Such light has been thrown upon the psychology of the gratuitous crime by the recently deceased novelist, André Gide, who was a profound and scrupulous student of "immoralism," and who made much of the *acte gratuit*, the motiveless crime done not for material gain but for its own sake, through sheer love of the art. (Variants of this concern also motivated French Existentialists such as Sartre, and the proto-Existentialist, Dostoevsky.)

Gide stresses the homosexual aspects of such motivation. Sartre and Dostoevsky (and another proto-Existentialist, Nietzsche) bring out the ways in which (as with the Superman, or the cult of suicide) a human being attains the technical equivalent of godhead (in being absolute master of one's destiny). The specifically sexual analogue of such independence, wherein one acts reflexively back upon the self, would be of narcissistic cast, as with the perverse pride described by Augustine in this book.

Reply to Objection 3. The stealing of the pears could not have been a peccadillo in Augustine's case. For if he was so predestined that subsequently he would lay great stress upon this offence, then he might have shown his election by already, as a youth, having some inkling of the importance he would later attribute to it. The offence must have had some strange importance then, a foreshadowing of the importance it would have later. Here we would link Augustinian predestination with a Leibnizian variant of the Aristotelian entelechy. Note also that Augustine's most succinct formulation of his motive flatly states it as the complete perversion of salvation: "*Amavi perire* (I loved to perish)," he says, in a near-pun that happens by accident to survive in the English translation (if we are entitled to hear "pear" in the "perish," and *pirum* in *perire*).

Review of relevant details in the text of Book II:

He was "turned away" (*aversus*) from God. (i) His pleasure was only in "loving and being loved" (*amare et amari*). (ii) God was "mercifully angry" (*misericorditer saeviens*). (iii) In iii, the theme of perversity is introduced in connection with his sexual development, purely from the standpoint of his physique, at the age of sixteen. The brambles of his lust (*vepres libidinum*) grew higher than his head. In the same chapter, when equating the perverse will with abject inclinations (as though affected by an "invisible wine"), he formulates in accordance with the mode of thought that leads him to distrust "curiosity," namely: the sin of becoming so attached to a creature of God's that one neglects the thought of God as the creator (a passage that leads into mention of a contrasting state: his mother's breast as a temple in which God already dwelt). Among his equals he was "ashamed to be less shameless." He took pleasure in his transgressions, not for the pleasure of the doing but for the praise. He lied, saying he had sinned when he hadn't, lest he appear more abject because he was more innocent, or might not seem more vile because he was more chaste.

He speaks of companions with whom he rolled in the filth (in *caeno*) of the streets of Babylon.*

Though neither hungry nor poor, he stole through sheer preference for injustice and an appetite for evil. (iv) He desired not the things he took, but the theft and sin as such

---

* In the dialogue with his son "Concerning the Teacher," Adeodatus is reported as noting that by but a single letter we can change the word for "filth," *caenum*, into the word for "heaven," *caelum*. (Note also that the *ae* of these two words is sometimes changed to *oe*.) The notion of "imitation" in the sense of parody or reduction to absurdity might be treated as the "grand" counterpart of Adeodatus' concern with such a slight difference that makes all the difference.

(*ipso furto et peccato*). The pear tree was heavily laden with
fruit (*pomis*) that had neither flavor nor appearance to recom-
mend it. They stole, not to eat, but to throw the stolen things
to the swine (*proicienda porcis*). The act was all the more
pleasing in that it was illicit (*quo non liceret*).

He was seeking only to be "gratuitously evil" (*gratis
malus*). Note that we have here a parody-like variant of his
word for "grace." The cause of his evil was nothing but the
evil itself (*malitiae meae causa nulla esset nisi malitia*). He
loved to perish (*amavi perire*). He loved his error (*amavi
defectum meum*—the noun here being, you will note, also the
word for "eclipse"). He loved not that for which he erred
(*deficiebam*), but the error as such. In his shame he sought
nothing but the shame itself. In chapter v he scans a broad
list of reasons for the committing of crimes: the various
honors, powers, goods, privileges, advantages, vengeance, etc.
that might tempt one to commit crimes. The implication is
that his own transgression in stealing the pears was not
motivated in this pragmatic or utilitarian sense. Hence its
ultimate perversity. Such an unmotivated act would be a
travesty of the divine since, according to Augustine, we can
assign no motive to God's act in creating the world. For any
motive would limit God's omnipotence.

In chapter vi there is a double jolt. The chapter begins
joltingly, "What, then, in my wretchedness, did I love in
Thee . . . !" But promptly thereafter, this jolt is rectified by
another jolt, this time corrective, as the next words make us
realize that he is not confessing to *God* but is apostrophizing
his *sin:* "O my Theft, O that Crime of mine at night" (*o furtum
meum, o facinus illud meum nocturnum*). Here again, in a
way, there is a shift like that between *caenum* and *caelum*,
or between "imitation" as humble obedience and "imitation"
as parody. Three lines further along, the object of address
has again become God. But now his "policy" towards the
pears changes somewhat, for they are referred to as beautiful.

(He is stressing their nature as creations of God, whereas previously, when recounting his theft of them despite their inferior quality, he was discussing them "in themselves" rather than in terms of their creator. The dialectics of the case has here led him to a different slant.) Further, in now stressing their appeal, he uses this emphasis as a way of reaffirming his main design, to the effect that he stole them, not to have the pears, but simply that he might be stealing (*tantum ut furarer*), the sole gratification being his own sin. Then he re-establishes the earlier pattern in saying that, if he ate any, it was only the crime itself that made them taste good (*condimentum ibi facinus erat*).

Next follows an impassioned passage restating his dialectic in its most direct form, as he asserts that all the aims we seek in our ambitions and our vices are to be attained only through the search for God. (Here, "curiosity" also comes in for its usual taking down, inasmuch as its search for knowledge lacks the proper stress on the comprehensiveness of God.) Then his formula attains completion: "So fornicates the soul" (*ita fornicatur anima*) when it is turned away from God (*cum avertitur abs te*) and seeks outside of God (*quaerit extra te*) those things which it finds limpid and pure only when it returns to God.* All things imitate God perversely (*perverse te imitantur*)—the clearest evidence for our proposed equation: "perversity" equals "parody"—when they put themselves apart from God and raise themselves up against him (*adversum te*). A few lines further along, he again returns to the statement that in his offence he had "perversely imitated" (*perverse imitatus*) the Lord. Such imitation was managed by his doing the impermissible "in a shadowy likeness to omnipotence" (*tenebrosa omnipotentiae similitudine*).

* "Fornication" is his word for any interest not directly motivated in terms of God as over-all motive. Thus, in the diagram that accompanies our next essay, this resonant "technical" word will be matched against "mortification," the term for the "slaying" of all such unruly trends.

In vii he introduces glancingly his theory of grace. God's grace melted his sins like ice, he says. And to God's grace he also ascribes whatever evils he did not do, an area that might otherwise have been vast, inasmuch as he had loved crime for its own sake (*gratuitum facinus amavi*). Next he "confesses" that he has been forgiven both the evils that he did of his own volition (*mea sponte*) and the ones he didn't do as the result of God's guidance (*te duce*). This is certainly a deployment worth noting. In the very thick of his concern with his "perversity," does he not here in effect announce to his readers (via a "confession" to God) that the charges against him have been "dismissed" (*dimissa*)?

The theory implicit in the remark is probably this: If man cannot turn to God unless or until God has first turned to man, then God must have turned to him, since he has turned to God. God's recent act of conversion whereby Augustine could become converted had been gratuitous, an act of grace and mercy, quite as Augustine's adolescent theft, in lacking advantageousness as a motive, had been a perverse imitation of such gratuitousness. A hint of his coming battles with the Pelagians enters, when he emphatically rejects the thought that a person could be virtuous by reason of his own strength; for one needs the mercy by which God forgives the transgressions of those turned to him (*conversis ad te*). Then Augustine suddenly considers another possible quarter that might deride him (*derideat*): persons who had been less sick than he, since they had received still more help from that same physician (*ab eo medico*).

In viii, he goes back to the formula in its simplicity: the theft which he loved only for the theft's sake (*in illo furto, in quo ipsum furtum amavi*), though it was *nihil*. Then he modifies his formula for the motivation by adding the element of conspiracy: He would not have done this alone—he so acted because he had accomplices, was in a band of sinners, a *consortium peccantium.* In ix, he settles on the theme of derision, laughter at the thought of deceiving those who did not know what he and his accomplices were doing, when one is ashamed not to be shameless (*pudet non esse impudentem*). And in the final lines of the chapter, he contrasts rest (*quies*) in God and that time of his adolescent perversity when he had become a region of dearth (*regio egestatis*).

Thus, the themes of evil sought for its own sake, of anything as evil when sought without reference to God, and of evil in the appeal to evil companions all add up to "imitation" in the sense of "parody."

Tentatively, also, when thinking of Augustine's grotesquely "godlike" theft, we might think at least glancingly of the Biblical reference to a benign kind of conspiracy, such furtiveness as would transform the early Christian plotters against paganism into the accepted authorities of a New Order: (II Peter 3:10) "But the day of the Lord will come as a thief in the night" (*adveniet autem dies Domini ut fur*).

IX   The Middle (Conversion, Turn, Peripety) in Detail

The year: A.D. 386. Augustine is thirty-two. Having watched the slow development of his questionings, we are now ready to consider Book VIII, in which things come to a head.

Currently, there is much talk of "decision-making." Often, the decisions are conceived after the analogy of voting, or purchasing, or giving answers to questionnaires, or the taking of risks calculated on the basis of probability.

Or there are the tense moments of decision in formal drama, when the protagonist debates whether to make a certain move, and finally makes the choice that shapes his

destiny, though he still has to discover what that destiny is.
Thus, for instance, at the end of Act I in *Macbeth*, there are
the steps from

> If it were done when 'tis done, then 'twere well
> It were done quickly

through Macbeth's hesitation and his prodding by Lady
Macbeth to the final

>   I am settled, and bend up
> Each corporal agent to this terrible feat.
> Away and mock the time with fairest show:
> False face must hide what the false heart doth know.

Or, at the corresponding "decision-making" moment at
the end of the first act in *Othello*, there is Iago's decision regarding his plot "to abuse Othello's ear." The expression
sounds perverse indeed when we recall Yeats's lines on the
annunciation in his poem "The Mother of God":

> The three-fold terror of love; a fallen flare
> Through the hollow of an ear.

Fittingly, in *Hamlet*, the usual moment of decision-making at the end of Act I is delayed until the end of Act II:

> The play's the thing
> Wherein I'll catch the conscience of the king.

But we are interested here in another kind of decision,
if it can be called decision at all: the kind of development
that usually takes place in the third act of a five-act drama.
Despite his great stress upon the will, and despite his ex-
traordinary energy in theological controversy, Augustine
seems to have felt rather that, at the critical moment of his
conversion, something was decided for him. Act III is the
point at which some new quality of motivation enters. And

however active one may be henceforth, the course is more like a rolling downhill than like a straining uphill. Perhaps the moment of decision that would correspond to the end of Act I was stated at the end of Book v, where he announces that he had decided to be a catechumen in the Catholic Church. (The Latin word is *statui,* from the root of which we get such words as "status" and "statute" and, as a compound, "constitution." Here he had first taken a "stand.")

The moment we are concerned with corresponds to the place in *Hamlet* where Hamlet, by his ruse of the play-within-a-play, has finally established the king's guilt, so that new motivational conditions are set up. It corresponds to the place in *Macbeth* where Banquo's ghost appears, and sits in Macbeth's place at table, invisible to all but Macbeth himself and, of course, the audience. It corresponds to the place in *Othello* where Othello is finally convinced by Iago's trickery:

> Come, go with me apart, I will withdraw
> To furnish me with some swift means of death
> For the fair devil. . . .

and from now on, new powers within him are unloosed. (The analogy to Augustine's views on "grace" holds even to the extent that, for all Othello's great energies, Iago's incentives are still needed, to keep Othello *persevering* in his suspiciousness. Yet, at the same time, Othello is acting not as a somnambulist, but "in character." His acts are his own. Indeed, in contrast with a hypnotized subject's mechanical obedience to the suggestions of the hypnotist, Othello does what Iago hypocritically asks him *not* to do.)

In our analogy, Othello's suspiciousness would correspond perversely to Augustine's state of conviction following his conversion. Othello's own actions, on the basis of his suspiciousness, would correspond perversely to Augustine's use of his "free will," as in his life of episcopacy and controversy. Iago's fatal suggestions to Othello would correspond perversely to the role of Monica in leading towards his conversion. The resolve to kill Desdemona would correspond perversely to Augustine's definitive dismissal of his mistresses. The role of the dramatist in shaping all the characters and their destinies would correspond to God's role as Providence and Predestinating Creator. The way in which, even though Othello had become "converted" to Iago's false interpretation, further goads on Iago's part were needed to "help" Othello persevere, would correspond perversely to the notion that man can "turn" to God only so long as God is "turned" to man.

The important point at which the analogy collapses involves the fact that in the case of Iago it is a man rather than a "mother-figure" who is leading Othello to renounce his sexual mate. However, this point at which the analogy breaks down has its own particular kind of perversity. The symmetry of our analogy is further impaired by the respects in which the role of Iago is also a parody of *Alypius'* place in the conversion. For though Iago is leading Othello, he gives Othello the impression of being a mere follower; and thus he parodies Alypius' conversion in his hypocritical avowal: "I am your own forever."

The word "conversion" itself has a certain ambiguity. Often we think of it as the abandoning of one faith for another (like St. Paul's drastic transformation on the road to Damascus). But there are also converts who merely change to a more exacting attitude towards the faith they had already believed in, as with persons who suddenly feel "called" to study for the ministry in a religion to which they already subscribed. ("Conversion" in the Old Testament is typically of this sort.) Insofar as an element of suspicion is indigenous to the "property structure" of monogamistic love, Othello's response to Iago's suggestions would correspond perversely to "conversion" in the Old Testament sense, an intensification of motives already there. It would correspond perversely to "conversion" of the New Testament sort insofar as it made explicit in Othello personally certain kinds of susceptibility that are otherwise but latent or implicit in the monogamistic situation as such. (Incidentally, despite the intensely devilish role of Iago, the play is not "Manichaean"—for Iago is allowed by his creator to exist only because of his contribution to the "good" of the play as a whole.)*

Turning now to Book vIII, let us consider its steps in a way designed as far as possible to bring out the *form* even though, from the purely theological point of view, such abstraction may be felt somewhat to slight the *matter*:

Chapter i. Decidedly *introductory*. Begins on theme of praise. Next, reference (from Job) to way in which God's words (*verba tua*) had stuck fast in his breast. (We'd take this as a usage midway between "words" and "The Word.") This suggestion of confinement next starts in the direction of *cleansing*: his heart had to be purged (*mundandum*). But he returns immediately to the theme of confinement, in a reference to the narrowness of the way (*angustias*) through which he would have to pass, a narrowness which he resisted. We take this as implying the problem of rebirth. Next follows a reference to a man clearly patriarchal, one Simplicianus, who is to guide him. (We might call him "grandfatherly" rather than "fatherly"; for Ambrose, who was said to have received Augustine *paterne*, is also said to have loved Simplicianus *ut patrem*.)

Next, specifically, the problem still to be solved: Though

* It may be asked why we have spent so much time and effort approaching the subject of *conversion* in terms of *perversity*. The answer is: First, the design is suggested by Augustine's own explicit contrast between these two forms of "turning." Second, we happen to believe that many forms of criminality might best be analyzed as *perverse religiosity*, whereas ordinary church-going might be better analyzed simply as a form of sociality far from the exacting rigors of either conversion or perversity. In our first book, *Counter-Statement* (in an essay on Thomas Mann and André Gide), we considered the respects in which "conscientiousness" and "corruption" can be treated as *Wechselbegriffe* —and we have found no reason to abandon that line of thought. The next essay will systematically consider the "logological" reasons why guilt is intrinsic to the nature of "Order."

he has lost his faith in worldly honors, he is still tenaciously
(*tenaciter*) bound by woman. Recalling that Paul permitted
marriage though rating it as an inferior state, he thinks long-
ingly of religious chastity.

Next comes a sentence we consider crucial to our theory
of what occurs at the moment of crisis in the garden. We take
it that he is here summing up the position at which he had
already arrived *before* that crisis. He says that he had transcended (*transcenderam*) the vanity of those who could not
see in this world the evidences of God. And he says that he
had added to his idea of God the belief in the divine Word.
"I had found Thee, our Creator, and Thy Word with Thee
God, and with Thee one God, by Which Thou hast created
all" (*inveneram te creatorem nostrum et verbum tuum apud
te deum tecumque unum deum, per quod creasti omnia*). In
brief, up to this point the passage has been concerned with
but the *first two* persons of the Trinity.

We are here following the text used in the Teubner edition. But other texts add: "and with Thee, with the Holy
Spirit" (*tecumque cum spiritu sancto*), thereby rounding
things out by listing *all three* persons of the Trinity.

As we have previously indicated, it was in puzzling over
this notable difference in the two versions that we came upon
our notion as to the possible distinction between "conversion
in general" and a "specifically *Trinitarian* conversion." And
we view the matter from the standpoint of Augustine's own
stress upon the equating of the Holy Spirit with *love*.

By this interpretation, when the introductory chapter of
Book vIII comes to the still unresolved problem of his relation
to women, Augustine pauses to say just how far along he had
come, as regards Christian doctrine. He had formed an idea
of one incorruptible substance from which all other substance
was derived. That is, he had abandoned the Manichaean doctrine that nature is intrinsically evil. He had formed an idea
of the relation between God and God's creative Word (in brief,

the relation between Father and Son). The reference to the third person of the Trinity would be omitted by him because this part of his conversion was still to take place, later in Book VIII. But a reference to the third person could quite conceivably be inserted by some later scribe who had in mind simply the usual Augustinian stress upon the Trinity, and who thus assumed that the omission here was sheerly an oversight.

Probably the point can never be settled. But in any case, had the words always been inserted or were they always missing, the point might more easily have escaped our attention, though we were already asking how one's responses to Father (as *potestas*), to Son (as Word, or Wisdom) and to Holy Spirit (as Love) might differ. And even if the reader does insist that all three persons should be mentioned at this stage in the development, the fact still remains that, as Book VIII at many points makes amply clear, the motivational transformation accompanying the crisis in the garden involves above all else Augustine's relation to *amor* and *caritas, eros* and *agape* (the difference between erotic affection and the sort that goes with parental or filial attachments, or with kindheartedness and the like). Our evidence for that need not depend on so frail a source as this one disagreement among codices, but can be based on testimony that all editions have in common.

Meanwhile, two other details should be noted, with regard to the introductory nature of the first chapter in Book VIII. (1) Including himself formerly among those who (Romans 1:21) "when they knew God, they glorified him not as God, neither were thankful," he cites from Job: "Behold, the fear of the Lord, that is wisdom." But the Latin is *ecce pietas est sapientia.* We have already referred to the connotations that *sapientia* had for Augustine. And as for *pietas:* To realize its strongly *filial* meanings in Latin, we need but recall Virgil's *pius Aeneas,* who merged the idea of familial loyalty with the idea of the Roman order in general. (2) The

chapter ends on an allusion to Matthew 13:46, the parable of
the merchant "Who, when he had found one pearl of great
price, went and sold all that he had, and bought it." By juxtaposing the chapters on perversity and conversion, we are led
to wonder whether this could be considered as complement
of the passage in II, iv, where Augustine says that he and his
fellow-conspirators stole things "to be flung to swine." The
swine are in Book II; the pearl is in Book VIII; both are in
Matthew 7:6: "Neither cast ye your pearls before swine."

Chapter ii begins the development proper. It hinges
around the personal example of one Victorinus, who had been
secretly a Christian for some time, and whom the grandfatherly Simplicianus had persuaded (after "derision" on Victorinus' part) to declare his beliefs in public. Victorinus had
been highly thought of in pagan circles; he had taught Sena-
tors, and even had his statue in the Roman Forum. Naturally,
he feared that his position would be compromised by a public
declaration of his submission to the "yoke of humility" and the
"disgrace (opprobrium) of the Cross." The earlier theme of
perverse imitation is replaced by what we might call "con-
verse" imitation. (Incidentally, the inference that only God
and the Logos belong in the mooted passage of chapter i gains
some slight corroboration from the fact that Simplicianus is
represented here as congratulating Augustine on having read
the Platonists, for in them "in all ways God and His Word
creep in." The Latin verb is the one from which we get "in-
sinuate.")

We might call chapter iii a meditation on the sheer *form*
of repentance. The extra rejoicing that comes with the finding
of the lost sheep is related to the general dialectical principle
that the intensity of a pleasure is proportionate to the pain
that precedes it (*ubique maius gaudium molestia maiore prae-
ceditur*).

In chapter iv Augustine develops this idea a step farther
in noting that the conversion of a prominent citizen like Vic-

torinus is of especial importance because of the influence it has with so many. Thus the Devil is the more outwitted, since pride is linked with nobility and nobility with authority. Here the mutual engrossment of the perverse adolescent band in Book II is replaced by thoughts of a congregation in which "all make one another fervid, in a mutual kindling" (*fervefaciunt se et inflammantur ex alterutro*). Augustine's cunning as a rhetorician is particularly noticeable in the opening sentence of this chapter. The attack here is breathless, precipitate, an effect that we might best suggest in translation by breaking the sentence into lines:

> Come, Lord,
> Act,
> Rouse and recall us;
> Inflame and seize;
> Be fragrant, be sweet;
> Let us love,
> Let us run.

Here a note of urgency is imparted to a section that might otherwise seem to be proceeding at too meditative a pace for this stage of the narrative.*

* *Age, domine, fac, excita et revoca nos, accende et rape, fragra, dulcesce: amemus, curramus.* It looks as though something might be made of the fact that the last two words in effect equate "love" and "run." There is a related passage in a letter by Jerome, the main translator of the Vulgate Bible. Jerome is contrasting fantasies of himself among dancing girls (*choris intereram puellarum*) with curative visions of himself among angelic hosts (*videbar mihi interesse agminibus angelorum*). And he imagines the angels singing a quotation from the Song of Solomon: "Because of the savour of Thy good ointments, we will run after Thee." Also there is a Latin proverb, *currentem instigare*, "to stir up someone who is already eager." And there is the famous line from Ovid, quoted in Marlowe's *Doctor Faustus*, where the lover calls upon the "horses of the night" to run *lente, lente*. All told, we are approaching a critical shift in Augustine's ideas of appetition, with corresponding transformations in the nature of his "will."

"Let us run." That is, "let us move." That is, "let us be motivated," and in terms of a motive now definitively emergent. Again, we might recall Joyce's *Portrait*, with its notable transformation in the

Chapter v begins on his burning desire to "imitate" Victorinus (a desire that is, in effect, a radical revision of such imitation as he censured in Book II). Perhaps we should also remember the high social standing of the convert with whom Augustine would thus identify himself; and he explicitly considers the matter of turning from his job as teacher of pagan rhetoric to a situation in which he would have "free time" for God (*occasionem vacandi tibi*). Then, after a brief account of a "chain" whereby perverse will leads to lust, indulgence in lust leads to bad habit (*consuetudo*) and habit leads to compulsion (*necessitas*), he introduces the theme of conflict which will mount to the point of the hysterically tearful release. At this stage the conflict is presented in terms of *two wills* battling within himself, both of them his, the old one "carnal," the new one "spiritual" (and different from the old in that it enabled him *gratis* to worship and enjoy God). However, he is still explicitly asking that the moment of transformation be delayed.

Chapter vi reasserts his detestation of his job as pagan rhetorician, a job that required him to "sell the power of speaking" (*ego vendebam dicendi facultatem*). Against this he pits stories of the Desert Fathers, and of Antony in particular. This is the previously mentioned chapter in which Pontitianus, on discovering that Augustine and Alypius are reading Paul's Epistles, tells them that he is secretly a Christian—and the three discuss the unpalatable life of the Court.

Chapter vii begins with a strong synonym for the idea of "turning." Augustine says that while Pontitianus was speak-

fourth chapter, when Stephen looks upon the birdlike bathing girl who stands enigmatically for his new vocation, his turn from The Word to words:

"Heavenly God! cried Stephen's soul, in an outburst of profane joy.

"He turned away from her suddenly and set off across the strand. His cheeks were aflame; his body was aglow; his limbs were trembling. On and on and on and on he strode. . . ."

A few lines later we are told that "the tide was near the turn."

ing, God "twisted" him back upon himself (*retorquebas me ad me ipsum*), setting him face to face with himself so that, while Pontitianus talked, whenever Augustine sought to turn (*avertere*) his gaze away from himself, God again opposed him to himself, putting him before his own eyes. The theme of delay continues, as he calls for "chastity and continence," but adds "not yet" (*noli modo*). While Pontitianus talked, Augustine was suffused "with a horrible sense of shame." And after Pontitianus had left, he beat himself (*flagellavi*) with mental scourges (*sententiarum verberibus*).

Chapter viii finds him "healthily sick and dying vitally" (*insaniebam salubriter et moriebar vitaliter*). The symptoms were a frenzy of shame at failure to act, and an unaccustomed violence that greatly disconcerted Alypius. Augustine retires into an adjoining garden (*abscessi in hortum*).* Loyal, "me, too" Alypius follows soon after (*pedem post pedem*). And in twenty lines, forms of the word "will" now turn up fourteen times, along with two similar-sounding words, *valent* and *vulsi*, while Augustine wrestles with himself, plagued in particular by the fact that, whereas the parts of his body move in obedience to his will, it was quite different as regards the will's own willingness to obey.

Incidentally, this very stress upon the will is almost enough in itself to indicate that Augustine is here involved preponderantly with the motives that he himself would relate to the third person of the Trinity. Thus, see xiii, xi, where he discusses the "trinity" of the human mind: To be, to know, to will (*esse, nosse, velle*). And see *De Trinitate*, xv, xxi, where he explicitly treats human *will* as synonymous with *love* and analogous to the Holy Spirit.

Perhaps the entire next chapter (ix) should be quoted here, to convey the jaggedness of the style at this point, and

---

* In IV, xii, he spoke of Christ as having "retired" (*abscessit*) from the world, though at the same time without having retired.

to show how the term "command" suddenly flares up, along
with incidences of "will":

> Whence this monster? And why? May Thy mercy give light,
> that I may ask, if I may find answer in the hiding-places of human
> punishment and the shadowy contritions of the sons of Adam.
> Whence this monster? And why? The mind commands the body,
> and is promptly obeyed. The mind commands itself, and is resisted.
> The mind commands the hand to move; and the obedience is so
> prompt, one can hardly know where the command left off. Yet the
> mind is mind, while the hand is body. The mind commands the
> mind to will; yet, though it is no other than itself, it does not do
> as told. Whence this monster? And why? That which would not
> command unless it willed, I say, commands the will, yet does not
> do what it commands. But it does not will entirely; hence does
> not command entirely. For it commands only to the extent that it
> wills. And insofar as what it commands is not done, to that extent
> it does not will. For the will commands that there be a will not
> other than itself. But it does not command entirely; therefore what
> it commands is not. For if it were whole, it would not command
> that it be, since it would be already. Accordingly it is not mon-
> strous partly to will and partly not to will, but it is mental sickness,
> since it does not wholly rise with the lift of truth, but is also
> weighted down by bad habit (*consuetudine*). And thus there are
> two wills, neither of them complete, each having what is lacking
> in the other.

As regards the sheer *form* of the developments in Book
VIII, what shall we make of the sudden turn in the tenth chapter? Beginning with a quotation from Psalms ("Let them
perish from Thy presence"), Augustine launches into an attack
upon the Manichaeans, who attributed such conflicts to the
action of "two different natures battling within us, one good
and the other evil." Rather, he says, each of us is one, but is
fighting within himself (as punishment for his own sins, and
for his guilt inherited from Adam). Evil is not "natural," but
is a product of our wills.

Augustine here refutes the Manichaeans by a reduction
to absurdity, in showing that, if you carried out their line of
reasoning, a person would have as many "natures" as he had
wishes. The interesting consideration from the formal point

of view, however, is that his sudden striking at the Manichaeans here serves to move him a step further along, from the quandary of chapter ix. *Logically*, the conflict between "command" and "will" seems to be quite as before. But *psychologically*, this venting of fury against the Manichaeans brings him nearer to the critical moment, when of a sudden he will feel unified.

To an extent, perhaps, this movement of opposition represents simply the kind of unifying force that we see in wars. when nations of diverse interests are brought together by resistance to a common enemy. But something else seems involved here, too. For if he still had the problem of his women to resolve, and if his "evil" attachment to women was "doctrinally" associated with his earlier views as a Manichaean, the particular form of his refutation at this point could be significant, too. In effect, he did not simply "refute" their position—he "dissolved" it by showing that, if you carried out the Manichaean position completely, it would imply that a person has as many "natures" as he has conflicting wishes.

In any case, whether or not the reader agrees that there is a peculiar formal implication in this particular kind of argument at this particular point, as the chapter ends the Manichaean distinction between "good" and "bad" principles in nature has been replaced by a distinction between eternity which attracts us upwards (*superius*) and temporal interests which hold us down (*inferius*).*

Chapter xi is remarkable in that, while repeatedly stressing the idea that he is being held in suspense, he details momentous transformations. He has already changed his slogan; now he is saying, "Let it be done—*now!*" And even at the end of the chapter, his "turn" word here is *controversia*, a controversy within his own heart, involving none other than himself against (*adversus*) himself. Yet in this chapter, detailing

* This distinction should be recalled in chapter xvii, on "Conversion of a Word."

a state of suspense in which there was something he all but touched and grasped (*adtingebam et tenebam*) yet did not touch and grasp (*nec adtingebam nec tenebam,* we stress the point for use later), there is a notable passage which, beginning with a reference to his mistresses ("toys of toys, vanities of vanities"), turns into a paean to "continency" personified as a "fecund mother of children and joys" who has God as her husband. She "smiled on him with encouraging derision" (*inridebat me inrisione hortatoria*), thereby giving us indeed a third reference where the idea of laughter is stated favorably, and like the only other two favorable ones, with child-mother connotations. Surely, if he could become a child of such a mother, so antithetical to the *nugae* he was about to abandon, he would go a long way towards fulfilling his mother's hope that, in becoming converted, he would have God as his Father. He says that he blushed greatly, still hearing his "toys" even while Continency called him, exhorting him that his unclean members be mortified (*obscurdesce adversus inmunda illa membra tua, ut mortificentur*). And so he "hung in suspense" (*pendebam*).

The twelfth and last chapter arrives at the critical moment itself, when "there arose a great storm, bringing a great downpour of tears" (*aborta est procella ingens ferens ingentem imbrem lacrimarum*). The Latin verb here has strong secondary connotations of birth, as evidenced by the fact that from it comes the word "abortion."

As we see it, the many possibilities had narrowed to the point where, *words* having been replaced by *The Word,* the intellectual aspect (the "Wisdom") of his conversion had already been accomplished. But there was left still unsolved the problem of "Love." And this could not be solved until the general lure of corporeal *mistresses* could be replaced by the single spiritual, dignified maternal figure of *Continentia,* who had God as her husband. Not until now would the problem of the third person in the Trinity be resolved. Also, note that such a person would be capable of straddling two identities, taking the role either of the Holy Spirit or of the Holy Mother, in exemplifying the principle of Maternal Love, conceived in the absolute.

Insofar as irresolution might remain, it could be resolved by controversy, quite as we have just seen how rage against the Manichaeans could in effect help to resolve an internal quandary as regards conflicting wishes. The *inner* controversy of chapter xi could be replaced by *outer* controversy, as notably in later struggles with Pelagians and Donatists.*

* The Pelagians were to be the opponents on the other side of his opposition to the Manichaeans. The Manichaeans made too much of evil, in treating it as a substance or principle rather than as a privation, or "eclipse." The Pelagians, on the other hand, so played down the doctrine of "original sin" that the mediatory role of Christ in the redemptive process was slighted. This position in effect threatened the great stress upon a *Christian* church. The Donatists in turn threatened the church by the excessive demands they made upon the *personal* virtue of churchmen. The efficacy of the churchly offices had to be proclaimed in their own right. Even if performed by sinners, the offices must be effective if they are performed properly, the efficacy being in the rite itself, *ex opere operato*. Augustine's position would be analogous to that of a modern medical doctor who might contend that if he prescribed the right medicine it would have the right effect, regardless of whether he personally happened to be a criminal in other respects.

Thus, in sum: From the book of Genesis, Augustine got the basic doctrine that all things of nature are intrinsically good. From Paul, the founder of Christian ecclesiastical *organization*, he got the stress on the corruption of human nature as a result of Adam's fall, and of the corresponding need for Christ as redemptive sacrifice.

Thereafter, he could fight the Manichaeans whenever he was beset by conflicting wishes. He could fight the Pelagians whenever his stress upon the importance of the individual will threatened to play down the role of Christ as necessary scapegoat, and hence as central pole about which the Christian doctrine would be organized. He could fight the Donatists whenever his insistence upon personal virtue got to the point where it endangered the church as an organization of churchmen, each of whom had human frailties.

However, in laying too great stress upon his anti-Donatist position, he would be threatened by the conclusion (later stressed by Lutherans) that "it is impossible to keep the commandments"—and while such a position might help him to stress the all-importance of Christ's sacrifice as divine antidote to human depravity, it in turn had to be fought lest it give too much weight to the Manichaean view that human nature *intrinsically* possessed an evil principle. But all such

He felt it more fitting that he should negotiate his weeping alone (*solitudo mihi ad negotium flendi aptior suggerebatur*). So, leaving even Alypius, he flung himself under a fig tree some distance away. Then, after a spell of outcries, his formula changed fatefully to "Why not now?" (*quare non modo*)—and might we be justified in noting how close the sound of his word for "why" here is to that of his typical word for "seek": *quaero?*

It was then that he heard the voice of the child of uncertain sex chanting repeatedly, "Take up and read" (*tolle, lege*). Though in IV, iii, he had scoffed at those who would determine their fortune by opening at random the book of some poet and chancing upon some sentence that seemed to fit their own case, he was now in a greatly different mood, and was profoundly affected when the first words his eyes fell upon were these, from Romans 13:13-14:

> Not in rioting and drunkenness, not in chambering and wantonness, not in strife and envying; but put ye on the Lord Jesus Christ, and make not provision for the flesh, to fulfil the lusts thereof,

and with this sentence, it was as though, with the light of security suffusing his heart, all shadows of doubt dispersed (*cum fine huiusce sententiae quasi luce securitatis infusa cordi meo omnes dubitationis tenebrae diffugerunt*).

The remaining lines of the chapter are perfect for our purposes: First, loyal, "me, too" Alypius tries the same experiment, encounters a line which he feels is particularly suited to his case, and is as promptly converted. (His line was from Romans, 14:1: "Him that is weak in faith, receive ye." There is something wonderfully symmetrical about the fact that his very uncertainties thus suddenly were made to form the basis of his new certainty.) Next step: Augustine and Alypius go

quandaries henceforth could be directed *outwards*, in controversies with rival sects, rather than being felt as a wrangle within. Such wars of words, it seems, were in order, once he had solved the problem of "love," in terms of The Word.

in together, to announce the news to his mother. (Note that
in the Latin sentence of five words, three of them begin with
in: inde ad matrem ingredimur, indicamus.) Then the book
ends on a kind of summarizing formula that refers to God as
having converted Augustine to Him (*conversisti enim me ad
te*) and having converted (*conversisti*) his mother's grief into
gladness, a more plentiful (*uberius*) gladness, dearer and more
chaste, than if he had married and had children.

As regards Augustine's theory of motives, by the way, it
is worth pointing out again that the converting is done by *God*.
His very stress upon the importance of the will had made him
especially sensitive to the fact that a change within had taken
place as though from without (or it would be more accurate
to say, "as though from more deeply within"). He had done
many things, and wanted many things, and wanted not to
want many things—but now he had *been* converted. The felt
difference in the quality of his motivation must have convinced
him that some power beyond him must have turned in order
for him to be turned.

He had the personal sense of the situation which the Old
Testament prophet had formulated thus: "Turn thou me, and
I shall be turned" (*converte me et convertar*—Jeremiah 31:18).

X   The Book of Monica

Yet perhaps it is not until the ninth book that Augustine
completes the process whereby the Holy Spirit attains final
incorporation into his psychic economy. We refer to chapter
x, which describes a conversation between himself and his
mother, a few days before her death.

In preceding chapters, he has announced the abandoning of his profession as "word merchant"; he has told of his
respiratory troubles (which are not described fully enough for
us to know whether they would now be called the symptoms

of a "psychogenic illness" connected with the exactions of his conversion); he has given us (IX, iv) a most Augustinian equation, the "internal Eternal" (*internum aeternum*); he has retired to a wealthy friend's estate, where he would have leisure to meditate on matters of religion; he has described his engrossment with the Psalms, and his unsuccessful attempts, at Ambrose's advice, to study Isaiah (a prophet that probably most attracted Ambrose, Augustine says, because Isaiah foreshadows the calling of the Gentiles); and he has told of his son's death, in chapter vi.

This last chapter is particularly interesting from the purely formalistic point of view. For though his mother died before his son (as we learn in IX, xii, where Adeodatus is ordered to stop weeping at her death), Augustine tells of his son's death first; and by this arrangement he brings it about that the strictly narrative portion of the autobiography ends on the subject of his mother, who died when Augustine was accompanying her from Milan back to Africa.

At the beginning of chapter viii, he announces her death. Through the remainder of this chapter, and all of the next, in the accents of a piously written obituary, he describes her scrupulous character. Thus in chapter x he details the remarkable conversation he had with her, speculating on the nature of the future life:

The day impending (*impendente autem die*) on which his mother was to die, Augustine was standing alone with her, leaning against a window that gave on the garden of a house they occupied in Ostia. They were tired after a long journey, and were conversing pleasantly (*dulciter*), speculatively groping (*quaerebamus*) towards the future, wondering about the eternal life of the saints, and what it might be like, though no one on this earth had experienced one bit of it in detail. They opened their mouths wide (*inhiabamus*) to receive the supernal flow of God's fountain (*superna fluenta fontis tui*). Going beyond all worldly things, "into the very Id" (*in id ipsum,* and we leave it for the reader to speculate as to how closely this ultimate Id might or might not correspond with the Freudian species), they ascended internally (*ascendebamus interius*) while thinking and speaking and wondering, until they came to the very roots of their own minds, and then transcended these, "to reach a realm of unremitting plenty" . . . but here, at almost every word, we must pause for comment.

"Reach" is *attingeremus*. Whereat we should recall (VIII, xi) that just before his talk of turning from his female "toys" to Continency, he had talked of almost touching and grasping and then neither touching nor grasping (*adtingebam et tenebam . . . nec adtingebam nec tenebam*). We should take it that the word in the late passage is concerned with the same thing as the earlier incidence, itself perhaps in the offing still earlier (VIII, ii) where Augustine had alluded to Psalm 144:5, addressing God: "Touch the mountains, and they shall smoke." The word for "plenty" is the breasty word, *ubertatis*. The word that we have translated "unremitting" is *indeficientis*, in Latin a double negative; perhaps the translation, "unfailing" is better. The idea might be conveyed by some such longer expression as "forever uneclipsed," if we would reaffirm that for Augustine after his break with Manichaeanism, evil was like the deprivation of light, conceived not as a power in itself but as the deficiency of a proficiency. The passage next equates divine wisdom with a food, the "food of truth" (*veritate pabulo*), a life-giving wisdom through which the world became created. But this reference serves as a bridge into talk of the Eternal, since the creative *Sapientia* must have forever preceded the creation of time, whereas souls that merely lived on after being created would not be eternal in this total sense.

From the logological point of view, the next words are exquisitely accurate. For they contrive to merge almost imperceptibly the two oral functions of speaking and feeding: *dum loquimur et inhiamus illi*. "While we *are* speaking" (the sentence shifts into what the grammarians would call the "historical" present, but what we would here call a sense of eternity as the forever now, the *nunc stans*), "and while we are open-mouthed towards her" (eternal truth), "we touch her modestly (*attingimus eam modice*)* with the whole thrust of the heart" (*toto ictu cordis*). Then, fittingly, follows an allusion to St. Paul's formula, "the first-fruits of the Spirit" (*primitias spiritus*). Here, we take it, the third person of the Trinity is being brought into the structure. Whereat, there is a flat contrast between Word in the theological sense and word as a temporal happening. Then comes what is, for our purposes, the most astoundingly perfect passage conceivable:

> So we were saying: If to someone the tumult of the flesh were silent, and all the images of earth and water and air silent, silent the poles, and silent even the soul to itself, going beyond itself by having no thought of self; if our dreams were silent, and unfoldings of the imagination, all speech and every sign and whatever comes into being by passing away; if all these were completely silent to someone (for if we could but hear them, all things are saying, "We did not make ourselves, but He made us who abides for ever"); if, having said as much, they would then say nothing, but turned their ears intently towards Him who made them (and He alone speaks not through them but through his very self, that we might hear His Word, not by the language of the flesh nor by the voice of an angel nor by sound of storms nor by the enigmas of similitudes, that we might hear Him Himself without them, only Him Whom in all these things we love); so now we are reaching out and in quick thought touching (*attingimus*) the eternal Wisdom that overarches all; if this state should be prolonged, and any visions of a greatly different sort withdrawn; and if precisely this one condition were to seize and absorb the beholder and wrap him in joys eternal, so that eternal life would be like this unique moment of recognition towards which we sighed; is not this to enter the joy of our Lord? And when might that be? Would it not be when we rise again but shall all be changed? †

* This is one of the passages that makes us want to see in *modica* a deflected name for Monica.

† Incidentally, in case any reader finds it hard to understand just how this so strongly monologue-like passage could have been developed by both Augustine and his mother together as per his introductory words

We have tried to make this passage run as fluently as possible. For we have in mind the thought that it should form a total contrast with the previously cited passage depicting an internal wrangle, just before his conversion. Logologically, we are endlessly enticed to speculate on the paradoxical knot of motives that must be involved when an inveterate wordman thus conceives of eternity under the sign of an ultimate, unchanging Word, itself conceived in terms of wordlessness, (wordless through having attained to the very Essence of words), while that wordlessness in turn is conveyed in a breathlessly long periodic sentence that, to be spoken aloud, would require many fresh intakes of breath. Our tentative assumption is that, though silence as so conceived requires the sophistication of a consummate word-man, it nonetheless ties in psychologically with motives vestigially "infantile." It would be a point at which great sophistication and great simplicity could meet.

The chapter ends with Monica's remark that she no longer felt a desire to go on living. Apparently, so great was her conviction of a future life under some such conditions as he has just been describing, now that her son was converted her purpose here had been fulfilled, and she was eager to begin her eternity of that rare postverbal silence about which the former word-merchant has been so eloquent. The chapter, we repeat, is written explicitly under the sign of her death, which is announced in the chapter immediately following, and took place only a few days after this conversation. We consider this an aspect of its motivational bearing upon his ideas of the Holy Spirit.

To sum up: Insofar as their imagining drew upon vague, vestigial memories of the infantile, it would seem to have in-

"we were saying" (*dicebamus*), note that the first words of the next paragraph may supply the answer. They are: "I spoke thus" (*dicebam talia*), though he goes on to explain that his words but give the gist of the things "we" said (*loqueremur*).

volved, not only his memories, or hers with relation to him, but also hers with relation to her own infancy.

In any case, as regards the motives of the Trinity: So far as his own psychic economy was concerned, this episode following his conversion seems to have been as basic to the processes of his conversion as was the incident of his hysterical weeping in the garden. Here, clearly, when the references to Wisdom in terms of food change into thoughts of "the first-fruits of the Spirit," our special concern with "firsts" admonishes us to note how radically the third person of the Trinity has come to figure here (if the reader accepts our tentative suggestion that, though the Holy Spirit is "grammatically" a male, it can also contain the lineaments of the maternal, material for a kind of "pre-Mariolatry," in its connotations of "Love," such Love as would be in the same category with the figure of "Continency" he had made antithetical to his mistresses, his "trifles" or "toys"). Here would be the completing of his major doctrinal design.

Two notable details regarding his description of his grief at his mother's death: first, there is a touch of the pattern displayed earlier in his reference to the death of his close friend. It is as though, he says, one life had been made of his and hers together, and were now being torn apart (*et quasi dilaniabatur vita, quae una facta erat ex mea et illius*). And there is a hint of the reflexive pattern, when he speaks of "another sorrow in which he sorrowed for his sorrow" (*alio dolore dolebam dolorem meum*), so that he was beset by a "twofold sadness" (*duplici tristitia*). But in the closing words of the book, this divisiveness clearly gives way to a new principle of unity, in a remarkable sentence that begins with a reference to his parents, next modulates into talk of union with his brothers under God as father, in "our Catholic mother," and ends on the transforming of the idea of citizenship from a political category to a religious one (the terministic development that attains its architectural completion in his *City of God*).

XI What All Is Memory

Whatever may have been Augustine's reasons for doing so, the reversal whereby he treats of his son's death before his mother's (though his mother died first) has the formal effect of terminating *his* autobiography with *her* death.

For the ninth book ends the account of his personal unfoldings in the *narrative* sense, involving a *temporal* series of steps. And the remaining four books (almost equal in length to the first nine) will embody a notably different kind of development. Having given us nine books of memories, Augustine now stops to ask what Memory itself might be. And since the scrutinizing of this term leads him progressively into a concern with other terms that cluster about it, we might say that the very method of his book here undergoes a kind of conversion. An "episcopal" role takes over—and the "confessions" gradually become more and more like "professions."

In general, the new style of unfolding proceeds thus: Meditations on the nature of Memory lead into thoughts on the role that Images play in the process of remembering. But the subject of Images quickly leads into thoughts on the nature of Sensation and Temptation. Next, scruples concerning the incessant nature of Temptation lead to thoughts on the function of a Redeemer, whose Mediatory role involves a relation between two realms, human and divine, temporal and eternal. But thoughts on the relation between temporal and eternal lead in turn to speculations on the problem of "beginnings" as such—and so Augustine ponders on the account of the Creation as given in the opening chapters of Genesis. His way of narrowing down to oneness (asking about an ultimate first) thus also leads to a multiplicity (the "plenitude" of the Creation, as infused with the unity of its authorship)—and thus in effect a Platonist dialectic underlies these steps and matches an infolding by an exfoliation.

Admittedly, our summary has reduced the last four books to a more clearly graduated progression than is actually the case. Since all the terms involve one another, the last step is partly present even in the first one. But the successive featuring of these various topics does follow such a pattern of development in the large. And, above all, the contrast between the first nine books and the last four is clear, and clearly involves the distinction between "rectilinear" and "circular" terminologies which will form the basis of our next essay, on "The First Three Chapters of Genesis." The turn from a *narrative of memories* to the *principles of Memory* is itself a technical, or "logological" equivalent of a turn from "time" to "eternity."

"Musically," the turn is announced at the beginning of Book x by a stress upon the idea of *knowing:* "Let me know Thee, my Knower, let me know, even as I am known" (*Cognoscam te, cognitor meus, cognoscam, sicut et cognitus sum*), such fourfold repetition in the opening sentence being the equivalent of the effect we might now get by a subtitle, such as: "The People of Knowledge with Relation to God." Recall, however, that his discussion of what we might now call infantile "instincts" involved the root form of this same verb. He had said that all he "knew" was to suck, rest and cry.

Perhaps we may also note, as a reflection of the change in motives, his explicit concern with the question: To whom are his Confessions addressed? His answer is: to a duality of audiences. He is confessing in his heart to God but in his writings before witnesses (x, i). He is confessing to men in God's presence (x, iii). He is confessing before God and those whom he has been "commanded to serve" (x, iv). In xi, i, he decides that he is confessing to help him and his readers love God.

In chapter vi, after a reference to his *conscientia* (a word that, like the French *conscience*, means both "conscious-

ness" and "conscience"),* leads into his terministic search
by speculating on the ways in which we derive knowledge
from the senses, as corrected by the judgments of reason. His
verb for the role of the senses in making contact with the
things that are stored in the memory is *attigerit,* the verb that
was used figuratively in connection with the discussion between Augustine and his mother just before her death. Then,
at the end of vii and the beginning of viii, he formally announces his desire to aim at a systematic transcending (*transibo*) of his natural powers ("ascending by degrees": *gradibus
ascendens*)—and immediately thereafter, he plunges into the
subject of the Memory, its "plains and vast mansions" (*campos
et lata praetoria*).

In the Memory, there are "treasures of innumerable
images" conveyed through the senses. The same word for
"treasure" had appeared in ix, vii, where the bodies of two
martyrs were spoken of as having lain hidden and forgotten
"in the treasure house of God's secret" (*in thesauro secreti
tui*), a sepulchral association that is reenforced a few lines later
by a reference to things that forgetfulness has not yet ab-
sorbed and buried (*sepelivit*).

As one might expect, references to the "inwardness" of
memory run throughout the section. Memory is an "inner
place not a place" where things are stored at varying depths
within. Here are such words as *penetralia, intus,* and various
synonyms for the remote and the hidden. There is the "great
recess" of the memory into which each of the senses pours its
particular kind of sensations; it has "innumerable fields and
caves and caverns"; there are the Memory's "many inexpres-
sible secret folds." Whereat we might recall that, in the opening chapter of Book ix, God was called "more inward than
every secret" (*omni secreto interior*); or see v, vi, for reference

---

* Though in this passage it should doubtless be translated as
"consciousness," see near the end of v, vi, when it should clearly be
translated as "conscience": *domine deus meus, arbiter conscientiae
meae.*

to the "secret" of God's providence; and the word for "folds" (*sinus*) which also appears again when the Memory is called a "vast *sinus*," is the word the Bible applies to "Abraham's bosom" (cited by Augustine in IX, iii), while in V, ii, it had appeared in a reference to weeping on God's bosom (literally "in" God's bosom). In XI, xxxi, he refers to the *sinus* of God's "deep secret," the place far from which he had been placed by the consequences of his transgressions. In the Latin dictionaries the range of the meanings for the word is given as: curve, fold, hollow, coil, bosom, lap, purse, money, bay, gulf, basin, valley; figuratively: love, affection, protection, intimacy, innermost part, heart, hiding-place. The Memory is also likened to a "vast *aula*," for which the range of meanings is: court, forecourt, inner court, yard, hall, palace, royal court, residence, courtiers, princely power, royalty.

There are many other references conveying connotations of great scope in connection with his ideas of the Memory. There is a "multitude" of things which he can recall if he so wishes. They are "poured in and heaped up" by the senses. He has a plenty (*copia*) of past experiences to draw on, when thinking of the future. Memory is a great power (*vis*). It is spacious and boundless. In it he can see the vastnesses of nature. It has "immense capacity." It is a "profound and infinite multiplicity." It is also something vaguely dreadful (*nescio quid horrendum*). Or again, remembered things are like crowds swarming in answer to one's call, coming in larger numbers than are wanted, and being dismissed by a wave of the hand.

Twice he likens things in the memory to foods in the stomach, really there, though beyond the experience of actual taste (x, ix, xiv).

So much for the imagery that hovers about his ideas of the Memory. As regards its technical operations, he stresses the notion of things presenting themselves in order as they

are called for, those in front ceding to those that follow.
Things are classed both by particulars and under general
heads (*distincte generatimque*), in accordance with the specific sense impression through which they were recorded. By
the Memory he can see colors in darkness, or listen to a song
in silence (an observation, by the way, which might serve to
remind us how the normal experience of memory can provide
the makings of that quasi-mystical figure, the oxymoron). The
role of Memory in promoting discriminations is treated in
terms of the notion that, while smelling nothing, one can distinguish the scent of lilies from that of violets, and thereby
have preferences, purely in the Memory. In Memory he can
confront himself and reflect on himself, forming plans and
hopes for the future on the basis of the past, inferring what
will follow what, and praying "God forbid." But, in sum,
though Memory is a power of his own mind and belongs to his
own nature, it is beyond his understanding.

So far, the emphasis has been upon the remembering of
sensory impressions. But there are also memories that he had
acquired not just as "images" but as the things themselves
(*res ipsas*). Interestingly enough, he refers here to things he
learned during the days of his liberal education (*doctrinis
liberalibus*): he cites in particular his early pagan training in
disputation, which he rightly says he has not forgotten (as
Manichaeans, Pelagians, and Donatists among others will have
many occasions to attest). Here also would belong (x, x) such
knowledge as answers questions whether a thing is, what it is,
and of what sort (*an sit, quid sit, quale sit*). Recognition of
the right answers to such questions could not have come from
the memory, he says, unless there is a still remoter kind of
memory, in caverns still farther back (*in cavis abditioribus*).
Presumably Augustine is here touching upon Platonist doctrines of *anamnesis?* Mathematical knowledge is also of this
sort, not acquired through the senses (x, xiii).

He is now ready for the reflexive stage, as with the thought that he remembers having remembered, puzzling as to how he can remember memory itself, how he truly remembers having heard things that were false, and how he even remembers forgetfulness, the "privation of memory." Without memory, he cannot even name his own name.

Later, in xi, ii, he will say: "Let me confess to Thee whatever I shall have found in Thy books, and let me hear the voice of praise and let me drink Thee" (*et te bibam*). Yet, surprisingly, when looking for traces of God in his Memory, he does not mention the fountain of Biblical quotations which he has stored up, to provide him with a constant source of ejaculations, and which in the last book will almost overwhelm his pages. Obviously, from the purely terministic point of view, "God" is in his Memory since "God" is either explicit or implicit in every one of those sentences. One can get out of a vocabulary only what one has put into it—and the Bible "solved" this problem by putting "God" into the first sentence. Hence, so far as the sheer dialectics of the case is concerned, his attempt at an ascent through Memory to God is solved in advance by the very nature of the terminology which, since his conversion, he had been committing to memory. And reinforcing such trends there would be a technical equivalent of "memory," the *forms* of language (the logic of internal consistency that comes to a head in a title of titles, or "god-term").

Logologically, there are only two ways in which a terminology can "transcend" itself: either by tautology or by *non sequitur*. If the operation is contrived by *non sequitur*, this means that the work is inconsistent with itself. But if it is consistent with itself, then the term for the transcendent function must be there at the start, either explicitly or implicitly. Usually it is implicit, and is gradually purged of its obscurities. But in theological terminology it is explicit from

the start, though there may be a certain craftiness in unveiling
it.

Also, as we have seen when considering the imagery
that Augustine associates with the Memory, there can be a
process of diffusion (a kind of ruminating or mulling over)
whereby images elsewhere applied to the transcendent term
may here be applied to a term that on its face makes far lesser
claims—and thus there is an imagistic bridge ambiguously aid-
ing in the transition to the term that is out-and-out transcendent. But insofar as several terms are consistently related,
they mutually imply one another—hence, in the last analysis,
the genius of the "highest" term will in some way pervade the
lot.

In any case, Augustine is now nearing the point where
he will abandon the term Memory, to take up other terms
technically beyond it. And chapter xvii breaks into a dithy-
ramb stating again that he will transcend (*transibo*) the Memory in his desire to reach (*attingere*) God from wherever He
can be reached (*attingi*), and cling to Him (*inhaerere*) from
wherever He can be clung to (*inhaereri*).

XII   To Cling (*Inhaerere*)

The strategic role of *attingere* in Augustine's account of
the conversation with his mother had been enough to make
us watch for this word in other contexts. But we owe to the
child psychologist, John Bowlby, the suggestions that led to
the observing of the Latin words for "cling" or "cleave." In a
paper on "The Nature of the Child's Tie to Its Mother," Dr.
Bowlby discusses five "instinctual responses" of infants;
namely: crying, smiling, sucking, clinging, and following. In
I, vi, Augustine had mentioned three of these: crying, smiling,
sucking. There is no mention of either clinging or following,

as infantile "responses," though the *principle* of following as
an adult becomes emphatically embodied in Augustine's devout relation to the Scriptures.*

Recall that in that same early chapter, Augustine also
mentioned one kind of infantile "knowledge" not on Dr.
Bowlby's list: resting. This addition is very important in Augustine's case, because of its relation to his great theological
stress upon hopes of an ultimate rest in God. And as we began
watching contexts in which the Latin equivalents of "cling"
appear, we inclined to the motion that for him the idea of
resting in God merges with the idea of *clinging to* God.

In VII, xi, Augustine had quoted from Psalms 73:28 the
"basic" passage using this term: "It is good, then, for me to
cleave unto God" (*mihi autem inhaerere bonum est*).
(Another English version somewhat conceals the meaning by
a less forceful expression: "But it is good for me to draw near
to God.") Other passages we have noted are:

IV, iv. He says there is no true friendship unless God
glues together (*agglutinas*), with the love of the Holy Ghost,
those who are clinging to each other (*haerentes sibi*).

---

* In II, vii, Augustine distinguishes between things he did of his
own volition (*mea sponte*) and things he didn't do as the result of God's
guidance (*te duce*). And in another passage we have already cited in
another connection (v, xiii), he gives the idea a twist by saying that he
was unconsciously being led to Ambrose by God that he might consciously be led by Ambrose to God.

Though we were not aware of either "leading" or "following" as
key terms, we do not mean to imply that they are absent. A further
search would be necessary, to check on this question. And at least it
is obvious that, owing to Augustine's attitude towards the authority of
the Bible, one could find many words that *strongly imply* the idea of
"following" (which in turn implies the follower's qualifications to be a
leader).

Incidentally, a writer in whom the specific term "to follow" (*sequi*)
plays a noticeably strategic role is Spinoza, with his great stress upon
the notion of ideas that "follow logically" from other ideas. It would be
interesting to see whether one could disclose an "infantile" strand of
motives underlying his high degree of rational sophistication. Also, there
is the notable fact that Spinoza's stress upon the notion of logical sequence (and thus his constant reference to the "*sequitur*") contrasts so
strikingly with Augustine's stress upon guidance of Biblical authority.

IV, xii. "Cling (or cleave) to Him Who made you" (*inhaerete illi, qui fecit vos*). The next sentence refers to standing with God and resting in God: *state cum eo et stabitis, requiescite in eo et quieti eritis.*

v, iv. Though having nothing one possesses all by clinging to God (*inhaerendo tibi*).

VI, xv. A reference to the sending of his mistress back to Africa, though his heart still clung to her (*adhaerebat*).

VII, v. Though he still had much to learn, the Catholic faith was already firmly fixed (*stabiliter . . . haerebat*) in his heart.

VII, xvii. He did not doubt to Whom he should cling (*cui cohaererem*) but he was not yet the kind that would so cling (*qui cohaererem*). The dative *cui* and the nominative *qui* are so nearly alike in pronunciation that this usage is doubtless intended to be felt as word-play.

VII, xix. On his imperfect understanding of the relation between Christ and the Word: he didn't understand how the flesh clung to the Word (*haesisse carnem illam verbo tuo*).

VIII, i. God's words had stuck fast (*inhaeserant*) in his breast.

VIII, vi. Concerning the stories of conversion which Pontitianus told and which had such an important effect as one stage in Augustine's conversion. One friend tells another that he is about to declare his faith, and the second answers that he will stick by him (*adhaerere*) in order to share in so great reward and service.

x, xxviii. On clinging to God with all his being (*cum inhaesero tibi ex omni me*).

XII, ix. The heaven of heavens, by clinging to God (*inhaerendo tibi*) passes beyond the vicissitudes of time.

XII, xi. The blessedness of clinging to God's blessedness (*inhaerendo beatitudini tuae*). Later in the same chapter: by incessantly and unfailingly clinging (*indesinenter et indeficienter tibi cohaerendo*).

XII, xv. Clinging to God "with so chaste a love" (*tam casto amore cohaerentem*). The word is repeated twice more in this chapter, the third instance being again the quotation from Psalms which we cited at the beginning of this list.

All these references in Book XII have concerned the relation between God and the heaven of heavens, which participates in His eternity by clinging to him. They merge into talk of Jerusalem and its peace, as that of the "dearest mother, where are the first-fruits of my spirit" (XII, xvi).* The word *sinus* appears (xxv) in a reference to God "in Whose bosom (*in cuius sinu*) there is no contradiction" and (xxviii) in a reference to primal matter holding in its vast bosom (*sinu grandi*) the various natures that are to be formed from it. Chapter xxvii begins by likening the words of Genesis to a fount that is full to overflowing, and it ends on the figure of a fledgling restored to a nest. Chapter xxviii changes the figure, saying that whereas to some the words are like a nest, to others they are like bushes (*frutecta*) about which they fly rejoicing (*volitant laetentes*), chirping and plucking.

In Book XIII, chapter ii, the idea of clinging is explicitly merged with the idea of conversion. Again alluding to the passage from the Psalms (though this time he uses *adhaerere* instead of *inhaerere*), he says that matter must cling to God lest by turning away (*aversione*) from God it lose the light it got by turning towards Him (*conversione*). The same notion is repeated in iii, the words here being *cohaerendo* and *conversa*. The last instance we noted occurs in XIII, viii, where every obedient intelligence of the heavenly city is described as clinging to God (*inhaereret tibi*); and the very next words refer to rest in God's Spirit (*requiesceret in spiritu tuo*). Thus, though the theme of rest and peace on which the work draws to a close does not explicitly use the word "cling," surely this list of citations we have been considering establishes it as

* See page 122, where there is a previous reference to "the first-fruits of the spirit."

there implicitly, in case one were to ask how it might be conveyed in terms of an "instinctual response."

We are not suggesting that Augustine's ideas of rest (and silent words) in the afterlife are reducible simply to terms of an infant clinging to its mother. But we are saying: As regards the sheerly *verbal behavior* of his pages, the references to *clinging* indicate that such associations characterize one notable strand in the complex of meanings that "eternity" represents in his particular terminology. It is even conceivable that an especially eloquent adult's use of the word "cling" in contexts of the mother-child type may be in a wholly different channel of motivation from the "instinctual response" which Dr. Bowlby has observed in infants. We must leave that for psychologists to decide. In the meantime, so far as sheerly verbal behavior is concerned, such use of the *word* "cling" (*inhaerere*) is here being taken as at least the articulatory analogue of the human infant's speechless *act* of clinging. And this view should be combined with our earlier comments on Augustine's eloquent description of silent verbalizing in the afterlife, a notion we interpret as the analogue of the infant's speechlessness itself, when such speechlessness is paradoxically conceived by an adult in terms of language.

XIII   Trinitarian Considerations
That Complicate the Ascent

In x, xx, Augustine gives an equation that is of major importance for logological purposes. Here he equates the search for God with the search for a happy life: *cum enim te, deum meum, quaero, vitam beatam quaero.* In brief, here "happiness" is the empirical equivalent of "God," a conversion made all the more possible by the fact that the word for "happy" also means "blessed." Next, in passing, he likens our knowledge of happiness to our appreciation of eloquence, an

awareness we can have even if we are not ourselves eloquent.
(The passage is in line with thoughts of stylistic felicity.)

Augustine's reasoning here is approximately thus: Each
man seeks joy (*gaudium*) in some form or other. Thus, each
man has a partial "memory" of happiness. And if happiness
equals God, then in this sense God is in the memory. As
regards the corollary (that even the wicked in their search
for joy are searching for God), a quick solution is offered
(xxii) in terms of a member of the *vert*-family: "Their will
is not turned away (*non avertitur*) from a certain *image* of
joy" (*ab aliqua imagine gaudii*).

Next, (xxiii) the happy life is equated with "joy in
truth" (*gaudium de veritate*). And God exists in Augustine's
memory inasmuch as he remembers having found the truth.
(He does not say whether he is referring here to the critical
moment in the garden or to his preparatory experiences as a
catechumen, when he was filling his memory to overflowing
with Biblical texts each one of which took God's existence
for granted.)

Chapter xxv has a twist that one should consider, when
trying to understand Augustine's psychology. Any contemporary psychologies that would use the words "mind" and
"memory" would probably treat of "memory" as a *part* of the
"mind." But in Augustine's usage "memory" is the more inclusive term, since the mind can remember itself. Thus he
says that, in entering the depths of memory, he is entering
the seat of the mind (*intravi ad ipsius animi mei sedem*).
And he concludes that, though God was not in his mind, God
was in his memory (xxvi). God had granted it this "dignity,"
though not before he "learned" God (*neque . . . priusquam
te discerem*). But he promptly adds: The memory is not a
place (*nusquam locus*). An often troublous member of the
vert-family is here used favorably, as God is called: Truth
everywhere replying to those who would consult Him on *diverse* things. Next (xxvii), atop the recent admonition about

place, Augustine uses words of place; he says that while God was within (*intus*), he had sought God without (*foris*). The idea of touching is now reversed: Instead of his touching upon the divine, the divine touches him (*tetegisti me*), and he burns towards God's peace (*exarsi in pacem tuam*). This leads to talk of clinging (*inhaesero,* xxviii).

However, the idea of clinging implies also the possibility of being torn away from that to which one would cling. And such is the turn the "climb" takes next. He warns against the *temptations* resulting from worldly *prosperity* that comes from fear of *adversity* (a *vert*-term that appears five times in seven lines).

This development is explainable in various ways. At the very least, it serves to make the last four books more of a piece with the first nine than they would be otherwise. Since he will deal with temptation primarily in terms of his own temptations, the sharpness of the turn from confession to profession is blunted by this confessional section.* As personal portraiture it is the most appealing section of the book. Here we can ironically watch Augustine apologizing for traits that many people today would be quite proud of. (What he thinks of as "temptation" they'd doubtless think of as "vitality" or "sensitivity," for he approaches the whole subject as a problem in *mortification,* the deliberate slaying of appetites and ambitions. And in the course of his regrets he indirectly reveals how exceptionally responsive he was to the pleasurable things of this world. The evidence thus given unintentionally is far more convincing than if he had boasted instead of apologizing.)

The interruption of the "ascent" (as he pauses to discuss temptation) also has the effect of good contrast. Without it, the whole four books would be unrelieved by such counter-

* To avoid possible misunderstanding, perhaps we should note that Augustine does not make this explicit distinction between "confessing" and "professing." The word "confession" is used for all purposes, being applied even to his "confessing" of God's goodness.

point as he derives from these pages in which he merges his personal problems with a systematic account of "temptation" in general.

Our notion about the psychological difference between his relation to the second person of the Trinity and his relation to the third suggests another function that may be performed by the chapters on Temptation. On its face, the emphasis in these last four books is upon *knowing*. But interwoven with it there is the kind of attachment that comes to a focus in the idea of absolute *rest*. *Knowing* is the more intellectual of the two; *rest* is the more *moral*, or purgative. Thus, the shift might reflect the difference between the motives that could be classed under the head of Wisdom (which is associated with the "Word") and those classed under the head of Love (which is associated with the Holy Spirit, and is primarily in the category of appetition), or "will."

This would mean that there is a kind of "double plot" underlying the dialectic of these four "episcopal" books. One strand would be essentially intellectual (hence most directly related to the Word); and the other would be essentially moral or purgative inasmuch as it would directly involve appetition or willing—and the ideal word for such appetition is Love (most directly related to the Holy Spirit). The *purgative* element would figure here to the extent that the appetites proved unruly, and thus required a regimen of mortification. And the principle of such mortification would be completed in the idea of Christ as perfect victim, whose sacrifice is curative absolutely quite as the nature of mortification is curative partially.

Thus, Christ would mediate in two senses: From the standpoint of *willing*, He would mediate as a ransom for men's guilt. This would be mediation in the sense of intercession. From the standpoint of *knowing*, He would be the principle of mediation between the two realms of nature and the supernatural, time and eternity. The role as ransom would be that of dramatic catharsis. But from the purely dialectical point of view, in His dual nature as both God and man, Christ would be an ambiguously middle term bringing these two different realms together, by "translating" back and forth between them. He would play the same role theologically as the idea of Keats's Urn plays poetically, insofar as the Urn is the Imagination's viaticum for conducting us from the world of sensory imagery into a "spiritual" realm that transcends sensation and that, like Abraham's bosom (xii, xxv) contains no contradiction. Just as the Word, in creating nature, thereby set up the distinction between natural and supernatural realms, so the Word is seen to function in the opposite direction, too, by serving as Mediator between these two realms.

As regards conversion to a triune God in which the first person is equatable with Power (which in turn is equatable with Authority), the second with Wisdom (the Word), and the third with Love (Spiritual union), might it not be necessary that the two steps we noted in the narrative portion of the *Confessions* show likewise in the Cycle of Terms that the "post-narrative" portion unfolds? Would there thus be a kind of "double plot," with the need at times for the exposition to go back and bring forward an element that had been allowed to lag? Indeed, might not the principle of double plot in Western drama itself be ultimately related to this same pattern of thought?

In any case, there is this simple development to recall, as regards the step from Memory to Temptation: When speculating on the nature of Memory, Augustine comes upon the role played by images both in remembering past things and in imagining future possibilities on the basis of past experiences. Next, the subject of images leads into the subject of Temptation, owing to the unruly nature of images in the episcopal convert's dreams. Thus, after a brief paragraph in which Augustine expands the literal meaning of the word "Continency," saying that by it we are collected, and led back

into a oneness from which we had been scattered, he turns
to the problem of his dreams, which had not fully shared in
his conversion.

XIV   Imagery, Sensation, Temptation
and Mediator

Chapter xxx of Book x discusses the illusory images and
corresponding lascivious motions that trouble Augustine's
sleep. The next several chapters catalogue the various temptations of the senses and the mind, along with a frank rating
of his susceptibility to each. Surely Joyce refreshed his
memory of these particular pages, before writing the passage
in *Portrait of the Artist as a Young Man* describing Stephen's
contrition after his fright at the hell-fire sermon:

Each of his senses was brought under a rigorous discipline. In
order to mortify the sense of sight he made it his rule to walk
in the street with downcast eyes, glancing neither to right nor
left and never behind him. His eyes shunned every encounter
with the eyes of women. From time to time also he balked them
by a sudden effort of the will, as by lifting them suddenly in
the middle of an unfinished sentence and closing the book. To
mortify his hearing he exerted no control over his voice which
was then breaking, neither sang nor whistled and made no attempt
to flee from noise which caused him painful nervous irritation
such as the sharpening of knives on the knifeboard, the gathering
of cinders on the fireshovel and the twigging of the carpet. To
mortify his smell was more difficult as he found in himself no
instinctive repugnance to bad odours, whether they were the
odours of the outdoor world such as those of dung or tar or the
odours of his own person among which he had made many curious
comparisons and experiments. He found in the end that the only
odour against which his sense of smell revolted was a certain
stale fishy stink like that of longstanding urine: and whenever it
was possible he subjected himself to this unpleasant odour. To
mortify the taste he practiced strict habits at table, observed to the
letter all the fasts of the church and sought by distraction to divert
his mind from the savours of different foods. But it was to the
mortification of touch that he brought the most assiduous ingenuity

of inventiveness. He never consciously changed his position in bed, sat in the most uncomfortable position, suffered patiently every itch and pain, kept away from the fire, remained on his knees all through the mass except at the gospels, left parts of his neck and face undried so that air might sting them and, whenever he was not saying his beads, carried his arms stiffly at his sides like a runner and never in his pockets or clasped behind him.

Some notable details of Augustine's self-assessment, which is much more complicated than Stephen's, are as follows: Though he had learned to take food like medicine, there is menace in the fact that the sheer sating of hunger is a pleasure. Also, pleasure in eating may be concealed under the guise of concern for one's health. He was not tempted by odors. He found it hard to resist a liking for the sound of words and music; but he inclined to think that singing might be permitted, so that the weaker minds might be put in a more devotional mood. He was greatly tempted by visual beauty, but sought to make amends by reminding himself that all beautiful things come from God. He gave his usual warnings against curiosity, a "lust of the eyes" due to love of knowledge for its own sake.

At another point he attaches to it the word "idle," *supervacuanea*, thereby using dyslogistically an expression which is essentially eulogistic in Veblen, who applies it to the disinterested attitude of the scientist. We may begin by tolerating some trivial piece of gossip, then before we know it we are paying attention (*advertimus*) willingly. Or the sight of a dog chasing a hare distracts him (*avertit*) even if he happens to be thinking of serious matters; and it "converts" him (*convertit*), the word here referring to the fact that he is "turned" in the direction of the excitement. He sought respite from the lust of self-vindication (*a libidine vindicandi me*), whereat we might recall his earlier notion that as an infant he had cried vengefully: *me flendo vindicabam*. The desire to be feared and loved raised problems; for certain offices in society required that one make oneself feared and

loved, and the temptation was to want to be feared and
loved not in behalf of God but instead of God. He had great
doubts (xxxvii) about himself as regards his addiction to
language which, following a Biblical usage, he calls a "fur-
nace." * In xxxviii he rounds the circle by admonishing
against vainly glorying in the very scorn of vainglory. The
final scruple is an admonition against those who seek neither
to please nor displease others because they are so preoccupied
with themselves.

In chapter xi he sums up by saying that, beginning with
the senses, he has advanced from there into the recesses of
his memory (*inde ingressus sum in recessus memoriae meae*),
an expression that is characteristically Augustinian in its *in-
ness*, and that might be said to match the summarizing
sentence of vɪɪɪ, xii where, following the conversions of himself
and Alypius, he says that they both went in to tell his mother
of the change: *inde ad matrem ingredimur, indicamus*. Memory here gets its most resonant description: "multiple ampli-
tudes in wondrous ways full of innumerable plenties"—and
talk of being held down by "weights" serves as transition into
his next subject, the idea of a curative Mediator.

Thus the analysis of memory leads via the imagery of
dreams to the subject of Temptation, which leads in turn to
the theme of a perfect sacrificial exemplar, combining in one
figure sacrifice and priest, victim and victor. The purgative
nature of the Mediator rounds out the principle of Mortification grandly. But since this also involves a dual nature, from
the strictly logological point of view we can say that the
Mediator joins two disparate realms. This sets the terministic
conditions for an inquiry into the relation between "time" and

* The word (*fornax*) is very close in look and sound to *fornix* (a
word which in Horace and Juvenal means "brothel," and from which is
derived the word: *fornicatio*). And though the reader may think it a
dubious kind of supererogation on our part to point out the similarity,
there is at least the fact that in the very next sentence Augustine repeats
the same sentence about continency which had been the burden of his
introduction to the subject of his unruly dreams.

"eternity"—and that in turn is reducible to an ambiguity in the meaning of the word "first," as with Augustine's efforts to decide what the Bible could mean when, at its beginning, it says, "In the beginning . . ."

XV   In the Beginning . . .

Note: Though this chapter is central to an account of the terministic developments in the last four "episcopal" books, we shall not go into the matter as thoroughly as we might otherwise have done, since it is the main point of the next essay. As regards the motives of the Trinity, this chapter relates more directly to the Word than to the Holy Spirit. That is, the underlying *formal* problem involved in the relation between words for "time" and words for "eternity" centers in the problem of the Creative Word as *principium*. By our interpretation, this dialectical matter does not directly involve the problem of Love that preponderantly figured at the moment of crisis in the garden, though we have already seen how Augustine's ideas of "eternity" were suffused with the motive of the Spirit. In fact, as Augustine himself notes (xiii, xi), being, knowing and willing all involve one another, and thus are essentially inseparable.

It required no great dialectical enterprise, though it did require much rhetorical vigor, for Augustine to endow with urgency and resonance his view of "Eternity" as a "heaven of heavens," with a free maternal city of peace related to God as wife is to husband, the whole equatable with Blessedness, Goodness, Plenitude, Love, Light, Wisdom, Righteousness, Mercy, Power and the characteristic Augustinian internality, along with the Word as Silence, and such cling-to-able predestinating power of conversion as held out hopes of eventual absolute rest *in sinu Abraham.* Whatever God might or might not be, Augustine's rich store of Biblical quotations was a fountain of superabundance, and kept pouring forth whenever needed to provide authority for fresh additions to his equations for Eternity, in its nature as a being immediately personal.

Our purpose here is to place stress rather on the technical problem involved in conceiving the relation between "Eternity" and "Time," and in trying as far as possible to translate
Augustine's views from theology into "logology." That is:
Given the resources of language, what might one say about
Eternity, even if eternity is not? And given the limitations
of language, how inadequate must such statements be, even
if eternity is? And finally, whether eternity is or isn't, what
might be the empirical logological applications of the theological doctrines? And how describe Augustine's "verbal action,"
with regard to the resources and limitations of words applied
to a realm of the "ineffable"?

As Augustine himself makes amply clear, the way of
conceiving eternity is after the analogy of time endlessly extended. However, it would not be like time extending out of
the past on and on into the "future"; it would be rather like
the momentary present made permanent, without past or
future. And in this respect it would be immutable.

The more the reader inclines to positivism, the more
likely he is to assert that such distinctions are meaningless.
Yet from the logological point of view, there is one area in
which we do experience, *formaliter*, in principle, the relation
between "time" and "timelessness." This is in the relation between the words of a sentence and its "meaning." The syllables of the words are "born" and "die." But the *meaning*
of those syllables "transcends" their sheer nature as temporal
motions. It is an *essence*, not reducible to any part of the
sentence, or even to the whole of it. For evidence that the
meaning is not in the matter as such, there is the fact that
the sentence in its sheer materiality can be meaningless to
us, in case we do not know the language in which it is
spoken or written. Matter *qua* matter, on the other hand,
exerts its effects on us whether we "understand" it or not.
We must know what the words "Step aside" mean, if we are
to obey them. But a push can have the same effect without

our having to understand its "meaning." The push is material, "temporal"; the sound of the words is material, "temporal"; but the meaning of the words is in another dimension—and from the logological point of view, the sheer materiality of a sentence is to this other dimension as "time" is to "timelessness." (We grant, however, that there is a sense in which the "meaning," too, is "material." Only insofar as the proper physical motions of the brain take place, can the sentence have any meaning. Thus, we are not trying to say that the meaning of the sentence is *intrinsically* "eternal." We are merely saying that the relation between the sentence as a sequence of "transitory" syllables and the sentence as a "fixed" unit of meaning provides the makings for a formal distinction that can serve to suggest an ontological distinction between time and eternity.)

At one notable point, however, the analogy breaks down. For if we speak the sentence, the analogue of "eternity" precedes the analogue of "time"; but if we hear the sentence, the relation is reversed. However, eternity must "precede" time; it must be like the sentence spoken. But no, that isn't the only order possible: Besides the *creative* "Word" that *precedes* the temporal syllables, there can also be the *doctrinal* words that, in their transient, disjunct syllabification, lead again to the silence of the internal Word, the unitary meaning.

But, in any case, we do confront a problem of *beginnings* here. Insofar as the sentence is an idea, or principle, it proceeds according to a plan that is one kind of "first," a sort of "final cause" that guides the actual choice of words. Yet the wording of the sentence, in its step-by-step temporal sequence, involves another kind of "first," since each part of the sentence is "prior" to the part that follows it.

The idea of priority can take many forms, and in the next essay, on Genesis, we shall make this matter the center of our inquiry. We shall there try to show how the logological counterpart of "eternity" is the way in which terms can "imply" one another, so that an expository procession from one to another is in effect "predestinated," by being implicit in the term taken as the point of departure. This we shall treat as a "cyclical" and "tautological" aspect of terminology. Similarly, the logological counterpart of "time" is said to be the one-directioned "rectilinearity" of narrative. And in particular, we shall analyze the Creation story of Genesis to show how its terms straddle these two aspects of placement.

In the meantime, the best way to approach the problem is by assembling in one place the various formulations that Augustine offers, when trying to decide how "time" and "eternity" might be related. All told, here is the range of "beginnings" or "firsts" that Augustine considers in his meditations on the possible meaning of the Bible's opening formula, "*in principio*," the truth of which he says he knows within (*intus*):

xi, vi. The "eternal Word" by which the world was created must have been in silence, for there was as yet no matter and time whereby the syllables could arise and fall in succession. (In this regard, he contrasts the creative fiat with the "voice out of the cloud which said, 'This is my beloved Son,'" Matthew 17:5. These syllables, he says, actually passed, one after the other, in temporal sequence.) God's creative fiat had no such succession, since it is coeternal with God Himself (xi, vii)—and is in fact synonymous with God's Wisdom (xi, ix). Thus this Wisdom (*Sapientia*) likewise is a *principium*. And it in turn is associated with renewal of youth, "like the eagle's" (Psalms 103:5). In xiii, xxix, he asks himself how the Bible could say eight times "God saw that it was good." For if God's creative Word is coeternal with God, by such a succession the creation of time would in effect be situated *in time* rather than in *eternity*. He solves the problem somewhat summarily by hearing in his "inner ear" (*in aure interiore*) God's answer along these lines: When we cite the Biblical texts, we are speaking through God's Spirit; but though we understand them and speak them in time, God does not.*

xi, viii. But the Word is also a beginning (*principium*) in another sense: As gospel it teaches people what to do. Thus, its nature as a Beginning is equatable with its nature as an End (literally, showing "where we might return," *quo rediremus*).

xi, x. The Word is also equatable with God's Will, which likewise is co-eternal with Him, pertaining to His very Substance. By this step, Augustine rounds out his Trinitarian pattern, and thereby asserts that God's Will must not have changed either; God's decision to create the world by his Word could not have "arisen" (*exortum est*), but would be a part of the eternal principle. This point would in effect bring the Holy Spirit into the design. (Here, by the way, is a line of thought that, as Spinoza shows, can lead to pantheism. For if a decision to create the world is coeternal with God Himself, then the "principle" of its creation is a "necessary" part of God's nature—and pantheism is technically reducible to the doctrine that the necessary relation between Creation and Creator applies in both directions, Creator needing the Creation as essentially as Creation needs the Creator.)

The next several chapters develop the notion that the *principium* or principle of eternity is like the absolute ex-

---

* Dialectically, the problem is reducible to this: If there are two distinct orders of terms, and the second is said to emerge out of the first, where situate the term at which these two orders touch (the term that would mark the *principium* of the emergent order)? In terms of narrative and personality, Christianity proposes to solve this dialectical problem by the doctrine of a "God-man" as Mediator between the two orders. But when this Mediatory role is viewed rather from the other side, *as the beginning of the distinction between the two orders* (the role of the creative Word as the *beginning* of time), then the personal, narrative idea of a *God-man* is replaced by the strictly logical idea of a *first term*. And this *temporally* first term must nonetheless lie outside the order of "temporal" firsts; otherwise it would not belong to the other order, the "eternal."

tension of that momentary present which, in time, is forever arising out of the future and receding into the past. The present would be eternity if all were but of this moment, "ever standing" (*semper stantis*), without past or future. (Might we say, paradoxically, that timelessness is here conceived as the very *essence* of time? One might get the point by a hypothetical contrast of this sort: Suppose one were to say, "It is *absolutely* true that in our kind of world, if *a* is greater than *b* and *b* is greater than *c*, then *a* is greater than *c*." Such a principle would not in itself be a *semper stans* of the kind Augustine is suggesting, despite its particular kind of "timelessness." Yet obviously, it would lack the spontaneous identification with ideas of *Living* which are inherent in Augustine's Eternity. (Do not Yeats's Byzantium poems play about the thought of an eternity that would transcend time by translation into such purely formal properties, as were we to ask not how a person might be said to live eternally, but how one might attribute an eternal validity to the *principles* which a great artist had embodied in making a portrait of that person, though the portrait too soon ceased to exist?)

Creation being by definition the creation of time, Augustine notes (xi, xiii) that we cannot properly speak of eternity as being before or after time. There could be no "then" when time was not. So, following the Biblical style, he says not that God *was* before all time, but that before all time God *is* (*ante omnia tempora tu es*).

As seen from the strictly logological point of view, Book xii is primarily involved in an embarrassment of this sort: If eternity is without the befores and afters of time, yet only the Word and the Holy Spirit are coeternal with the Father, just what relation does the heaven of heavens (*caelum caeli*) bear to eternity? In xii, xv, the stress is upon the thought that this creature, like "the rational and intellectual mind" of God's "chaste city, our mother," is "clinging to the true and truly eternal God with so chaste a love" (*tam casto amore*

cohaerentem deo vero et vere aeterno). At the same time,
the heaven of heavens is "not without a beginning" (*non
sine initio*), since God made it. The "solution" is particularly
interesting, from the standpoint of the problem which we shall
consider in the next essay. The heaven of heavens which God
made, as it were, for His environs and chaste spouse, is said
to be a participant (*particeps*) in God's eternity. Though
there is no time before eternity, and though eternity is timeless,
God's eternity is "before" (*ante*) the city and its heavenly
scene. Thus, even in heaven, there is a principle of divisiveness, however benign. And when Augustine says that the
city is *abs te*, the grammatical form in itself does not indicate
whether we should translate this as "by" God or "from" God.
The sense clearly indicates "by," in the sense that we are here
dealing with something which God created, outside His creating of time. But in vii, vii, the sense of this preposition is
wholly divisive: "I was separated from Thee" (*separabar abs
te*). Thus, the statement that the city is *abs* God introduces
an inchoately divisive principle, though under unitary guise.
The stress is not upon the *partitive* nature of participation,
but upon the oneness of that eternity in which the creature
participates. Yet participation does imply partition. (Going
a step farther back, we can discern such an inchoate divisiveness even in the idea of the Trinity, as is made apparent by
the Hegelian variant, in which the analogue of the second
person is treated as "antithetical" to the analogue of the first
person, though this division between "father thesis" and "antithetical son" is healed again, on a "higher level," in the "synthesis" of the third term that corresponds to the Holy Spirit.)

This same chapter xv also uses another word for "beginning," as regards the heaven of heavens and the maternal
heavenly city: *exordium*. Etymologically, the word reinforces
perfectly our point about the ambiguity of *abs*. *Exordium* is
composed of the words for "out of" and "order"—and the
word for "order" itself apparently derives from roots meaning

"grow" or "rise"! (Etymologically, the word *initium* comes
from roots meaning "in" and "go." *Principium* is from words
meaning "first" and "take," a *princeps* thus being a chief, ruler,
leader, the word from which we derive "prince.")

From the sheerly logological point of view, there would
be no great problem in trying to explain how the heaven of
heavens could be said to be created and "take part" in God's
eternity, even though eternity is by definition without before
and after. "God" would "come first" in a purely *logical* sense
of antecedence, as a more inclusive term. Similarly, when we
come to the next essay, we shall consider the equivalent of
the six "days" in which, according to the Biblical narrative,
the world was "created." Logologically, we need but distinguish between logical priority and temporal priority. But
insofar as logical entities are endowed with the principles
of personal life, they must be translated into terms of time
(which must in turn be translated into terms of timelessness)
—and from there on we necessarily encounter the paradox of
an eternity in which something is said to have been before
something else. The assumption of these essays is that the
problem is not by any means confined to theology, but lies
at the roots of all terminology.

Meanwhile, we list quickly the various other points that
bear most directly on Augustine's puzzlings over the formula,
"in principio":

xi, xiii. God's day being eternity, Augustine finds no
difficulty in explaining the Father's words to the Son: "This
day have I begotten Thee."

xi, xviii. The past and future can only be thought of as
present. (That is: To think of something is to think of it *now*.
The film of a modern motion picture seems to be the most
perfect instance of what Augustine has in mind here. "Flash-
backs" to "past" incidents are just as immediate as incidents
occuring "now." But isn't there still a notable difference between thinking of something when it is present and thinking of

it when it is absent? The English empiricists' distinction between "ideas" and "sensations" seems to have been based on a distinction of this sort, as with the difference between the "image" of a fire we now burn and the "image" we *now* have of a fire we intend to make *tomorrow*.)

xi, xxii and xxiii. Augustine's outcries, begging for an ability to understand the nature of time, show that he spontaneously places this kind of inquiry outside the realm of sheer "curiosity," though in xi, xii he shows awareness that the objection might be raised—for he indirectly defends himself by defending someone else who might have asked such questions and been ridiculed.

xii, xv. By the use of active and passive (light which lightens and light which is lit, etc.), he gets three distinctions which would correspond to a distinction between "eternal" and "temporal" referents for the same term. In standard English usage the same distinction is got by the use of capitals and lower case: Light, light; Wisdom, wisdom; Righteousness, righteousness. (These would all be variants of the Word-words pair.)

xii, vii. "In the beginning, which is from Thee" (or "of Thee"—*de te*), "in Thy Wisdom, which is born of (*de*) Thy substance, Thou didst create something, and out of nothing" (*aliquid et de nihilo*). From the logological point of view, this is an exceptionally packed sentence. The "creating of something out of nothing" might be called the very essence of an *act*. For an act can be an act only if it is *free* (if it is not free, it is but compulsive motion); and it can be free only insofar as it has novelty, in adding something to the previous total of necessary conditions (a contribution that can properly be described as the "creating of something out of nothing"). The Spinozistic equating of freedom with the doing of the rationally necessary may seem at first to oppose this view, but not when we consider the innovative ingredient in the discovery of "adequate ideas." God's creative fiat, then, is the paradigm of all action: It is creation "in principle." Since Wisdom is the Word, the equating of this principle with Wisdom is in effect the equating of "action" with "the verbal," or more generally, with symbol-using (of which the "rational" is a species). "God" thus becomes analyzable as the word for the idea of a wholly free act, though the locus is transferred from *act* to the idea of an agent of such a nature as to be capable of such an act.

xII, xx. Augustine lists five minor differences in answers to the question of just where God did begin. Apparently they all hinge about a paradoxical problem of this sort: If matter is formless, and formlessness is "almost nothing" (xix), and creation is the establishing of forms, just what is the relation between such prime matter and the creative acts enumerated in Genesis? Though these and related speculations later exercised scholastic philosophy, we might legitimately cut corners here, for our purposes, by saying merely that, in creating all the actualities of the world, God must somehow also have created all the potentialities. Or, as Augustine puts it (xix): God must also have made the "creatable" and the "formable" (*creabile atque formabile*).

xII, xxix. On possibilities of understanding "in the beginning" as "first" (*primo*). This leads to the enumeration of four ways in which there can be precedence: (1) by eternity, as God precedes all things; (2) by time, as the flower precedes the fruit; (3) by choice (*electione*), as the fruit precedes the flower; (4) by origin, as the sound precedes the song. The first of these expresses in terms of time the relation between time and timelessness. From the strictly logological point of view, "eternity" would be considered as a quasi-positive synonym for "timelessness." And terms for "timelessness" might be said to "precede" terms for "time" in the sense that the orbit of terms for "timelessness" would "lie outside" the orbit of terms for "time." Or, otherwise put: "timelessness" is an even more highly generalized term than "time." By the dialectics of the case, "timelessness" becomes the "ground" of time, quite as Kant named the "unconditioned" as the ground of the "conditioned." If you define the world of time as "positive," then any term for anything else would be "negative"—whereat we find things pointing in the direction of "negative theology." Whereas "eternity" ("timelessness") is *dialectically* a negative, it is far from such in Augustine's *rhetoric*.

As Augustine himself points out, there is no difficulty understanding his second and third kinds of priority, the second referring to the temporally prior in the purely empirical sense of today as preceding tomorrow, and the third equally empirical, as with the choice of one thing rather than another. But though he does not say so, ambiguities lurk around the edges of both these kinds. Thus, though the flower precedes the fruit, there is a sense in which both flower and fruit could be viewed as working towards culmination in a seed—and that point of view could suggest another kind of "first." And the notion of preference as a "first" can lead into such methodological preferences as the choice of a term that will serve as point of departure in a logical sequence.

By the fourth kind of priority, Augustine means what Aristotle would have called a "material cause." If you would sing a song by making sounds, the sounds are "prior" to the song in the sense that you can't make the song without making the sounds. (We might suggest the idea somewhat punningly thus: The sounds are formed *in order that* the song may come to be.)

In xiii, v, there occurs what in contemporary usage would be called a "breakthrough." It has to do with Augustine's conviction that he had seen, "in an enigma," how the first two verses of Genesis mention all three persons of the Trinity. By his interpretation, "In the beginning God created . . ." would mean: "In the Son (God's Word, His Wisdom) God created . . ." And the Spirit that hovered over the waters would be the third person of the Trinity, thus rounding out the pattern.

The equating of Son with Beginning has such manifold possibilities dialectically, one can understand why Augustine called this calculus an "enigma." One might say that, by his interpretation, the world's very beginnings would be not just "Elohist" and "Jehovist," but "Christian." Indeed, as regards "firsts," note that in this "enigma" the term for the Son would even precede the term for the Father, so far as the opening sentence of Genesis was concerned.

Logologically, such an arrangement would be in keeping with the further paradox that there is a sense in which we should properly speak of the Son rather than the Father as a "beginning." For the second person of the Trinity would be, as it were, the "first distinction," or "departure," the very essence or principle of divisiveness, though in a "happy" sense of the term. There is also the dialectical fact that, only by the Son's being a Son, can the Father be a Father—and in this sense the Son would be the "beginning" of the Father as well as of "divisiveness," and thus the principle of Creation itself, in the Creation's role as the Creator's offal (or "off-fall"). Note also that, as *sheer title*, Christ would be a "beginning" for Augustine, inasmuch as his name sums up the logic of "Christianity."

In the *De Trinitate*, v, xiv, where the Father is called the *principium* of the Son, and the Father and Son together are called the *principium* of the Holy Spirit, the entire Trinity is called the *principium* of things created. The first two of these firsts would exemplify wholly non-temporal kinds of priority. The third would mark the point where terms for non-temporal and terms for temporal meet. As we indicated in the previous paragraph, the "familial" process involved in the Father's generating of the Son is particularly notable from the standpoint of logical-temporal ambiguities. For though there is a sense in which a father precedes a son, there is also a sense in which the two terms are logically "co-eternal," inasmuch as they are reciprocals, and "simultaneously" imply each other. Chapter xv, which asserts that the Holy Spirit exists as a Gift "before" being given would amount logologically to the statement that the term "Holy Spirit" is intrinsically equatable with the term "Gift," without reference to any particular time or occasion on which He has been, is being, or will be "given."

Augustine's speculations concerning time also involve an imagery of stretching that is probably due to the idea of linearity in connection with time's irreversible direction. In xi, xiv, he says that time exists only insofar as it "tends (*tendit*) not to be. The primary meanings of this verb are: to stretch, make tense, stretch out, spread out, distend, extend. Other relevant meanings: press, strain, reach, aim, strive, be directed, be inclined, exert oneself, endeavor. In xi, xxiii: Time is a kind of distention, or extension (*distentionem*). In xi, xxviii: There is constant attention (*attentio*) to the present. When one is about to sing a psalm, expectation is extended (*tenditur*) towards the psalm in its entirety. As one sings, more and more of the psalm becomes extended (*tenditur*) in one's memory, and the life of this action is distended (*distenditur*) both ways between the memory of what has been sung and the expectation of what is yet to be sung. Always present is the attention, through which the future elements become past.

In xi, xxix, this set of usages takes on a new dimension. Augustine begins using *distentio* in the sense of "distraction." Our thinking of time in terms of the many distracts us from thoughts of the One (Christ here being called the Mediator between the One and the many). Augustine would be not distracted (*distentus*) but drawn out (*extentus*); he would strive not distractedly (*secundum distractionem*) but intently (*secundum intentionem*).

In xi, xxvi: When reducing time to extension (*dis-*

tentionem), he goes on to say that it may be an extension of
the mind itself (*ipsius animi*). Here, surely, is a hint of
Kantianism. The equating of mind with *distentio* is also
notable in comparison with the Cartesian distinction between
res extensa and *res cogitans*, though in the Cartesian dialectic
extension is equated with space, and time is equated with
consciousness (that would correspond to "mind" in Augustine's tentative alignment).

Also, running through the *Confessions*, there are references to "space of time." For instance (vii, xv) all "spaces
of times" (*spatia temporum*) are said to come and go only
through the "working and abiding" of God (*nisi te operante et
manente*). In xi, xxvii, he says that while time was passing
it was being extended (*tendebatur*) into a certain space of
time (*in aliquod spatium temporis*), since the present has
no space (*praesens nullum habet spatium*). In vii, i, when
describing his earlier belief in the corporeality of God, he
says that the absence of space seemed to him absolutely
nothing, not even like such a "spacious nothing" (*spatiosum
nihil*) as emptiness is. (*Prorsus*, the word here translated
"absolutely," happens to be a genuine, though not readily
noticeable member of the *vert*-family, a telescoping of *pro*
and *versus*, thus meaning literally: turned forward or straight
ahead.) In x, xxiv, when exclaiming how he has expanded
in his memory while seeking God, he uses a verb form of
the word for space: *spatiatus sum*. And recall that, though
the word *spatium* does not appear in his introductory remarks on God's ubiquity, the subject of those passages is the
way in which God "fills" everything, so that he is in God
and God is in him; this is the pattern of thinking he also
embodies when on the subject of the memory.

All told, one might say that Augustine's idea of God is
essentially temporal rather than spatial, inasmuch as it combines ideas of consciousness and the "eternal present." But
though space may suggest the "outside" and mind, memory,

and the like the "inside," there remains the blunt logological fact that "in" is as spatial a concept as "out." Eternity is a perpetual present, and "the present has no space" (*praesens nullum habet spatium*, xi, xxvii). But "space" here is meant in the sense of "interval"; and the expression for "perpetual present" is *semper stans* (that is, "ever *standing*"), an idea involving an image of substantiality that is definitely spatial.

XVI   Multitudes and Abundances (*Ubertates*) and Increases

In sum: These last four "episcopal" books have a form of their own. This form has its special kind of "conversion," a development quite different from the one described in the first nine narrative books.

Viewing the Trinity as a form, we might say that Augustine had arrived at the idea of a monotheistic "Father" (equated with Power, or Authority) as soon as he had come to a decision about the origin of evil. For his proposed "solution" made it possible for him to reject the Manichaean doctrine of competing deities (one a god of light, the other of darkness, and the dark one imbuing nature with a principle intrinsically evil). This "solution" ultimately involved theological doctrines of predestination and "original sin" which we shall consider logologically in the essay on Genesis. The Platonists' stress upon the divinity of the Logos had prepared him for the second person of the Trinity, the Son (equated with Wisdom). This could link well with the creative fiats of Genesis, The Word as the "beginning" of time. His emotional crisis in the garden, when he had shamefully turned from the remembrance of his mistresses to dutiful reverence for a chaste, dignified, maternal Continentia, had added the third person to the design, the Holy Spirit (equatable with Love, and thus most directly bearing on the moment at

which he had become moved by a new quality of "will").
And the incident of rebirth in the garden had been completed
by the conversation with his mother, just before her death.

The last four books "recapitulate" this story in a totally
different kind of development. In Book x, where he "enters"
the memory, with the expressed intention of "transcending"
it, Augustine begins the kind of dialectical progression that
is traditionally, in Neo-Platonist thought, called the Upward
Way. By the steps we have been charting, this development
brings him to speculation on the relation between "eternity"
and the "heaven of heavens" (which is said to be a "participant" in such eternity, without being co-eternal with it).
Rhetorically, this movement came to a head in thoughts of
clinging. Dialectically, it came to a head in ambiguities
whereby temporal terms had to be used for the discussion of
a realm that by definition transcended the temporal. And this
problem led to speculations on the very idea of a "first."
Formally, this amounts to the reduction of everything to a
concern with *oneness,* though there is the notable difference
that the idea of unity as *ordinal* rather than *cardinal* suggests not just reduction *to* a center but also the possibility of
subsequent radiation *from* that center. In this particular
dialectic, the development can be from words for "eternity"
to words for "time," which in effect means that "time" can
come to be viewed *in terms* of "eternity."

It is formally fitting that this stress upon beginnings
comes to a head in Book xii. This would be analogous to a
peripety occurring in Act iii of a four-act drama. About the
scene in the garden, the whole work hinges. But the second
half, considered in itself, hinges about the talk of beginnings.
And whereas the Upward Way had led to talk of eternity, the
complementary Downward Way leads from "eternity" back
into "time." Thus, inasmuch as the idea of a beginning is
permeated with the idea of divine unity, this principle of
divinity suffuses the idea of the manifoldness, or *plenitude,*

which Augustine stresses in Book XIII, throughout his comments on the account of the Creation as narrated in Genesis.

The movement of infoliation now becomes a movement
of exfoliation. From its origins in unitary timelessness (a
timelessness conceived as a kind of time made immutable,
with a spatiality rather like that of images in the memory than
like that of things perceived in the world, for the heaven of
heavens is called an "intellectual creature"), the world of
time is spread open like a fan, as Augustine comments on the
work of the various "days." But the stress is placed not just
upon natural plenitude, but rather upon the idea that it all
arises from a plenitude of the Creator's goodness.

This last book also shows signs of a more specifically
"episcopal" purpose, though it's hard to bring out this point
sufficiently without seeming to overstress it. We have in mind
problems to do with ecclesiastical administration. Compared
with works like Cicero's *De Officiis*, or Ambrose's Christianized
counterpart, *De Officiis Ministrorum*, the concern with ad-
ministrative matters is slight. Yet we'd miss an important
motivational strand if we did not mention it.

Augustine's own emphasis upon the question of beginnings might give us the best lead. As seen from this point of
view, the best way to approach the contents of this final
book is by an analogy: As the narrative section of the *Confessions* ended on what we proposed to call the "Book of
Monica," so this episcopal section ends on what we might
call the "Book of the Holy Spirit."

But to say as much is forthwith to be reminded that
the theme of the Spirit has many strands. Thus, increasingly
as we near the end, there is the stress on the theme of rest.
And inasmuch as the third person of the Trinity is equatable
with Love, Augustine's idea of rest in the Holy Spirit will
be equatable with the idea of rest in absolute familial love
(*caritas* or *agape* as distinct from *amor* or *eros*, though Augustine does not explicitly draw this distinction). Here would be

the motivational area that fits most directly with talk of
"clinging." (Near the end of chapter xxxi, Augustine also
uses a variant of the predestinatory notion that man cannot
turn to God unless God has first turned to man: Following
Paul, Romans 5:5, he says that we love God by the love which
"is shed abroad in our hearts by the Holy Ghost.")

Similarly, the idea of the Spirit also has direct bearing on
the *Scriptures*. Thus, the statement (xiii, iv) that God's Spirit
can be said to rest in those whom God has caused to rest in
Him, introduces a principle of convertibility which amounts
to saying that we interpret things in God's Spirit when we
interpret Biblically. And since the former "word merchant"
has already stated (xi, ii) that it is now his office to "preach
the Word" (*praedicare Verbum*), the idea of seeing things
in terms of Scripture glides into the idea of seeing them in
terms of the Church (and here would belong such views on
ordination and giving as went best with ecclesiastical organization).

In this connection, there is another kind of "first" (xiii,
xxiii), as he derives from the Spirit of God that ecclesiastical
order whereby some are "spiritually subject" (*spiritaliter sub-
duntur*) to those who "spiritually precede" them (*spiritaliter
praesunt*). The humble obedience which one learns as a
follower has become rather the humble obedience which one
teaches as a leader. And whereas the matter of "gifts" obviously has direct bearing upon fiscal problems (the costs of
administration), this topic, too, can be derived from thoughts
on the Holy Spirit since in Christian theology the Holy
Spirit is pre-eminently associated with the idea of a gift. (Cf.
Aquinas, *Summa Theologica, Prima Q 38, Art. 2: Donum est
proprium nomen Spiritus sancti*. Or see *Confessions*, xiii, ix:
"in Thy gift we rest.") The terministic element becomes
clear when (xiii, xxvi), following Paul, he stresses the difference between merely giving and giving *in the name of* (a
prophet, a righteous man or a disciple).

To view nature in the Spirit of the Scriptures is wholly to avoid such natural history as Augustine would have classed under "curiosity." His approach readily leads to *allegorical* interpretations of words for natural phenomena, *e.g.*, interpreting light as illumination (hence as faith: xii), or fishes and whales as surrogates for miracles. It is a mode of thought to which logology is always, though somewhat coyly, prone. In particular, logology would lay much store by Augustine's chapter xv, on the "firmament of authority," since it forms a perfect terministic bridge linking ideas of sky, Scriptures and ecclesiastical leadership.

The purely methodological aspect of this book's stress upon Spirit attains a notable formulation in chapter xxiv. Here, when considering the difference between literal and figurative interpretations, Augustine says that something which is indicated by the body in many ways can be understood by the mind in one way, or something which is indicated by the body in one way can be understood by the mind in many ways. Or, more briefly: One thing can be stated in many ways, or one statement can be understood in many ways. Or again: We can say something in many ways and understand it in one, or we can understand in many ways what has been obscurely said in one.

From the standpoint of textual analysis in general, Augustine might here be taken as falling in line with the proposition that one idea can be conveyed by various images, or one image can sum up various ideas. Augustine uses his formula in connection with references in Genesis to the fruitfulness and multiplication of species. He wants to interpret these references figuratively, as symbolizing the multiplication of good things generally—and he proposes to include within the class of "human generations" various thoughts developed by the fertility of reason. Primarily, such observations would seem to be in line with the notions of spiritual offspring he mentioned in connection with his con-

version, at the end of Book VIII. But behind that there also
lurks the possibility of an etymological association of ideas
linking the word for logical classification, "genus," with the
word for biological progeny, "generation." Such a concern
with *families* of concepts would ultimately involve another
variant of the subtle and elusive relation between logical and
temporal terminologies.

XVII   Conversion of a Word

By its own weight a body strives towards its proper place.
Weight leads not just downwards, but also towards its place. Fire
tends up, stone down. By their weights, things are acted upon,
and seek their places. Oil poured under water rises above the water.
Water poured on oil sinks beneath the oil. . . . When not in order,
things are restless; when in order, they come to rest. My weight
is my love; by it I am borne wherever I am borne. By Thy gift
we are inflamed (*accendimur*) and are borne upwards. We grow
ardent and advance. We ascend (*ascendimus*) . . . and sing the
song of degrees.

One could linger long over this passage, in which Augustine adapts to his theological purposes Aristotle's hierarchal
notion that each thing in nature seeks its proper level. From
the logological point of view it particularly strikes our fancy
because of the formula equating "weight" and "love" (*pondus
meum, amor meus*). Clearly this almost epigrammatic statement of motives suggests that we should add *pondus* to the
list of words worth special watching.

A few lines previously Augustine had said, "In Thy
gift we rest" and "Our rest is our place." Then he develops
the thought that rest in Spirit is equatable with placement in
the universal order. The expression, "song of degrees," borrowed from the Psalms, is used to suggest rather the rungs of
a ladder than the original meaning, of stages along a course;
and thus it serves more directly to introduce connotations of
hierarchy into this view of restful placement. (Recall also,

page 113, the distinction between eternity that draws us up and temporal interests that hold us down.)

The talk of being "borne upwards" could lead us back to his concerns in chapter vi, where eight instances of the word "borne over" (*superferri*) occur in nine lines. Concern with the Spirit as "borne above" the waters, and with a passage through unsubstantial waters to rest in Spirit, leads by transitions into the lines we have quoted on placement by the weight of love.

But our primary interest here is in the word *pondus* itself. For if we watch it in various contexts throughout the text, we find that in this particular context it undergoes a conversion all its own. But first, glancing back at previous entries, here is what we find:

Surprisingly enough, the makings of this final statement appear in a passage (IV, xiv) where Augustine is discussing the books on aesthetics he wrote in his early years at Carthage. Here he refers to the "weights" (*pondera*) of "various and diverse loves" that are all "distributed in our souls." (Note, incidentally, that the word for "diverse" here, *diversorum*, is a member of the *vert*-family.) It is also notable that, just a few paragraphs previously (IV, xii), he had written of "descending to ascend," and of falling by ascending "against" God. Thus, when discussing beauty in terms of fitness, he already had the various pieces that could be assembled as he has finally assembled them in xiii, ix.

In IV, xv, he is sinking from the weight of his own pride (*pondere superbiae meae*).

v, iv. He quotes a reference from the Book of Wisdom (11:20) on God's ordering of all things by number, weight, and measure (*in mensura et numero et pondere*).

VII, xvii. He speaks of being torn away from God by his own weight (*deripiebar abs te pondere meo*). He meant here the weight of carnal habits.

vⅢ, vi. He is groaning under the weight of his worldly business.

(As an aside, we might note ⅸ, ii, where he is ascending from the valley of tears, singing a song of degrees. Similarly, in x, viii, there is a reference to "ascending by degrees," *gradibus ascendens.*)

x, xl. Having just finished his catalogue of sensory, intellectual, and spiritual temptations, he speaks of lapses due to his "troublesome weights" (*aerumnosis ponderibus*).

And as late as xⅢ, vii, there is a reference to the weight of lust (*pondere cupiditatis*). This appears just after the lines associating love (*caritas*) with the Holy Spirit.*

To be sure, if we also consider some of the forms that the same root takes as a verb, the contrast is lost. Here is an area of overlap, that obscures the distinction between weights as something that holds one down and such "weight of love" as can rise.

For instance, there are the references to Augustine's being held in suspense just before his conversion: the verbs *suspendebat* and *pendebam* in vⅢ, xi. (Recall that the critical moment in the garden takes place in xii.) In vⅠ, iv, he says that, when he had first learned from Ambrose the ways of interpreting some Biblical texts figuratively, he began to assent, but he was still hanging back, in a suspense (*suspendio*) that was in effect killing him. A fate-laden incidence occurs in ⅸ, x, which opens with the ablative absolute: *impedente autem die* (the day impending, on which his mother was to die). This is the chapter that describes their enrapt conversation about the silence of eternity.

In its first and simplest form the verb figures (ⅰ, viii) when Augustine is speculating on the way he had come to

---

* Such a reference as this, to the "weight of lust," incidentally reminds us that, among the Latin meanings for *pondus*, is also one plural form which, in Biblical parlance, is translated as "stones."

learn language while depending (*pendens*) on the authority
of his parents and the nods of adults. We wonder whether
we are justified in pairing it with a passage (XIII, ii) that refers
to things depending (*penderent*) on God's Word. In VIII, vi,
the idea of the impending is presented favorably, when he
speaks of bestowing (*impendere*) much care upon works that
deal with conversion and monasticism.

We have given but a small fraction of the entries having
verb forms of this fate-laden word. And even these few spoil
the symmetry of our position somewhat, since in these forms
the word is "converted" before we get to the notable passage
in XIII, ix. But as regards the noun forms, if any references are
missing the omission is due solely to inadvertency. And the
notion we have in mind, as regards this passage, is that, of a
sudden, the word "weight" must have conveyed to Augustine
rather the sense of *lightness*, somewhat as though a stone were
to levitate. This is contrived by adapting the traditional metaphor of love as a flame which ascends. And the likeness between kindling and ascension is made still closer by the tonal
similarity of the two verbs: *accendimur, ascendimus.*

XVIII   In Conclusion

When we first began this analysis of the *Confessions*, we
had about so much in mind: (1) Augustine's change from
teacher of pagan rhetoric to Christian bishop should provide
a focal point of study with regard to our concern with the
possible relation between terms for "God" and terms for language. (2) The stress upon *conversion*, in contrast with the
chapter on *perversity*, would probably make terms in the "*vert*-
family" particular candidates for observation, and might provide good grounds for comparing (however contrastingly)
the motives of delinquency and religious dedication. (3)

From the standpoint of form, everything should be considered as leading up to and away from the critical moment of conversion in the garden. (4) There was a notable difference between the narrative method of the first nine books and the dialectical structure of the last four books. (5) This difference pointed to two modes of placement, and these might be more directly studied by a "logological" analysis of the same text in Genesis which Augustine analyzes theologically.

As we proceeded, these plans became altered in one major respect. We began to see that the strong Trinitarian emphasis in Augustine's thinking had radical bearing upon his conversion, in shaping its nature as a form. In particular, the strand of motivation most directly related to the Word (in Plato) seemed qualitatively different from the strand of motivation most directly related to the Holy Spirit. The one was in the category of the "intellect," the other in the category of "love" or "will."

However, this simple alignment was complicated by the fact that, once the idea of the Word as Mediator in the Platonic sense of a bond between disparate realms became fused with the idea of Mediator as willing sacrifice, then the ingredient of love (or will) also infused the Word with its nature. Augustine deals with this point explicitly (xiii, xi) when he observes that being, knowing and willing are inseparable. (And in the light of the important role he assigns to Memory in Book x of the *Confessions*, it is interesting to note that in the *De Trinitate*, iv, xxi, when discussing how the Father, Son and Holy Spirit are inseparable even though he in speech thus separates them, he next notes that the same is true of "memory, intellect and will.")

We proceed on the assumption that, regardless of the theological significance one might attach to such analogies, they might indicate distinctions in the purely empirical realm of motives. That is: Where Augustine assigns a triune nature to God, without either affirming or denying his position theologically we might view it from the purely empirical point of view as indicating that Augustine had a sense of triple motivation within himself. In brief, "God" would stand for a kind of motive he associated with *being* (which in turn he equated with *memory*), in fusion with a kind of motive he associated with intellect (Wisdom, the Word), and in further fusion with the kind of motives he associated with love (will); and the psychological counterpart of such theological Trinitarianism would involve a "triune" response on his own part (insofar as his own personality might be conceived as "made in the image of" his idea of God).

Such psychic economy might be expected to operate approximately as follows:

(1) Beginning with the thought of his individual identity (which in turn depended upon the kind of continuity that is made possible by memory), he thought of this identity as being grounded in a comprehensive "allness" ultimately reducible to terms of *potestas*. Such *potestas* would combine ideas of both natural power and personal authority. The idea of God's relation to natural power would correspond to the idea of the self as a body. And the idea of God as a superpersonal authority would correspond to the idea of the self as an individual user of symbols. (God would be an absolute "Father," to match Augustine's notion of his own identity as a "son.")

(2) The terministic element here could be considered in itself as the absolute Word, the Logos, analogous to his own empirical use of words. It would be "derivative" (and thus could be said to be "generated" as a Son is generated by a Father) in the sense that there must "first" be *being* in order for that being to be *known*. Yet such a "first" need not be conceived purely in terms of *temporal* sequence. For there is a sense in which the *being* and the *being-known* are one, as with Berkeley's equating of *esse* with *percipi*. If, for instance, color exists only because our senses are so constructed that we experience certain vibrations in terms of color, then the "exist-

ence" of the color is identical with the "perceiving" of it. Logologically, "Father" is related to "Son" as a *tree* is related to the *word* "tree"—yet its identity as precisely a tree is not just in the thing itself but also in the name we assign to it. So, in this sense, its identity (as precisely a tree and nothing else) requires both the thing and its name, "simultaneously." Such a Logos would be a first in its own right, in the sense that from its genius is derived the universe of rational discourse, with the various distinctions, classifications, negations and the like that go with such a realm.

(2a) One may think of the Word as Mediatory, in the sense that it interposes itself between one's nature as an individual body and one's ideas of that body's ultimate ground. Such Mediation would be "creative" in the sense that to it are due the individual person's ways of "hearing" what other persons have to tell him, and of developing his own body of beliefs. But the other side of Mediation would be still missing: the idea of Mediator as curative victim.

(3) But one's views on *potestas,* as developed by the "intellection" of the verbal principle (or symbols in general), are found to involve problems of "will." From the standpoint of supernatural Trinitarian identity, there is no such problem of "will." Insofar as the thing and its name correspond, in that very correspondence there is the kind of perfect communication (or, more accurately, "communion") that is meant by the "Holy Spirit" (as a term "proceeding" from *both* "Father" and "Son"). It is the name for the principle of identity between thing and name. And the *personal* term for perfect correspondence between the named and its name (*nominatum* and *nomen*) would be "Love."

However: The empirical analogue of such a "Love" in the absolute is *will* (that is, desire, appetition). And insofar as the empirical resources of the word enable us to build doctrinal structures that put us variously at odds with ourselves, the principle of perfect Love has as its empirical analogue a condition of conflicting loves ("wishes" that are at war with one another). In Augustine's case, such conflict was reduced primarily, though not wholly, to terms of sexual appetite (a special emphasis that he also justified in part by his linguistic observation that, though there are many "lusts," if we don't specify the object of the lust the object is assumed to be sexual).

Here was a problem that, arising from the continuities of memory, and shaped as a problem by doctrinal considerations (themselves rooted in symbol-using) was "resolved" by the resources of symbol-using. This change took place when he substituted for the physicality of his mistresses a loyalty to the matronly figure of Continentia, conceived in keeping with the norms of the doctrines to which he would be vowed.

However, such substitution, which was made possible by the resources of the verbal (or of symbol-using in general), left attendant problems unresolved. We learn from his own testimony, for instance, that his dreams were not converted. In this sense, the attempted coercing of appetite (as per the ideals of *wollen sollen*) still made him a victim of guilt. And the Word took over this victimage, by becoming Mediator in the cathartic sense. In the role of *willing* sacrifice (a sacrifice done through *love*) the Second Person thus became infused with the motive of the Third Person (the term analogous to will or appetition, with corresponding problems). Similarly, just as Holy Spirit is pre-eminently identified with the idea of a "Gift," so the sacrificial Son becomes a Gift *sent* by God.

By this arrangement, the world is "Christianized" at three strategic spots: The *emergence* of "time" out of "eternity" is through the Word as creative; *present* communication between "time" and "eternity" is maintained by the Word as Mediatory (in the Logos' role as "God-man"); and the *return* from "time" back to "eternity" is through the Mediatory God-man in the role of sacrificial victim the fruits of Whose sacrifice the believer shares by believing in the teachings of the

Word, as spread by the words of Scriptures and Churchmen.

However, the principle of victimage is not confined to the idea of an absolute victim. There is also the relation to theological enemies and to persons such as his mistresses, to whom he was related as to objects of temptation. Thus, just before the chapter in which the notable change takes place, with all the parts of his motivation clicking into Trinitarian shape, there is his flare-up of rage against the Manichaeans, a flare-up that should probably be interpreted as also involving the implied "dissolution" of his mistresses (when he denied the reality of evil by reducing the Manichaeans' theory to absurdity).

The attempt to unravel the strands here is complicated by a kind of "trinitarianism" within the book's terminology itself. For though, in one sense, the conversion takes place in Book viii, there is another sense in which it has already taken place in the very first words of the incantatory introduction. For instance, insofar as praise equals love, and love equals the Holy Spirit, then the principle of the Spirit is implicit in the theme of praise. Similarly, though the theme of "knowledge" announced at the beginning of Book x would fall primarily under the heading of the Word, the search involves an entrance into "Memory," which is analogous to the Father in the memory-intellect-will triad, and implies the theme of Spirit in ways we have already indicated. In this sense, there is a cyclical identity "eternally and changelessly present" on every page of both the narrative section and the later "episcopal" unfolding. So, even while we try to analyze its transformations "in time," there is a motivational constant infusing it as a whole.

Still another kind of "predestination" is conceivable here, as regards Augustine's own life. If one is going to develop in a certain way, conceivably the logic of this ultimate development would manifest itself, however roundabout, at much earlier stages, in his peculiar way of assimilating experiences.

For the things that happen to us do not acquire their identity from themselves alone, but also reflect the character of the way in which we confront them. In this regard, Augustine might be said to have assimilated his earlier experiences in a way that already "implicitly contained" his conversion, which would be the proper "extrapolation" or "logical conclusion" of his trends. The nearest one can come to glimpsing this kind of "predestination" is in his account of the theft, which he apparently committed with an exactingly "conscientious" kind of corruption, a "spirit" that would eventually mature into a different view of spirit.

As regards our concern with key terms (and with such possible etymological cognates as the *vert*-family, the *pondus* set, the *in* of place and negation, and range of words bearing upon the "stretching" of time and variants of the words for quest and questing that run like an *idée fixe* throughout the text), our charting begins in a kind of documentation that makes our statements as nearly irrefutable as statements can be. But at the same time, such study points experimentally towards an aspect of language that has still largely eluded analysis, namely, the search for the possible reduction of a writer's terminology to a few basic "designs," which might be taken as "class names" for many terms not on their face belonging under these heads.

As regards Augustine's terminology in particular, our general notion is that, via his remarks on *Continentia*, he endows the Holy Spirit with a strongly maternal strand of motives. This would include on one side the kind of responses that later writers would tend rather to express with reference to Mary, and the kind of responses that in his personal relations would seem most directly associated with Monica. Terms that we would treat as especially containing this strand are: *Continentia, attingere, inhaerere, requies, modica, casta, dignitas, sinus, memoria,* heaven of heavens, the heavenly city of peace, eternity and the various words with connotations of food or plenty, such as God's fountain, God's milk, *ubertas,* *plenitudo, sapientia* and *primitiae Spiritus.* "Laughter" in the *Confessions* is a dyslogistic term (used in the sense of "derision") except in three places where it involves the mother-child relation.

Though we take it that theology has its beginnings in religion, we also assume that there is an important one-to-one relation between the growth of a complex theology and the high development of social institutions. In this sense, Augustinian theology would be as much an expression of the Roman Empire as of an "I-Thou" relation between man and God.

The resources of dialectics being what they are, one can make out a good case either for the thesis that modern science grew up outside the rationalizations of theology or for the thesis that modern science is but the translating of theology into a secular counterpart. Much of one's choice will depend upon the relative importance one attaches to experimentation and rationalization in the development of modern science, while money also played an important part—its nature as a device of accountancy contributing both to the facilitating of exchange and to the rationalizing of motives for exchange.

A logological calculus inclines to look rather for the *continuities* in the development from Western theology to the order of modern accountancy and modern technology, particularly since such a calculus helps keep us ever on the alert to spot the role of *symbolism* as the motivating genius of secular enterprise. Otherwise, our world looks too purely "pragmatic," whereas its recently much-accelerated dreams of unlimited power and interplanetary empire become so hard to distinguish from paranoia—we should do best to watch for purely symbolic motivations here, despite the undeniable material reality and might of the technologist's engines.

Insofar as "technologism" is a "religion" (and it is a "religion" to the extent that technology is viewed as an intrinsic good, so that its underlying, unspoken assumption is:

"The more technology, the higher the culture"), we had better favor a calculus that keeps us always aware of technology's possible relation to theology's vast motivational Cathedrals, and particularly such as Augustine's, which is so tirelessly concerned with problems of words and The Word.

3 The First Three Chapters of Genesis

Outline of the Inquiry

unfolded quasi-narratively. (m) Simplest known instance of the temporizing of essence. (n) Theodor Reik's *Myth and Guilt, the Crime and Punishment of Mankind.*   242-272

I   On Covenant and Order

Hobbes's *Leviathan* well serves our purposes here, if we can bring ourselves to discount the cantankerousness of his "Christian politics." The important thing about his book for our purposes is that it makes us acutely conscious of the Biblical stress upon *Covenants* as motives. And we want to so relate the ideas of Creation, Covenant and Fall that they can be seen to implicate one another inextricably, along with ideas of Sacrifice and Redemption.

Creation implies authority in the sense of originator, the designer or author of the things created.

Covenant implies authority in the sense of power, sovereignty—the highest or most radical sovereignty in case the Covenant is made by God.

The possibility of a "Fall" is implied in the idea of a Covenant insofar as the idea of a Covenant implies the possibility of its being violated. One does not make a covenant with stones or trees or fire—for such things cannot break agreements or defy commands, since they cannot even understand agreements or commands.

Also, the possibility of a "Fall" is implied in the idea of the Creation, insofar as the Creation was a kind of "divisiveness," since it set up different categories of things which could be variously at odds with one another and which accordingly lack the proto-Edenic simplicity of absolute unity. Thus Coleridge observes (*Table Talk,* May 1, 1830):

A Fall of some sort or other—the creation, as it were, of the non-absolute—is the fundamental postulate of the moral history of man. Without this hypothesis, man is unintelligible; with it, every phenomenon is explicable. The mystery itself is too profound for human insight.

Though this may be a mystery theologically, its logological analogue is not mysterious. Logologically, there is a "fall" from a prior state of unity, whenever some one term is broken into two or more terms, so that we have the "divisiveness" of "classification" where we formerly had had a "vision of perfect oneness." Insofar as the title of a book could be said to sum up the nature of that book, then the breakdown of the book into parts, chapters, paragraphs, sentences, words would be technically a "fall" from the Edenic unity of the title, or epitomizing "god-term." The *parts* of the book reduce its "idea" to "matter." Or, as Coleridge said (*Table Talk*, October 15, 1833): "The Trinity is the Idea: the Incarnation, which implies the Fall, is the Fact: the redemption is the mesothesis of the two—that is—the Religion."

Presumably he is thinking of "religion" here in the sense of *religare* (to bind, connect, fasten)—and the logological analogue to his theory in this instance would concern our way of tying the particulars of a work together in accordance with the over-all spirit signalized by its unitary and unifying title.

Narratively, there was the Creation; then came the "Edenic" Covenant (which included the injunction against eating of the tree of the knowledge of good and evil); then the Fall; and then the "Adamic" Covenant (3:14-19) which included punishments for Adam's first disobedience. But though this order is irreversible from the standpoint of narrative, there is a sense in which we can reverse the order. For instance, we could "begin" with the idea of a punishment; next we could note that the idea of punishment implies the idea of some infraction which makes the punishment relevant; and such infraction implies the need for a set of conditions that make the infraction possible; and insofar as we looked for a "first" set of such conditions, the idea of them would imply the idea of the kind of Creation that allowed for disobedience.

Again, in the idea of punishment, we might discern another kind of implication. Insofar as punishment is a kind of "payment" for wrong, we can see flickering about the edges of the idea of punishment the idea of redemption. To "pay" for one's wrongdoing by suffering punishment is to "redeem" oneself, to cancel one's debt, to ransom or "buy back."

Next, since the idea of an *agent* is implicit in the idea of an *act*, we can say that in the idea of *redemption* there is implicit the idea of a personal *redeemer*. Or, if you think of redemption as a condition or situation (a "scene"), then you may extract the same implication by thinking of a redeemer as an instrument, or agency, for bringing about the condition. And this step, you will note, automatically includes the idea of a substitution: the possibility that one character may be redeemed through the act or agency of another.

The idea of such substitution, or vicarage, neatly parallels at one end of the series an idea at the other: the notion that, as one character can redeem another by suffering in his stead, so one character can impute guilt to another by sinning in his stead. This would be true of the Pauline logic whereby Adam's disobedience represents a guiltiness in Everyman with regard to Covenants ("In Adam's fall, We sinned all"), and there is introduced a principle of representation whereby a "second Adam" can serve as sacrificial substitute for mankind when the categorical guiltiness is being "paid for."

More specifically, the conditions for such a doctrine of "original sin" are set up when our "first" parent who commits the crucial sin has a name at once individual and generic, a name that can be translated either as "Adam" or as "man." Thus, in his sin as "Adam," he can personate mankind in general. We shall later consider other ways in which the purely narrative style operates here, but this shift between individual and generic should be enough for the moment.

The other six great Covenants mentioned in the Bible are the Noachian, Abrahamic, Mosaic, Palestinian, Davidic and the New (as per Hebrews 8:8). But the two mentioned in the first three chapters (the Edenic and the Adamic) are sufficient for our purposes, except that the step from punishment to redemption is tenuous. There are the ceremony of redemption by vicarious atonement in connection with the feast of the Passover (Exodus 12) and the sacrificial slaying of the goat set apart for Azazel (Leviticus 16). Earlier, the principle of a personal redeemer was clearly present in Abraham's offering of Isaac (Genesis 22). And as early as Genesis 8:20-21 (in connection with the third Covenant), Noah makes burnt-offerings "of every clean fowl" (whereat the Lord "smelled a sweet savour" and "said in his heart, I will not again curse the ground any more for man's sake").

Though the idea of a redemptive sacrifice is clear enough as regards the Biblical idea of a Covenant in general, it is but inchoately there, as regards the two Covenants in the first three chapters of Genesis. We have tried to argue for its implicit presence by showing that the idea of redemption is a further stage in the idea of punishment, and the idea of a redeemer (hence, of vicarious atonement) is implicit in the idea of redemption. And as regards our over-all concern (with the notion that the idea of a redeemer is implicit in the idea of a Covenant in general), the later developments of the Bible itself with relation to God's "peculiar people" make this relation clear enough.

But I might add, incidentally, that one Bible I happen to be consulting, The Scofield Reference Bible, professes to find "the first promise of a Redeemer" in Genesis 3:15, where the Lord God, in cursing the serpent for having tempted Eve, decrees: "And I will put enmity between thee and the woman, and between thy seed and her seed; and it shall bruise thy head, and thou shalt bruise his heel." The editor asserts that here begins "the highway of the Seed," which he traces through Abel, Seth, Noah (Genesis 6:8-10), Shem (Genesis 9:26-27), Abraham (Genesis 12:1-4), Isaac (Genesis 17:19-21), Jacob (Genesis 28:10-14), Judah (Genesis 49:10), David (II Samuel 7:5-17), Immanuel-Christ (Isaiah 7:9-14; Matthew 1:1, 20-23;

I John 3:8; John 12:31). Thus, however strained the point
may seem, it should apply insofar as there is a continuity between the idea of temptation and the idea of a redeemer, when
this continuity is expressed in terms of a continuity of "the
Seed," from the locus of "original sin" to the locus of its can-
cellation by redemptive sacrifice. Or, otherwise put: the hered-
itary line here listed would represent at every stage a contact
with the principle of a Covenant, and the principle of a
Covenant contains within itself the principles of both temptation (on the part of one who might break the Covenant) and
"repayment" (or "redemption") insofar as the aggrieved party
is willing to impose and accept a fine or forfeit. (The thought,
incidentally, suggests how the ideas of "justice" and "mercy"
will also be found implicit in the idea of a Covenant—"justice"
being but the idea of a proper repayment, and "mercy" the
"good" word for the idea of a willingness to accept a repayment that in some notable respect is disproportionate to the
gravity of the offense.)

In Rashi's Commentary on the Pentateuch, with regard
to the opening formula ("In the beginning") another commentator is quoted to this effect: The main object of the Law
(or Torah) being to teach commandments (mitzvoth), if this
were the only consideration involved the Bible could have
begun with the second verse of Exodus 12 ("This month shall
be unto you the beginning of months: it shall be the first
month of the year to you"). Notably for our purposes, the
passage he mentions deals with the rite of the paschal lamb
sacrificed at Passover, and thus contains the thought that in
a notable respect this book of beginnings might have begun
with the principle of sacrifice.

For our purposes, this is a most important consideration.
For we are to deal above all with "firsts" (or "principles").
More specifically, we are to be concerned with the "firsts" or
"principles" of Covenants. And we are to be on the lookout
for the important role played by the sacrificial principle in the

cycle of terms that cluster about the idea of a Covenant. So it's notable that the most famous Jewish commentary on Genesis begins by considering a possible alternative first, to do with the instituting of a sacrifice as regards the Lord's governmental contract with His chosen people.

However, we are told in the Rashi commentary, the Bible begins as it does rather than with the establishing of a paschal ceremony because the first words of Genesis, by showing all the world to be the property of God, make clear Israel's right to seize the lands of the Canaanites, since God could dispose of His property as He chose, and He chose to give the lands of Canaan to the Israelites. (Incidentally, there is a sense in which the beginning of Genesis as we now have it would be the proper "pre-first," even for the commentator's claim: it sets up the conditions of division and dominion necessary for the idea of a Covenant by which Canaan became a promised land.)

Rashi also cites a Rabbinical interpretation to the effect that God created the world for the sake of the Law (the Torah). And in connection with this position (as against the notion that the Bible is attempting to say what came first *in time*), he notes that there were waters before the creating of heaven and earth. (Also, the very word for "heavens" is a combination of words for "fire" and "water.")

Rashi is interested in bringing out the notion that the world was created by God not solely to the ends of justice, but first of all to the ends of mercy combined with justice. As regards our cycle of the terms implicit in the idea of a Covenant, we need but note that the ideas of both justice and mercy are present in the idea of repayment for the breaking of a contract (justice when the penalty is proportionate to the offense, mercy when the penalty is favorably disproportionate, while injustice would involve a penalty unfavorably disproportionate).

As regards Rashi's questioning of the notion that the

Creation story in Genesis is dealing strictly with firsts *in time,* we should find his reservations logologically much to our purposes. Logologically, Genesis would be interpreted as dealing with *principles* (with *logical* "firsts," rather than sheerly *temporal* ones). From the very start it is dealing with the *principles of governance* (firsts expressed in quasi-temporal terms since they are the kind most natural to the narrative style). That is, the account of the Creation should be interpreted as saying in effect: This is, in principle, a statement of what the natural order must be like if it is to be a perfect fit with the conditions of human socio-political order (conditions that come to a focus in the idea of a basic Covenant backed by a perfect authority).

To get the point, turn now to Pope's line, "Order is Heaven's first law." In Pope's formula, the idea of a "first" is ambiguous. The reader is not quite sure (nor need he be) whether it means first in time, or first in importance, or first in the sense of a logical grounding for all other laws, a kind of "causal ancestor" from which all other "laws" could be deduced or derived as lineal descendants.

Once we have brought out the strategic importance of the part played by the Biblical stress upon the idea of a Covenant, there are advantages to be gained by locating our cycle of Dramatistic terms about this term "Order," rather than about the term "Covenant."

The most general starting point for the Dramatistic cycle of terms would be in the term "act." Under this head would belong God's creative acts in the first chapter of Genesis, God's enactment of the first Covenant (largely permissive, but with one crucial negative command), Adam's act of disobedience and God's enactment of a second Covenant imposing penalties upon all mankind.

Also, of course, there would be terms for the many kinds of "rationally" purposive motion, along with their corresponding "passions," which characterize human life in all its aspects.

These would be without such stress upon "sin" or "guilt" as necessarily arises when we deal with the story of a *first temptation*. But for this very reason, such a general approach to a Dramatistic cycle of terms would not serve our present purpose. Frankly, it would not be morbid enough. We need an approach that, like the Bible itself, leads us from a first Adam in whom all vicariously "sinned," to a "second Adam" by whom all might vicariously make atonement. For we are trying to analyze the respects in which the ideas of both guilt and redemption by vicarious sacrifice are intrinsic to the idea of a Covenant (which in turn is intrinsic to the idea of governance).

Yet the term "Covenant" is not wholly convenient for our purposes. Having no opposite in standard usage, it seems as purely "positive" as words like "stone," "tree" or "table," which are not matched by companion words like "counter-stone," "anti-tree," or "un-table" (except sometimes in the dialectic of E. E. Cummings). And perhaps the notion of "positive law" secretly contributes to one's feeling that "Covenants" can be treated as "positive," despite the all-importance of the negative in defining the conditions of Adam's fall. The term "Order," on the other hand, clearly reveals its dialectical or "polar" nature, on its face. "Order" implies "disorder," and vice versa. And that's the kind of term we need.

However, when putting it in place of the word "Covenant," we should try never to forget Hobbes's emphasis upon the severities of *sovereignty* as integral to the kind of Order we shall be studying. The idea of "Order" is ambiguous not only in the sense that it contains an idea of "Disorder." The term "Order" is ambiguous also since it can be applied to two quite different areas, either to such natural regularities as tides and seasons, or to socio-political structures in which people can give or receive orders, in which orders can be obeyed or disobeyed, in which offices are said to pyramid in an orderly arrangement of powers and responsibilities. The double notion of God's authority (in his roles as both originator and sovereign) obviously combines both of these meanings. It joins the idea of the creative verbal fiats by which God brought the natural order into existence, and the idea of a divine ruler laying down the law by words, in keeping with Hobbes's stout statement: "He only is properly said to reign, that governs his subjects by his word, and by promise of rewards to those that obey it, and by threatening them with punishment that obey it not."

Our task, then, is to examine the term "Order," by asking what cluster of ideas is "tautologically" present in the idea of Order. Such a cycle of terms follows no one sequence. That is, we may say either that the idea of Disorder is implicit in the idea of Order, or that the idea of Order is implicit in the idea of Disorder. Or we might say that the idea of Order implies the ideas of Obedience and Disobedience, or that either of them implies the other, or that either or both imply the idea of an Order, etc.

However, when such terministic interrelationships are embodied in the narrative style (involving acts, images and personalities) an irreversibility of the sequence can become of major importance. For instance, the implications of a story that proceeds from order to disorder (or from obedience to disobedience) differ greatly from those of a story that proceeds in the other direction. We may say that "success" and "failure" imply each other, without equating the step from success to failure with the step from failure to success. There are also paradoxical complications whereby, for instance, a step from success to failure in some respects is at the same time a step from failure to success in other respects. And there is the possibility of a story so self-consistent in structure that an analyst could, ideally, begin at the end and deductively "prophesy" what earlier developments must have taken place, for things to culminate as they did. But such considerations merely subtilize the narrative or temporal principle of irreversibility; they do not eliminate it.

The plan, then, is first to evolve a cluster of interrelated key terms implicit in the idea of "Order." Then we shall ask how the narrative, or "rectilinear," style of Genesis compares with the "cycle of terms" we have found to revolve "endlessly" about the idea of "Order." And finally, we shall draw some conclusions from the comparison of the two styles (the "timeless" terministic cluster and the kind of "temporal" sequence embodied in the Biblical myth). The distinction is one touched upon by Coleridge ("Idea of the Prometheus of Aeschylus," in Vol. IV of the Shedd edition of his *Complete Works*), where he speaks of the Biblical method as "sacred narrative" and "Hebrew archaeology," in contrast with Greek "philosopheme."

II   Tautological Cycle of Terms for "Order"

When reading this chapter, and later references to the same subject, the reader might find it helpful to consult the accompanying chart—Cycle of Terms Implicit in the Idea of "Order"—outlining the "Terministic Conditions for 'Original Sin' and 'Redemption' (intrinsic to the Idea of 'Order')."

First, consider the strategic ambiguity whereby the term "Order" may apply both to the realm of nature in general and to the special realm of human socio-political organizations (an ambiguity whereby, so far as sheerly empirical things are concerned, a natural order could be thought to go on existing even if all human beings, with their various socio-political orders, were obliterated). This is a kind of logical pun whereby our ideas of the natural order can become secretly infused by our ideas of the socio-political order.

One might ask: Is not the opposite possibility just as likely? Might not the terms for the socio-political order become infused by the genius of the terms for the natural order?

Cycle of Terms Implicit in the Idea of "Order"

God as Author and Authority

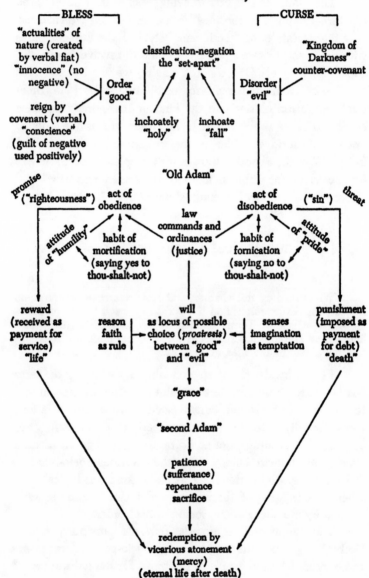

They do, every time we metaphorically extend the literal meaning of a natural image to the realm of the socio-political. It is the point that Bentham made much of, in his Theory of Fictions, his systematic procedure ("archetypation") for locating the natural images that may lurk undetected in our ideas, and so may mislead us into attempting to deal too strictly in terms of the irrelevant image. For instance, if Churchillian rhetoric gets us to thinking of international relations in such terms as "iron curtains" and "power vacuums," then we must guard lest we respond to the terms too literally —otherwise we shall not conceive of the political situation accurately enough. The nations of the Near East are no "vacuum." Theologians have made similar observations about the use of natural images to express the idea of godhead.

But it is much more important, for our present purposes, to spot the movement in the other direction. We need to stress how a vision of the natural order can become infused with the genius of the verbal and socio-political orders.

Thus, from the purely logological point of view, we note how, inasmuch as the account of the Creation in Genesis involves on each "day" a kind of enactment done through the medium of God's "Word," the sheerly "natural" order contains a verbal element or principle that, from the purely empirical point of view, could belong only in the socio-political order. Empirically, the natural order of sheerly astrophysical motion depends upon no verbal principle for its existence. But theologically, it does depend upon a verbal principle. And even though one might say that God's creative fiats and his words to Adam and Eve are to be conceived as but *analogous* to ordinary human verbal communication, our point remains the same. For, from the empirical point of view, there would not even be an *analogy* between natural origins and responses to the power of words. The world of natural, non-verbal motions must be empirically the kind of world that could continue with its motions even if it contained no species, such as man, capable of verbal action; and it must be described without any reference to a Creation by verbal fiat, whether or not there had been such.

By a Dramatistic ambiguity, standard usage bridges this distinction between the realms of verbal action and non-verbal motion when it speaks of sheerly natural objects or processes as "actualities." Here even in a purely secular usage we can discern a trace of the theological view that sees nature as the sign of God's action—and thus by another route we see the theological way of merging the principle of the natural order with the principle of verbal contract or covenant intrinsic to legal enactment in the socio-political order.

But to proceed with the "tautologies":

If, by "Order," we have in mind the idea of a command, then obviously the corresponding word for the proper response would be "Obey." Or, there would be the alternative, "Disobey." Thus we have the proportion: Order is to Disorder as Obedience is to Disobedience. However, there is a logological sense in which the things of nature could be called "innocent." They cannot disobey commands, since they cannot understand commands. They do not have a "sense of right and wrong," or, more generically, a "sense of yes and no." They simply do as they do—and that's that. Such would be the *non posse peccare* of natural things, or even of humans insofar as their "natural" state was not bound by moralistic negatives. All was permissive in Eden but the eating of the one forbidden fruit, the single negative that set the conditions for the Fall (since, St. Paul pointed out, only the law can make sin, as Bentham was later to point out that only the law can make crime). The Biblical myth pictures natural things as coming into being through the agency of God's Word; but they can merely do as they were designed to do, whereas with God's permission though not without his resentment, the seed of Adam can do even what it has been explicitly told not to do. The word-using animal not only understands a thou-shalt-not;

it can carry the principle of the negative a step further, and answer the thou-shalt-not with a disobedient No. Logologically, the distinction between natural innocence and fallen man hinges about this problem of language and the negative. Eliminate language from nature, and there can be no moral disobedience. In this sense, moral disobedience is "doctrinal." Like faith, it is grounded in language.

"Things" can but *move* or *be moved*. "Persons" by definition can "act." In being endowed with words (symbols) by which they can frame responses to questions and commands, by the same token they have "responsibility."

Looking into the *act* of Disobedience, we come upon the need for some such term as "Pride," to name the corresponding *attitude* that precedes the act. And some such term as "Humility" names the idea of the attitude that leads into the act of Obedience.

But implicit in the distinction between Obedience and Disobedience there is the idea of some dividing line, some "watershed" that is itself midway between the two slopes. Often a word used for naming this ambiguous moment is "Will," or more fully, "Free Will," which is thought of as a faculty that makes possible the choice between the yea-saying of Humble Obedience or the nay-saying of Prideful Disobedience (the choice between *serviam* and *non serviam*).

Ontologically, and theologically, we say that this locus of freedom makes possible the kind of personal choice we have in mind when we speak of "Action." But note that, logologically, the statement should be made the other way round. That is, whereas ontologically or theologically we say that by being endowed with free will man is able to act morally, the corresponding logological statement would be: Implicit in the idea of an act is the idea of free will. (Another version of the formula would be: Implicit in the idea of an act is the idea of freedom).

The ontological and theological statements may or may

not be true. The logological statement would be "true logologically" even if it were not true ontologically. That is, even
if we hypothetically suppose, with strict behaviorists, cyber-
neticists and the like, that there is no such thing as "free will,"
that all "action" is reducible to terms of mechanical "motion,"
it would still remain true that implicit in the idea of action
there is the idea of freedom. If one cannot make a choice, one
is not acting, one is but being moved, like a billiard ball tapped
with a cue and behaving mechanically in conformity with the
resistances it encounters. But even if men are doing nothing
more than that, the *word* "act" *implies* that they are doing
more—and we are now concerned solely with the implications
of terms.

As regards the Dramatistic tautology in general, an act
is done by an agent in a scene. But such an act is usually
preceded by a corresponding attitude, or "incipient act" (as
when an act of friendliness grows out of a friendly attitude
on the part of the agent). The scene is motivational locus of
the act insofar as the act represents a scene-act ratio (as, for
instance, when an "emergency situation" is said to justify an
"emergency measure"). But insofar as the act derives from an
attitude of the agent, the agent-act ratio can be narrowed to
an attitude-act ratio, as when a friendly agent does a friendly
act. The term "Will" is apparently designed to assign a "place"
to the choice between different possibilities of attitude-act
development. Here a verb is thought of as a noun; the idea of
"the will" as willing is conceived after the analogy of rain
raining, though we do not speak of fear as fearing. But the
idea of such a locus for "the Will" brings up a further problem: What in turn influences "the Will"?

On the Disorder side, this role is assigned to the Imagination, insofar as the imagination's close connection with sensory images is thought both to make it highly responsive to
the sensory appetites and to make sensory appetites more en-
ticing. In brief, the combination of Imagination and the

Senses, by affecting the Will from the side of Disorder, is said to predispose towards Temptation, *except* insofar as Imagination in turn is corrected from the side of Order by the controls of Reason and Faith (which can also be thought of as having a controlling effect upon each other). Another refinement here is the notion that, once Imagination is on the side of Reason, it can contribute to Order, rather than to Disorder, by making reasonable things seem sensible, and thus inducing the Wills of persons weak in Reason to nonetheless freely choose, as it were reasonably, and thus to act on the side of Order, eschewing Temptation.

The idea of Reason, in such a system, is obviously permeated with ideas of Dominion, owing to its identification with ideas of control, and as indicated in the formula, "the Rule of Reason." So it brings us clearly back to the principle of sovereignty underlying the general idea of Order by Covenant. The relation between Reason and Faith becomes ambiguous because of the possible shift between the natural order and the socio-political order as grounds of Reason. For if the socio-political Order is conceived in "ultimate" terms (as it is in the idea of a Covenant derived from God), then Faith must be a higher kind of control than Reason, insofar as Reason is identified with "Natural Law" and with purely worldly rules of governance. (Incidentally, we might note the strongly verbal element in both, as indicated by the close relation between Rational and Logical, and by St. Paul's statement that the doctrines of the Faith are learned "by hearing." However, there is said to be a further stage of supernatural awareness, called by St. Anselm *contemplatio* and by Spinoza *scientia intuitiva*, which would, by definition, transcend the verbal.)

There is also an act-agent ratio, as with the Aristotelian notion of *hexis, habitus*, the notion that a person may develop a virtuous Disposition by the practices of virtue, or a vicious Disposition by repeated indulgence in vice. And this brings us to the subtlest term of all, as regards the set of major Dramatistic terms clustering about the idea of Order, namely: Mortification.

Of all theology-tinged terms that need logological reclamation and refurbishment, this is perhaps the most crucial. Here the motives of sacrifice and dominion come to a head in every-day living. The possibility is that most ailments now said to be of "psychogenic" origin are but secularized variants of what might be called "mortification in spite of itself." That is, if we are right in assuming that governance makes "naturally" for victimage, either of others (homicidally) or of ourselves (suicidally), then we may expect to encounter many situations in which a man, by attitudes of self-repression, often causes or aggravates his own bodily and mental ills.

The derived meaning (humiliation, vexation, chagrin) would figure here. But mainly we have in mind the Grand Meaning, "subjection of the passions and appetites, by penance, abstinence or painful severities inflicted on the body," mortification as a kind of governance, an extreme form of "self-control," the deliberate, disciplinary "slaying" of any motive that, for "doctrinal" reasons, one thinks of as unruly. In an emphatic way, mortification is the exercising of oneself in "virtue"; it is a systematic way of saying no to Disorder, or obediently saying yes to Order. Its opposite is license, *luxuria*, "fornication," saying yes to Disorder, or disobediently saying no to Order.

The principle of Mortification is particularly crucial to conditions of empire, which act simultaneouly to awaken all sorts of odd and exacting appetites, while at the same time imposing equally odd and exacting obstacles to their fulfillment. For "mortification" does not occur when one is merely "frustrated" by some external interference. It must come from within. The mortified must, with one aspect of himself, be saying no to another aspect of himself—hence the urgent incentive to be "purified" by "projecting" his conflict upon a scapegoat, by "passing the buck," by seeking a sacrificial vessel upon which he can vent, as from without, a turmoil that is actually within. "Psychogenic illness" would occur in cases where one is scrupulous enough to deny oneself such easy outgoing relief, and instead, in all sorts of roundabout ways, scrupulously circles back upon himself, unintentionally making his own constitution the victim of his hierarchically goaded entanglements. At least, that's the idea.

To complete the pattern: On the side of Order, where the natural actualities created by verbal fiat are completed in sovereignty and subjection by Covenant, with Obedience goes promise of reward (as payment for service), while on the other side goes Disobedience, with threat of punishment as enforced payment for disservice.

Then comes the Grand Rounding Out, where the principle of reward as payment (from the Order side) merges with the principle of punishment as payment (from the Disorder side), to promise redemption by vicarious atonement. Sovereignty and subjection (the two poles of governance) are brought together in the same figure (Christ as King and Christ as Servant respectively)—and the contradiction between these principles is logically resolved by a narrative device, the notion of two advents whereby Christ could appear once as servant and the second time as king. Here is the idea of a "perfect" victim to cancel (or "cover") what was in effect the "perfect" sin (its technical perfection residing in the fact that it was the first transgression of the first man against the first and foremost authority).

However, the symmetry of the design does not resolve the problem of the "watershed moment," the puzzle of the relation between "determinism" and "free will." The search for a cause is itself the search for a scapegoat, as Adam blames Eve, Eve blames the serpent, the serpent could have blamed Lucifer, and Lucifer could have blamed the temptations implicit in the idea of Order (the inchoate "fall" that, as we saw

in the quotation from Coleridge, is intrinsic to the "creation
of the non-absolute"). Adam himself has a hint of the Luci-
ferian rejoinder when he says to the Lord God that he received
the fruit from "the woman whom thou gavest to be with me."
Also, from the purely imagistic point of view, there is a sense
in which the Lord God has caused Adam to be tempted by
an aspect of himself, in accordance with the original obstetri-
cal paradox whereby woman was born of man.

Here would be a purely "grammatical" way of stating
the case: If order, implying the possibility of disorder, implies
a possible *act* of disobedience, then there must be an agent
so endowed, or so minded, that such an act is possible to him
—and the *motives* for such an act must eventually somehow
be referred to the *scene* out of which he arose, and which thus
somehow contains the principles that in their way make a
"bad" act possible.

Arrived at this point, we might shift the problem of the
"watershed moment" to another plane, by recalling that the
same conditions of divisiveness also make for the inchoately
"holy," inasmuch as the Hebrew word for "holy," *qodesh*,
means literally the "separate," the "set apart," as does the word
qadesh, which means "Sodomite." This verbal tangle has
often been commented on, and applies also to the New Testament word, *hagios*, which means both "holy" and "accursed,"
like its Latin counterpart, *sacer*. Here, we might say, is a
purely terministic equivalent of the problem of choice, or motivational slope. The question of de-terminism narrows down
to a kind of term that within itself contains two slopes (two
different judgments or "crises").

As regards the matter of terms, we could move into the
area of personality proper by equating human personality
with the ability to use symbol-systems (centering in the feeling for the negative, since "reason," in its role as the "sense
of right and wrong," is but a special case of the "sense of yes
and no"). Thus, more broadly, we could say that the concep-

tion of the creative verbal fiat in Genesis is essentially the *personal principle*. But insofar as personal character is defined by choice (cf. Aristotle on *proairesis**), the question then becomes one of deciding how far back the grounds of choice must be traced (atop the primary logological fact that the *perfection* of choice comes to a head in the formal distinction between Yes and No.) Insofar as Genesis would depict us as arising from a scene that is the act of a super-person, and insofar as redemption is thought to be got by voluntary enlistment on the side of Order, conceived sacrificially, then the ultimate formula becomes that of Jeremiah 31:18: "Turn thou me, and I shall be turned" (*converte me, et convertar*). Here the indeterminate watershed of "free" choice is reducible to a question of this sort: Though all men are given enough "grace" to be saved, how can anyone be saved but by being given enough grace to be sure of using it? Yet how could he have as much saving grace as that, without in effect being *compelled* to be saved (in which case he would not, in the last analysis, have "free will")?

Fortunately, it is not our duty, as logologers, to attempt solving this ultimate theological riddle, entangled in ideas of providence, predestination, and the possibilities of an elect, chosen from among the depraved, all of whom deserve eternal damnation, but some of whom are saved by God in his mysterious mercy, and may attest to their future glory by becoming a kind of materially prosperous elite here and now (or at least by being able to answer without question).

Fortunately, as logologers, we need but consider the ways in which such ideas are interwoven with the conditions of dominion, as they prevail among human symbol-using animals. As seen in this light, the thought of all such issues leads us to revision of our initial dialectical pattern. That is, the Order-Disorder pair is not enough. And what we need now

---

* *Poetics*, VI, 24.

is another kind of antithesis, setting Order against Counter-Order.

Methodologically, we might say that we have now come upon the penalties resulting from our earlier decision to approach this problem in terms of "Order" rather than in terms of "Covenant." For the idea of a "Counter-Covenant" would have been somewhat different from the idea of such a mere disintegration as is usually suggested by the term "Disorder."

In sum, there is a notable qualitative difference between the idea of a mere "fall" from a position in which one still believes but to which one is at times unequal, and the idea of a deliberate turn to an alternative allegiance. It would be a difference between being "weak in virtue" and being "strong in sin."

But perhaps we should try to sum up the line of reasoning we have been pursuing in these last paragraphs. We have been considering the problem of a possible ultimate ground for "Temptation." Logologically, "Temptation" is but a tautological aspect of the idea of "Order." It is grounded in the idea of a verbal command, which by its very nature contains possibilities of both obedience and disobedience. We don't "command" the non-verbalizing things of nature. To the best of our ability, we simply set up conditions which we think likely to bring about the kind of situation we desire. We reserve our commands (or requests!) for language-using entities that can, to varying degrees, resist. And the command is backed, explicitly or implicitly, by promises or threats. However:

Ontologically, or theologically, such a purely "tautological" point of view would not be enough. And we confront such problems as St. Augustine was concerned with, in his battles with the Manichaeans. We may, like the Manichaeans, conceive of an ultimate Tempter, existing in his own right, and with powers rivaling those of God. Or we may derive everything from a God who is by definition merciful, and good, the author of a wholly good Creation, yet who not only lets man sin, but permits the existence and incessant schemings of a supernatural tempter endowed with diabolical ingenuity and persuasiveness. Hence arises the "problem of evil," (as with Augustine's urgent question, *"Unde malum?"*). We have considered in the previous talk how Augustine proposed to solve the problem theologically by his notion of evil as a "deficient cause," a kind of "eclipse."

But logologically, the question takes on a different form. Logologically, moral "evil" is a species of *negative,* a purely linguistic (or "rational") principle. And insofar as natural calamities are viewed in terms of moral retribution, we should say that the positive events of nature are being seen through the eyes of moral negativity (another instance of ways whereby the genius of the verbal and socio-political orders can come to permeate our ideas of the natural order). All told, "evil" is implicit in the idea of "Order" because "Order" is a polar, or dialectical term, implying an idea of "Disorder."

But there can be two kinds of "Disorder": (1) a tendency towards failure to obey completely always; (2) disobedience due to an out-and-out enrollment in the ranks of a rival force. We might call this a distinction between mere Disorder and deliberate allegiance to a Counter-Order. (There is an analogous situation in contemporary politics, since a person's disagreements with those in authority may be interpreted either as temperamental deviation from the prevailing orthodoxy or as sinister, secret adherence to an organized enemy alien power.)

Theologically, perhaps the analogous distinction would be between the kind of "Temptation" that is intrinsic to the possibility of choice and the kind that attains its ideal perfection in the notion of a Faustian pact with the Devil—the difference between ordinary "backsliding" and "heresy" or "black magic." In Joyce's *Portrait,* it would correspond to the distinction between Stephen's sexual fall despite himself in the second section, and his deliberate choice of a "proud" aesthetic calling, as "priest of the imagination," in section four. Problems of "predestination" lie in the offing, inasmuch as different people are differently tempted or differently enlightened, and such differences are not of their own choosing but arise in connection with the accidents of each man's unique, particular destiny. (In the *Confessions*, for instance, we see St. Augustine interpreting as God's will many decisions which he had made for quite different personal reasons. And no man could sell his soul to the Devil, if God—who was necessarily present at the signing of the contract—but chose that moment to flood the victim's imagination with the full realization of his danger.)

At this point, we should look at Hobbes's *Leviathan*, since it illustrates so well the idea of Disorder in this more aggressive sense, of a Covenant matched by a "Counter-Covenant." And in the course of doing so, it well illustrates the role of the sacrificial principle which we believe to be "logologically inseparable" from the idea of dominion.

III Covenant and "Counter-Covenant" in Hobbes's *Leviathan*

Part I of the *Leviathan* is "Of Man." But this subtitle can easily mislead us. For Part I is not just "Of Man." It is *of man in the commonwealth.* That is, the principle of Part II, which explicitly concerns commonwealth, is already implicit as a germ in Part I. Thus there is no break in continuity as we turn from Part I to Part II. The quickest way to make it obvious that the motives of commonwealth are already operating in the first section, and coloring the philosopher's view of man *qua* man, is to cite such chapter headings as: "Of Power, Worth, Dignity, Honour, and Worthiness," and "Of Persons, Authors, and Things Personated." Perhaps you can't explicitly write just "of man" without implicitly writing of man in the commonwealth (or at least, of man in the tribe), since man is, as Aristotle puts it in good Athenian fashion, a "political animal."

Similarly, in Genesis, though the first three Covenants have to do with man and woman, brothers, parents, children, and though it is not until the fourth, or Abrahamic Covenant, that God deals with *Israel as a nation,* yet the generic and familial motives exemplified in these early Covenants are but the beginnings of such motives as come clear in terms of dominion, however theocratically conceived. This is to say that man's notion of his "pre-political" self will necessarily be seen in the light of a socio-political perspective. And all the more so, because "pre-political" childhood is experienced in terms of family relationships that are themselves shaped by tribal or national conditions as a whole.

As regards Part II, "Of Commonwealth": If you read this section, along the lines of our notion that the first section is "in principle" saying the same thing, you get the essence of Hobbes's politics. Here, near the end of chapter xvii, occurs an almost gloriously resonant passage succinctly summing up the Hobbesian notion of a Covenant, made with a "common power," and designed to keep the covenanters "in awe, and to direct their actions to the common benefit":

> The only way to erect such a common power, as may be able to defend them from the invasion of foreigners, and the injuries of one another, and thereby to secure them in such sort, as that by their own industry, and by the fruits of the earth, they may nourish themselves and live contentedly; is, to confer all their power and strength upon one man, or upon one assembly of men, that may reduce all their wills, by plurality of voices, unto one will: which is as much as to say, to appoint one man, or assembly of men, to bear their person; and every one to own, and acknowledge himself to be author of whatsoever he that so beareth their person, shall act, or cause to be acted, in those things which concern the common peace and safety; and therein to submit their wills, every one to his will, and their judgments, to his judgment. This is more than consent, or concord; it is a real unity of them

all, in one and the same person, made by covenant of every man with every man, in such manner, as if * every man should say to every man, *I authorize and give up my right of governing myself, to this man, or to this assembly of men, on this condition, that thou give up thy right to him, and authorize all his actions in like manner.* This done, the multitude so united in one person, is called a COMMONWEALTH, in Latin CIVITAS. This is the generation of that great LEVIATHAN, or rather, to speak more reverently, of that *mortal god,* to which we owe under the *immortal God,* our peace and defence. For by this authority, given him by every particular man in the commonwealth, he hath the use of so much power and strength conferred on him, that by terror thereof, he is enabled to form the wills of them all, to peace at home, and mutual aid against their enemies abroad. And in him consisteth the essence of the commonwealth; which, to define it, is *one person, of whose acts a great multitude, by mutual covenants one with another, have made themselves every one the author, to the end he may use the strength and means of them all, as he shall think expedient, for their peace and common defence.*

And he that carrieth this person, is called SOVEREIGN, and said to have *sovereign power;* and every one besides, his SUBJECT.

In Part III ("Of a Christian Commonwealth") Hobbes adds a dimension, by introducing from the Bible his terms for what he calls "Christian politics." Essentially, this section involves his devices for subjecting priest-rule to the powers of secular sovereignty. That is to say: In another way, by new ingenuities, he reaffirms the principles of the commonwealth that were adumbrated in Part I and explicitly expounded in Part II. Perhaps the most quotable passage for our purposes is the last paragraph of chapter xxviii:

> Hitherto I have set forth the nature of man, whose pride and other passions have compelled him to submit himself to government: together with the great power of his governor, whom I compared to *Leviathan,* taking that comparison out of the two last verses of the one-and-fortieth of *Job;* where God having set forth the great power of *Leviathan,* calleth him King of the Proud. *There is nothing,* saith he, *on earth, to be compared with him. He is made so as not to be afraid. He seeth every high thing below him; and is king of all the children of pride.* But because he is

---

* Ever keep in mind that pre-Kantian "as if," and the Hobbesian idea of a primal social covenant gains greatly in relevance.

mortal, and subject to decay, as all other earthly creatures are; and because there is that in heaven, though not on earth, that he should stand in fear of, and whose laws he ought to obey; I shall in the next following chapters speak of his diseases, and the causes of his mortality; and of what laws of nature he is bound to obey.

The reference to Leviathan as "King of the Proud" is perfect for our purposes. However, we have said that, where Governance is, there is the goad to scapegoats. And that brings us to:

Part IV ("Of the Kingdom of Darkness"). The curative victim here is not Christ, but Popery, conceived as Anti-Christ.

At this point (praise Logology!) we most decidedly need not enter the fray on Hobbesian terms. But we most decidedly should be admonished by Hobbes, in accordance with our ways of translating. And his methodologically fundamental admonition gets down to the fact that, in the light of his title for Part IV, "Of the Kingdom of Darkness," we must shift from Order-thinking back to Covenant-thinking, and thereby concern ourselves with the sheerly dialectical possibilities of a Counter-Covenant, though the word itself is not in Hobbes.

Viewed here not as doctrine, but sheerly as design, Hobbes helps us realize that, implicit in the idea of a Covenant is the idea not just of obedience or disobedience to that Covenant, but also of obedience or disobedience to a *rival* Covenant. The choice thus becomes not just a difference between seeking the light and not seeking the light, but rather the difference between eagerly seeking the light and just as eagerly seeking darkness (a "Disorder" having an "Order" all its own, however insistent the orthodoxy must be that the Satanic counter-realm can exist only by the sufferance of the One Ultimate Authority).

About the edges of all such speculations lie variants of the Manichaean "heresy," according to which Evil is a power in its own right. As we have observed before, logology must side with Augustine's attacks upon this position. For logology looks upon "evil" as a species of the negative, and looks upon the negative as a sheerly linguistic invention. This would be the logological analogue of Augustine's theological doctrine that *malum* is a *causa deficiens*, a mere deficiency, like an eclipse. And from the purely dialectical point of view, we take it that all admonishments against the temptations of a Counter-Covenant are a recognition of the moral certainty that the mere stating of a position is likely to call forth some opposition. Hobbes's strongly nationalist position made it inevitable that Catholicism would be his scapegoat.

But whether the scapegoat principle be conceived after the analogy of a villain, or after the analogy of an arbitrarily chosen vessel that gets its function purely by appointment, or after the analogy of divine paraclete combining exhortation and guidance with victimage, the principle of Mortification is basic to the pattern of governance, as summed up in Paul's paradox (II Corinthians 12:10): "Therefore I take pleasure in infirmities, in reproaches, in necessities, in persecutions, in distresses for Christ's sake: for when I am weak, then I am strong."

The idea of the Sacrificial Redeemer, in bringing together ideas of patience, repentance, and obedience to the verbalities of the faith, reproduces in the large the same principle that prevails in the minute scruples of Mortification. Here also would belong the idea of the "remnant," those especially good Jews who maintained the continuity of a blessed relation to the deity despite the backsliding of the people as a whole. And the priesthood, too, would be an extension of the principle of sacrifice, in that it involves special persons set apart for the sacrificial services. The priests extend the sacrificial principle to themselves insofar as they practice special acts of mortification deemed to fit them for their special office.

The companion principle to such an idea of graceful, voluntary subjection being, of course, sovereignty, the other side of the sovereign-subject relation is presented in terms of the ultimate rewards in store for those of good will who subject themselves to the principle of governance. That is, as with the two advents of Christ, the logical contrast between sovereignty and subjection is resolved by translation into terms of narrative sequence whereby the principle of subjection, of mortification first prevails, but is finally followed by the sovereign principle of boundless rejoicing. And in the meantime, the notion of "grace" itself (as a way of goading the sluggish Imagination to the proper fears) is extended to include the idea that natural calamities are "acts of God," designed to warn or chasten—whereupon the principle of Mortification is introduced under another guise.

Mortification is as true of Order as mortmain is of contract.

IV Principles of Governance Stated Narratively

Imagine that you wanted to say, "The world can be divided into six major classifications." That is, you wanted to deal with "the principles of Order," beginning with the natural order, and placing man's socio-political order with reference to it. But you wanted to treat of these matters in *narrative* terms, which necessarily involve *temporal* sequence (in contrast with the cycle of terms for "Order," that merely cluster about one another, variously implying one another, but in no one fixed sequence).

Stated narratively (in the style of Genesis, *Bereshith*, Beginning), such an idea of principles, or "firsts" would not be stated simply in terms of classification, as were we to say "The first of six primary classes would be such-and-such, the second such-and-such" and so on. Rather, a completely narrative style would properly translate the idea of six classes

or categories into terms of time, as were we to assign each of
the classes to a separate "day." Thus, instead of saying "And
that completes the first broad division, or classification, of our
subject-matter," we'd say: "And the evening and the morn-
ing were the first day" (or, more accurately, the "One" Day).
And so on, through the six broad classes, ending "last but
not least," on the category of man and his dominion.*

Further, a completely narrative style would *personalize*
the principle of classification. This role is performed by the
references to God's creative fiat, which from the very start
infuses the sheerly natural order with the verbal principle
(the makings of that "reason" which we take to be so essential an aspect of human personality).

Logologically, the statement that God made man in his
image would be translated as: The principle of personality
implicit in the idea of the first creative fiats, whereby all
things are approached in terms of the word, applies also to
the feeling for symbol-systems on the part of the human animal, who would come to read nature as if it were a book.
Insofar as God's words infused the natural order with their
genius, and insofar as God is represented as speaking words
to the first man and woman, the principle of human personality (which is at the very start identified with *dominion*)
has its analogue in the notion of God as a super-person, and
of nature as the act of such a super-agent. (That is, we

* The clearest evidence that this principle of "divisiveness" is
itself a kind of "proto-fall" is to be seen in the use made of it by the
segregationists of the South's Bible Belt. Members of the Ku Klux Klan
refer to the classificatory system of Genesis as justification for their stress
upon the separation of Negroes and whites. In an ironic sense, they are
"right." For when nature is approached via the principle of differentiation embodied in the notion of Social Order, then "Creation" itself is
found to contain implicitly the guiltiness of "discrimination." Furthermore, the Word mediates between these two realms. And the Word
is social in the sense that language is a collective means of expression,
while its sociality is extended to the realm of wordless nature insofar
as this non-verbal kind of order is treated in terms of such verbal order
as goes with the element of command intrinsic to dominion.

take symbol-using to be a distinctive ingredient of "personality.")

Though technically there is a kind of "proto-fall" implicit in the principle of divisiveness that characterizes the Bible's view of the Creation, and though the principle of subjection is already present (in the general outlines of a government with God at its head, and mankind as subject to His authority while in turn having dominion over all else in the natural realm), the Covenant (as first announced in the first chapter) is necessarily Edenic, in a state of "innocence," since no negative command has yet been pronounced. From the dialectical point of view (in line with the Order-Disorder pair) we may note that there is a possibility of "evil" implicit in the reference to all six primary classifications as "good." But in all three points (the divisiveness, the order of dominion, and the universal goodness) the explicit negative is lacking. In fact, the nearest approach to an outright negative (and that not of a moralistic, hortatory sort) is in the reference to the "void" (*bohu*) which preceded God's classificatory acts. Rashi says that the word translated as "formless" (*tohu*) "has the meaning of astonishment and amazement." Incidentally, in connection with Genesis 1:29, *The Interpreter's Bible* suggests another implicit negative, in that the explicit permitting of a vegetarian diet implies that Adam may *not* eat flesh.

In the first chapter of Genesis, the stress is upon the creative fiat as a means of classification. It says in effect, "What hath God wrought (by his Word)?" The second chapter's revised account of the Creation shifts the emphasis to matters of dominion, saying in effect, "What hath God ordained (by his words)?" The seventh "day" (or category), which is placed at the beginning of the second chapter, has a special dialectical interest in its role as a transition between the two emphases.

In one sense, the idea of the Sabbath is implicitly a

negative, being conceived as antithetical to all the six foregoing categories, which are classifiable together under the
single head of "work," in contrast with this seventh category,
of "rest." That is, work and rest are "polar" terms, dialectical
opposites. (In his *Politics*, Aristotle's terms bring out this
negative relation explicitly, since his word for business activity is *ascholein*, that is, *"not* to be at leisure," though we
should tend rather to use the negative the other way round,
defining "rest" as "not to be at work.")

This seventh category (of rest after toil) obviously
serves well as transition between Order (of God as principle
of origination) and Order (of God as principle of sovereignty). *Leisure* arises as an "institution" only when conditions of dominion have regularized the patterns of *work*.
And fittingly, just after this transitional passage, the very
name of God undergoes a change (the quality of which is
well indicated in our translations by a shift from "God" to
"Lord God." * Here, whereas in 1:29, *God* tells the man and
woman that the fruit of "every tree" is permitted them, the
Lord God (2:17) notably revises thus: "But of the tree of
the knowledge of good and evil, thou shalt not eat of it: for
in the day that thou eatest thereof thou shalt surely die."
Here, with the stress upon governance, enters the negative of
command.

* Grammatically, the word for God in the first chapter, "Elohim,"
is a plural. Philologists may interpret this as indicating a usage that
survives from an earlier polytheistic period in the development of Jewish
Monotheism. Or Christian theologians can interpret it as the first emergence of a Trinitarian position, thus early in the text, with the Creator
as first person of the Trinity, the Spirit that hovered over the waters as
third person, and the creative Word as second person. (Incidentally, the
words translated as "Lord God" in chapter II are *Jehovah-Elohim*.
Later, in connection with the Abrahamic Covenant, the words translated
as "Lord God" are *Adonai Jehovah*. *Adonai*, which means "master,"
applies to both God and man—and when applied to man it also includes
the idea of husband as master.) The distinction between authority and
authorship is approached from another angle in Augustine's *Confessions* I, where God is called the *ordinator* and *creator* of all natural
things; but of sin he is said to be only the *ordinator*.

When, later, the serpent tempts "the woman" (3:4), saying that "Ye shall not surely die," his statement is proved partially correct, to the extent that they did not die on the day on which they ate of the forbidden fruit. In any case, 3:19 pronounces the formula that has been theologically interpreted as deriving mankind's physical death from our first parents' first disobedience: "In the sweat of thy face shalt thou eat bread, till thou return unto the ground; for out of it wast thou taken: for dust thou art, and unto dust shalt thou return."

The Interpreter's Bible (p. 512) denies there is any suggestion that man would have lived forever had he not eaten of the forbidden fruit. Chapter 3, verse 20 is taken to imply simply that man would have regarded death as his natural end, rather than as "the last fearful frustration." Thus, the fear of death is said to be "the consequence of the disorder in man's relationships," when they are characterized "by domination" (along with the fear that the subject will break free of their subjection). This seems to be at odds with the position taken by the Scofield Bible which, in the light of Paul's statements in Romans 5:12-21 ("by one man sin entered the world, and death by sin"—and "by one man's offence death reigned by one") interprets the passage as meaning that "physical death" is due to a "universal sinful *state*, or nature" which is "our heritage from Adam."

It is within neither our present purpose nor our competency to interpret this verse theologically. But here's how it would look logologically:

First, we would note that in referring to "disorder" and "domination," *The Interpreter's Bible* is but referring to "Order" and "Dominion," as seen from another angle. For a mode of domination is a mode of dominion; and a sociopolitical order is by nature a ziggurat-like structure which, as the story of the Tower makes obvious, can stand for the principle of Disorder.

If we are right in our notion that the idea of Mortification is integral to the idea of Dominion (as the scrupulous
subject must seek to "slay" within himself whatever impulses
run counter to the authoritative demands of sovereignty),
then all about a story of the "first" dominion and the "first"
disobedience there should hover the theme of the "first" mortification.

But "mortification" is a weak term, as compared with
"death." And thus, in the essentializing ways proper to the
narrative style, this stronger, more dramatic term replaces
the weaker, more "philosophic" one. "Death" would be the
proper narrative-dramatic way of saying "Mortification." By
this arrangement, the natural order is once again seen through
the eyes of the socio-political order, as the idea of mortification
in the toil and subjection of Governance is replaced by the
image of death in nature.

From the standpoint sheerly of imagery (once the idea
of mortification has been reduced to the idea of death, and
the idea of death has been reduced to the image of a dead
body rotting back into the ground), we now note a kind of
"imagistic proto-fall," in the pun of 2:7, where the Lord God
is shown creating man (*adham*) out of the ground (*adhamah*).
Here would be an imagistic way of saying that man in his
physical nature is essentially but earth, the sort of thing a
body becomes when it decays; or that man is *first of all* but
earth, as regards his place in the sheerly natural order. You'd
define in narrative or temporal terms by showing what he
came from. But insofar as he is what he came from, then
such a definition would be completed in narrative terms by
the image of his return to his origins. In this sense, the account of man's forming (in 2:7) ambiguously lays the conditions for his "return" to such origins, as the Lord God makes
explicit in 3:19, when again the subject is the relation between *adham* and the *adhamah*: "For dust thou art, and
unto dust shalt thou return." Here would be a matter of

sheer imagistic consistency, for making the stages of a narrative be all of one piece.

But the death motif here is explicitly related to another aspect of Order or Dominion: the sweat of toil. And looking back a bit further, we find that this severe second Covenant (the "Adamic") also subjected woman to the rule of the husband—another aspect of Dominion. And there is to be an eternal enmity between man and the serpent (the image, or narrative personification, of the principle of Temptation, which we have also found to be intrinsic to the motives clustering about the idea of Order).

Logologically, then, the narrative would seem to be saying something like this: Even if you begin by thinking of death as a merely natural phenomenon, once you come to approach it in terms of conscience-laden *mortification* you get a new slant on it. For death then becomes seen, in terms of the socio-political order, as a kind of *capital punishment*. But something of so eschatological a nature is essentially a "first" (since "ends," too, are principles—and here is a place at which firsts and lasts meet, so far as narrative terms for the defining of essences are concerned). Accordingly death in the natural order becomes conceived as the fulfillment or completion of mortification in the socio-political order, but with the difference that, as with capital punishment in the sentencing of transgressions against sovereignty, it is not in itself deemed wholly "redemptive," since it needs further modifications, along the lines of placement in an undying Heavenly Kingdom after death. And this completes the pattern of Order: the symmetry of the socio-political (*cum* verbal), the natural, and the supernatural.

V Restatement, on Death
and Mortification

If the point about the relation between Death and
Mortification is already clear, the reader should skip this
section. But in case the point is not yet clear, we should
make one more try, in the effort to show how the step from
conscience-laden guiltiness to a regimen of mortification can
be narratively translated into terms of the step from "sin" to
"death." It is important, because the principle of mortification
is integral to the idea of redemptive sacrifice which we have
associated with the idea of Order. The secular variants of
mortification, we might say, lie on the "suicidal" slope of
human motivation, while the secular variants of redemption
by sacrifice of a chosen victim are on the slope of homicide.

Conscience-laden repression is the symbol-using animal's
response to conditions in the socio-political order. The *physical* symptoms that go with it seem like a kind of death. Thus,
though the *word* for the attitude called "mortification" is borrowed from the *natural* order, the *feeling* itself is a response
to various situations of dominion in the socio-political order.
This terministic bridge leading from the natural order to the
socio-political order thus can serve in reverse as a route from
the socio-political order to the natural order. Then, instead
of saying that "conscience-laden repression is *like* death," we
turn the equation into a quasi-temporal sequence, saying that
death "comes from" sin. We shall revert to the matter later,
when considering formally how terms that are logically synonymous or that tautologically imply one another can be
treated narratively as proceeding from one to the other, like
cause to effect.

Logologically, one would identify the principle of personality with the ability to master symbol-systems. Intrinsic

to such a personality is the "moral sense," that is, the sense of "yes and no" that goes with the thou-shalt-not's of Order. Grounded in language (as the makings of "reason") such conscience gets its high development from the commands and ordinances of governance. A corresponding logological analogue of personal immortality could be derived from the nature of a *personal name*, that can be said to survive the physical death of the particular person who bore it, as the idea of Napoleon's essence (the character summed up in his name) can be verbally distinguished from the idea of his "existence." So long as we can "recall" a departed ancestor by name in recalling the quality of the personality associated with his name, he can be said to "still be with us in spirit." And from the strictly logological point of view, the proposition that man necessarily conceives of God in accordance with the personal principle of the verbal would be statable in narrative style as the statement that God is an order-giving superperson who created man in His image. This is how the proposition should be put narratively, regardless of whether or not it is believed theologically.

Similarly, like St. Paul, we may choose to interpret the Biblical account of the Creation and Fall as saying literally that, whereas other animals die naturally (even without being subject to the kind of covenant that, by verbally defining sin, makes "sin" possible), all members of the human species die not as the result of a natural process but because the first member of the species "sinned." That is, death in man's case is primarily associated with the principle of personality (or "conscience"), such as the Bible explicitly relates to a verbal Covenant made by the first and foremost exponent of the creative verbal principle, in its relation to the idea of Order. Otherwise put: When death is viewed "personally," in moralistic terms colored by conditions of governance (the moral order), it is conceived not just as a natural process, but as a kind of "capital punishment."

But a strictly logological analysis of the mythic idiom (of the style natural to narrative) suggests a possibility of this sort: Even if one did not believe in Paul's theological interpretation of the story, even if one did not literally believe that all men's physical death is the result of the first man's disobedience, the Biblical narrative's way of associating "sin" with "death" would be the correct way of telling this story.

Suppose you wanted to say merely: "Order gives rise to a sense of guilt, and insofar as one conscientiously seeks to obey the law by policing his impulses from within, he has the feel of killing these impulses." Then, within the resources proper to narrative, your proper course would be to look for the strongest possible way of saying, "It is as though even physical death were a kind of capital punishment laid upon the human conscience." And that's what the story does, as starkly as can be. And that's how it should be stated narratively in either case, whether you give it the literal theological interpretation that Paul did, or interpret it metaphorically.

Theology is under the sign of what Coleridge would call the "Greek philosopheme." The narrative style of Genesis is under the sign of what Coleridge would call "Hebrew archaeology." Each style is concerned with "principles," after its fashion, Genesis appropriately using the "mythic" language of *temporal* firsts. (Coleridge's special use of the word "archaeology" is particularly apt here, inasmuch as *archai* are either philosophic first principles or beginnings in time.)

I discussed this ambiguity on the section of "The Temporizing of Motives" in my *A Grammar of Motives*. But now we are attempting to bring out a slightly different aspect of the question. We are suggesting that, as regards the logological approach to the relation between Order and Guilt, the Biblical narrative as it now is would be "correctly" couched, whether you agree with Paul's theological interpretation of "original sin," or whether you view the narrative simply as a narrative, mythic way of describing a purely secular experience: the sense of "mortification" that goes with any scrupulous ("essential") attempt at the voluntary suppression of unruly appetites.

Such a speculation would suggest that the "archaeological" mode of expression allows naturally for a wider range of interpretation than does the "philosopheme" and its equivalents in formal theology. The narrative is naturally more "liberal." Yet this very liberality may in the end goad to theological controversy, insofar as theological attempts are made to force upon the narrative utterance a stricter frame of interpretation than the style is naturally adapted to. (A further step here is the possibility whereby the theologian may be said to be inspired in his own way; and thus, whereas he cites the original narrative as authority from God, his narrowing of the possible interpretation may later be viewed as itself done on authority from God.)

If you wanted to say, "It's essentially as though this were killing us," your narrative way of stating such an essence or principle would be the same, whether you meant it literally or figuratively. In either case, you wouldn't just say "The sense of *mortification* is profoundly interwoven with the sense of guilt." Rather, you'd say: "The *very meaning of death itself* derives from such guilt." Or, more accurately still, you'd simply show man sinning, then you'd show the outraged sovereign telling him that he's going to die. And if he was the "first" man, then the tie-up between the idea of guilt and the imagery of death in his case would *stand for* such a "primal" tie-up in general.

However, note how this ambiguous quality of narrative firsts can tend to get things turned around, when theologically translated into the abstract principles of "philosophemes." For whereas narratively you would use a natural image (death —return to dust) to suggest a spiritual idea (guilt as regards the temptations implicit in a Covenant), now in effect the idea permeates the condition of nature, and in this reversal

the idea of natural *death* becomes infused with the idea of
moral *mortification,* whereas you had begun by borrowing
the idea of physical death as a term for naming the mental
condition which seemed analogous to it.

VI The Narrative Principle in Imagery

Besides discussing the way in which the narrative style
translates principles into terms of temporal priority and personality, we should consider the peculiar role of imagery in
such "archaeology."

One problem here is in trying to decide just how the
concept of imagery should be limited. There is a sense in
which all the things listed in the account of the Creation
could be considered as images (lists of positive natural things
deemed permeated by the principle or idea of divine authorship and authority). Here would be waters, sun, land, moon,
stars, the various living things, etc., as defined by the "Spirit
of God."

The formula, "Let there be light," could be said to introduce (in terms of an act and an image) the "principle of
elucidation" at the very start, and in terms of a darkness-light
pair that, though both are in their way "positive" so far as their
sheer physical character is concerned, are related dialectically
as the flat negation of each other. Incidentally, also, the relation between the pre-Creative darkness and the Creative
light also at the very start introduces, in actual imagery, the
idea of the Order-Disorder pair—and it sets the conditions
for expressing the imagistic treatment of the Counter-Order as
a "Kingdom of Darkness."

The explicit statement that man is made in God's image
would be logologically translated: "God and man are characterized by a common motivational principle," which we would
take to be the principle of personality that goes with skill

at symbol-using. This kinship is reaffirmed in the account of Adam's naming the various animals, though also there is a notable difference in the degree of authority and authorship, as befits this hierarchal view of Order.

The reference to the mist in chapter 2, we are told in *The Interpreter's Bible,* once followed verse 8, on the Lord God's planting of the garden, and originally read: ". . . and a mist used to go up from the earth and water the garden." The same comment adds: "This is a statement to the effect that the garden was irrigated supernaturally—the word rendered *mist* has probably a mythological connotation*— not by human labor." Whatever such a mist may be mythologically or theologically (where it has sometimes been interpreted as standing for "error") there is a possible logological explanation for it, in keeping with the fact that an account of "firsts" naturally favors imagery associated with childhood. Such an image could well stand narratively, or "mythically," for the word-using animal's vague memory of that early period in his life when he was emerging into speech out of infancy. For at that time, the very growth of his feeling for words would be felt as a kind of confusion, or indistinctness, while a bit of linguistic cosmos (or verbal light) was gradually being separated from a comparative chaos (or inarticulate darkness) of one's infantile beginnings. That is, whereas speechlessness probably has not the slightest suggestion of confusion or deprivation to an animal that is not born with the aptitude for speaking, the speechless state should be quite different with the human being's period of emergency from infancy into articulacy. Yet, at the same time, it could be endowed with "promissory" or "fertile" connotations, insofar as the mist-wanderer was moving towards clarity.

At least, there is a notable example of such a mist in Flaubert's *Temptation of Saint Anthony.* For as the work

* "The Book of Genesis. Exegesis" by Cuthbert A. Simpson, in *The Interpreter's Bible* (Nashville: Abingdon Press, 1900), I, 493.

proceeds, it develops after the fashion of a swiftly accelerating
regression, going back finally to the imagining of an initial
source in "pure" matter (as maternal principle). Quite as
we saw, in connection with Augustine, the final procession
from a "first" to its unfolding in plenitude, Flaubert's book
traces plenitude back to its beginnings in a principle of
heretic, unitary matter. In this reverse development, the fog
of a monster's breath marks the line of division between the
realm of the verbal and the realm of infantile formlessness
(where all things are patchy combinations wholly alien to
the realm of Order as we know it). Similarly the fog-people
of Wagner's *Niebelungen* cycle seem to have such a quality
(particularly in the *Nebelheim* of *Das Rheingold*, surely the
most "infantile" of the plays, though all are somewhat like
fairy stories).

The complicating element to do with images, when used
as the narrative embodying of principles, or ideas, is that the
images bring up possibilities of development in their own
right. Thus, there is a kind of "deathiness" implicit in the
very term, "tree of life." One might think of it as being cut
down, for instance. The Biblical story relates it contrastingly
to the forbidden fruit (which turns out to be a tree of death).
But there is still the business of denying access to the tree
as a tree; hence the arrangement whereby, after the expulsion,
a flaming sword is set up, "which turned every way, to keep
the way of the tree of life." The sword would seem most
directly related to the idea of keeping people away from a
tree; yet it also would fit with the idea of "protecting" life
(though here, ironically, its kind of "protection" involves a
denial, and thus another aspect of the negatives of dominion,
with its principle of "capital punishment," or in general "mortification").

We shall elsewhere discuss the implications of the
imagery to do with the unnatural obstetrics of Genesis, the
possible logological interpretation of nakedness, the imagery

of eating and the role of the serpent as simultaneously the image and personal representative of the principle of temptation.

Perhaps the only other major imaginal deployment in the first three chapters concerns the Lord God's irate words to Adam (3:17): "Cursed is the ground for thy sake." On this point, our Scofield Bible says the earth is cursed because "It is better for fallen man to battle with a reluctant earth than to live without toil." But from the strictly logological point of view, Rashi's commentary seems more in keeping with the principle of firstness that infuses these chapters: "This is similar to one who goes forth to do evil; and people curse the breasts from which he suckled." Rashi here treats of a symmetry involving scene, agent, and act. The Lord God, to curse this agent thoroughly, curses the very ground he walks on. We might also remember, as regards the *adham-adhamah* pun, that this is the deathy, dominion-spirited ground from which he came.

To be sure, images also hover about ideas, as stated in the style of philosophemes. Also, ideas contain an element of personality always, as Plato's dialogues make apparent. And the Hobbesian notion of a quasi-original Covenant indicates how the pressure of narrative thinking affects our ideas of laws, principles, summations. But though the "archaeological" style cannot be distinguished categorically from the "philosopheme," one can at least distinguish their different slopes, or trends, and can in time spot the kinds of development that are specific to each.

VII   Dominion, Guilt, Sacrifice

In sum, when we turn from the consideration of a terministic cycle in which the various terms mutually imply one another, to the consideration of the narrative terminology in these opening chapters of Genesis, we note that the narrative terms allow the idea of Order to be "processed." Here one can start with the creation of a natural order (though conceiving it as infused with a verbal principle); one can next proceed to an idea of innocence untroubled by thou-shalt-not's; one can next introduce a thou-shalt-not; one can next depict the thou-shalt-not as violated; one can next depict a new Covenant propounded on the basis of this violation, and with capital punishment; one can later introduce the principle of sacrifice, as would become wholly clear when we came to the Noachian Covenant where, after the great cleansing by water, God gave Noah the rainbow sign, "And Noah builded an altar unto the Lord; and took of every clean beast, and of every clean fowl, and offered burnt-offerings on the altar." (8:20). Then gradually thereafter, more and more clearly, comes the emergence of the turn from mere sacrifice to the idea of outright redemption by victimage.

The Scofield editor says of the Noachian Covenant: "It's distinctive feature is the institution, for the first time, of human government—the government of man by man. The highest function of government is the judicial taking of life. All other governmental powers are implied in that. It follows that the third dispensation is distinctively that of human government."

Still, there is a notable difference between the idea of the kill in the sacrifice of an animal and the idea of the kill as per 9:6: "Whoso sheddeth man's blood, by man shall his blood be shed." This is the *lex talionis*, the principle of human justice, conceived after the nature of the scales, and grounded in the idea of an ultimate authority. It is not the idea of vicarious sacrifice. That is found implicitly in Noah's sacrifice of the clean animals as burnt-offerings.

But ultimately the idea of cleanliness attains its full modicum of *personality*, in the idea of a fitting personal sacrifice. The principle of personal victimage was introduced incipiently, so far as theology goes, in connection with the next Covenant, involving Abraham's willingness to sacrifice his beloved son, Isaac, on the Altar of God's Governance—while the principle of personal victimage was also clearly there, in the idea of Israel itself as victim. It was completed in Paul's view of Christ, and the New Kingdom.

We should also note that, in proportion as the idea of a *personal* victim developed, there arose the incentives to provide a judicial rationale for the sacrifice more in line with the kind of thinking represented by the *lex talionis*. Thus the idea of a personally fit victim could lead to many different notions, such as: (1) the ideal of a perfect victim (Christ); (2) the Greeks' "enlightened" use of criminals who had been condemned to death, but were kept on reserve for state occasions when some ritual sacrifice was deemed necessary; (3) Hitler's "idealizing" of the Jew as "perfect" enemy.

Whereas, the terms of Order, considered tautologically, go round and round like the wheel seen by Ezekiel, endlessly implicating one another, when their functions are embodied in narrative style the cycle can be translated into terms of an irreversible linear progression. But with the principle of authority personalized as God, the principle of disobedience as Adam (the "old Adam in all of us"), the principle of temptation as an Aesopian serpent, Eve as mediator in the bad sense of the word, and the idea of temptation reduced imagistically to terms of eating (the perfect image of a "first" appetite, or essential temptation, beginning as it does with the infantile, yet surviving in the adult), such reduction of the tautological cycle to a narrative linear progression makes possible the notion of an *outcome*.

Thus when we read of one broken covenant after another, and see the sacrificial principle forever reaffirmed anew, narratively this succession may be interpreted as movement towards a fulfillment, though from the standpoint of the tautological cycle they "go on endlessly" implicating one another.

Logologically many forms of victimage are seen as variants of the sacrificial motive. Burnt offerings, Azazel, Isaac, Israel in exile and the various "remnants" who undergo tribulations in behalf of righteousness can all be listed, along with Christ, as "reindividuations of the sacrificial principle." But a theological view of the narrative can lead to a more "promissory" kind of classification, whereby all sacrifices and sufferings preceding the Crucifixion can be classed as "types of Christ." When the devout admonish that "Christ's Crucifixion is repeated endlessly each time we sin," they are stating a theological equivalent of our logological point about the relation between the linear-temporal and the cyclical-tautological.

Logologically, the "fall" and the "redemption" are but parts of the same cycle, with each implying the other. The order can be reversed, for the terms in which we conceive of redemption can help shape the terms in which we conceive of the guilt that is to be redeemed. In this sense, it is "prior" to the guilt which it is thought to follow (quite as the quality of a "cure" can qualify our idea of the "disease" for which it is thought to be the cure—or as a mode of "wish-fulfillment" can paradoxically serve to reinforce the intensity of the wishes). But narratively, they stand at opposite ends of a long development, that makes one "Book" of the two Testaments taken together.

Thus, whereas narratively the Lord God's thou-shalt-not preceded the serpent's tempting of Eve, by appealing to the imagination, in mixing imagery of food with imagery of rule ("and ye shall be as *Elohim*"), and whereas the tempting preceded the fall, logologically the thou-shalt-not is itself implicitly a condition of temptation, since the negative contains the principle of its own annihilation. For insofar as a thou-shalt-not, which is intrinsic to Order verbally guided, introduces the principle of negativity, here technically is the inducement to round out the symmetry by carrying the same principle of negativity one step farther, and negating the negation. That is the only kind of "self-corrective" the negative as such has.

This principle of yes and no, so essential to the personal, verbal, "doctrinal," "sense of right and wrong," is potentially a problem from the very start. And when you add to it the "No trespassing" signs of empire, that both stimulate desires and demand their repression, you see why we hold that guilt is intrinsic to the idea of a Covenant. The question then becomes: Is victimage (redemption by vicarious atonement) equally intrinsic to the idea of guilt? The Bible, viewed either logologically or theologically, seems to be saying that it is.

One notable misfortune of the narrative is its ambiguities with regard to the relations between the sexes, unless logologically discounted. If man, as seen from the standpoint of a patriarchal society, is deemed "essentially superior" to woman, of whom he is "lord and master," it follows that, so far as the narrative way of stating such social superiority is concerned, man must be shown to "come first." Accordingly, as regards the *first* parturition, in contrast with ordinary childbirth, woman must be depicted as being born of man. This is the only way to make him absolutely first in narrative terms. Thus the punishment pronounced on Eve (3:16): "Thy desire shall be to thy husband, and he shall rule over thee" was ambiguously foretold (2:21, 22) where Eve is derived from Adam's rib.

A similar narrative mode of proclaiming man's essential social superiority appears in Aeschylus' *Eumenides.* Here, Athena, in her role as Goddess of Justice, gives her deciding vote at the "first" trial in the "first" law court—and appropriately she remarks that, though she is a woman, she was born not of woman but from the head of Zeus. (Her decision, incidentally, involves in another way the socio-political modifying of natural childbirth, since she frees Orestes of the charge of matricide by holding that he could not really have a mother, descent being through the male line, with the woman acting but as a kind of incubator for the male seed.)

The consciousness of nakedness as the result of the fall likewise seems to have been interpreted too simply, without reference to the major stress upon the matter of a *Covenant.* The approach from the standpoint of "Order" would be somewhat roundabout, along these lines: Social order leads to differentiations of status, which are indicated by differences in *clothing.* Thus, the same socio-political conditions that go with a Covenant would also go with clothing, thereby making one conscious of nakedness. The Biblical narrative itself makes clear that, under the conditions of Governance, sexual differentiation was primarily a matter of relative status. In a situation where man is to woman as master is to servant, and where the differences between the sexes were attested by clothes, nakedness would be too equalitarian.

But after sexual differentiation by clothing had been continued for a sufficient length of time, people began to assume a far greater difference between "social" and "sexual" motives than actually exists, and this is true also of modern psychoanalysis—until now we'd need a kind of ironic dissociation such as Marx proposed in connection with the "fetishism of commodities," before we could come even remotely near to realizing the extent of the social motives hidden in our ideas of sheerly "physical" sexuality. However, this marvelously accurate image of nakedness as interpreted from the standpoint of the estrangements resulting from Order in the sense of divergent rank, has been interpreted so greatly in purely sexual terms that often people seem even to think of Adam's original transgression as essentially sexual. Insofar as clothes imply social estrangement or differentiation by status, they are by the same token a kind of "fall." In themselves they are at odds with the natural order; yet nakedness is at odds with the order of our "second nature."

One final point, and our discussion of the specifically narrative resources here is finished. The opening sentence of

Aristotle's *Nichomachaean Ethics* can serve best as our text: "Every art and every inquiry, and likewise every action and practical pursuit, is thought to aim at some good: hence it has rightly been said that the Good is that at which all things aim." Thus, whenever the Biblical account says, "And God saw that it was good," we might take the formula as having, for its purely technical equivalent some such statement as, "And it was endowed with the principle of purpose." Since words like "aim," "end," "purpose" are our most generalized terms for such an idea, it follows that the equating of "to be" with "to be good" (as in the first chapter of Genesis) is a way of stating ethically, dramatically, narratively that a thing's "purpose" is technically one with its *esse*. Natural things, by their nature as creatures, are to be viewed as the *actualities* of God, hence as embodying a "design" (and they fit perfectly with Aristotle's stress, which is concerned with the varieties of "action," rather than with objects or things or processes in the sheerly neutral sense in which wholly impersonal, pragmatic science might view them).

All told, the idea of *purpose*, so essential to the narrative principle of *personality*, is here ingrained in the idea of Order, by being identified with the "good," whereby all things, by their mere act of being, contained in themselves the aim of their being.

No, that isn't quite the case. For their nature as "actualities" depends upon their nature as God's acts. Accordingly, in the last analysis, their aim involves their relation to the aims of their author (as the words in a well-formed book derive their aim from the purpose of the book as a whole— the Bible being a quite "bookish" view of the creative process).

Two further observations: (1) To recall, once more, that by the sheer dialectics of the case, this pronouncing of things as "good" brought up the possibilities of "evil." (2) It is interesting to think how Spinoza's *Ethics* in effect restated the Biblical narrative (though translating it from terms of "archae-

ology" into the circular terms of the "philosopheme," treating
of Creation "in principle"). Think of his word for purpose,
conatus, the endeavor of each thing to go on being itself, unless or until prevented by the determinations imposed upon
it by other things likewise endeavoring to go on being themselves. And he also had his technical equivalent of the particular thing's relation to an over-all principle at once outside
itself and permeating its very essence. The sacrificial principle
in Spinoza would seem to take the form of a benign mortification, a peaceful systematic distrust of the goads of the gods
of empire.

VIII   Final Comparing of Cyclical
and Rectilinear Styles

Theologically, there are two kinds of "sin," "original"
and "actual." "Actual" sins are those committed by an individual sinner, in his own right. But "original" sin is that of
the "old Adam" in us. It is sin "in principle." Hence it is the
kind of guiltiness that, as translated into terms of temporal
sequence, we "inherit" from our "first" ancestor in the male
line, as the result of his "first" disobedience to the "first" thou-
shalt-not imposed upon him by the first and foremost authority
(to whom he was subject, but from whom he inherited dominion over all created things, including his woman). For
that's the way to say "in principle" in narrative terms.

And why do we all always commit this sin "in principle"?
Because "temptation" is intrinsic to the tautological cycle of
terms implicit in the idea of Order (the most "crucial" condition of all being the principle of negativity which "inevitably" implies the "freedom" to negate a negation, to disobey
a thou-shalt-not).

And the thou-shalt-not is intrinsic to Order, inasmuch
as Order, or Dominion, involves the negativities of Law, the

"No trespassing" signs that go with the development of Property and its Rights.

Obedience says no to the self from within, "conscientiously," not merely through fear of policing from without.

And here arise the modes of sacrifice that express themselves either "suicidally," as Mortification, or "homicidally," in the slaying of scapegoats more or less clearly identified with the traits of human personality. Hence, the idea of a primary transgression is rounded out by the idea of an ultimate redemption (both the first and last steps involving the principle of *substitution*, the "old Adam" having sinned for us, and a corresponding Redeemer or Mediator of some sort being required to intercede for us).

The narrative, interpreted theologically, promises an ultimate linear progression to end all linear progressions (as time or narrative sequence ends, and the realm of eternity or "principles" takes over).

However, whether or not one believes in such a development theologically, there still remains the logological admonition with which we have here been concerned: the reason to believe that, while the era of temporal dominion continues, the cycle of terms implicit in the idea of worldly order continues, forever circling back upon itself, thus forever "guilty," thus forever demanding "redemption," thus forever inciting anew to the search for a curative victim. For it seems that, even if one believes in the idea of a perfect, supernatural, superpersonal victim, by identification with whose voluntary sacrifice one can be eternally saved, there is still the goad to look for victims here on earth as well, who should be punished for their part, real or imaginary, in blocking the believer's path to felicity, or perhaps in threatening to send him on his heavenly way too soon.

Thus, of Exodus, the book that "sets forth, in type, all redemption," and is, in type, "the book of the conditions upon which all relationships with God exist" (priesthood, sacrifice, forgiveness, cleansing, restoration, worship), our Scofield Bible also says: "Broadly, the book teaches that redemption is essential to any relationship with a holy God; and that even a redeemed people cannot have fellowship with Him unless constantly cleansed from defilement."

Our strictly logological equivalent of this theological statement would be based on the fact that the idea of a "Lord" (or Master) applies equally to supernatural and worldly governance. Thus, for a purely worldly order of motives, we should expect a correspondingly worldly kind of "defilement," with its call for a correspondingly worldly need of cleansing by sacrifice. Nazism provides the most drastically obvious instance of the ways in which such "cleansing" operates, by an ideology depicting a "perfect" victim in the guise of a "total" enemy (a scheme involving redemption both by blood and by power). Thus, where the Scofield Bible comments, "The history of Israel in the wilderness and in the land is one long record of the violation of the law," we should interpret this logologically to mean that the Biblical narrative is but continually restating the principle of circularity intrinsic to the idea of Order, continually coming upon this circular situation despite the rectilinearity of the narrative method.

Further, we should recall that the circularity is reversible, allowing not just for a progression from crime to guilt, but also for a progression from guilt to crime. That is, insofar as there is guilt intrinsic to the social order, it would not in itself be "actual," but would be analogous to "original sin," an offense somehow done "in principle." Here the sense of "criminality" could induce to the kind of crime that would "rationalize" it in terms of the subject's individual responsibility. The offender would feel guilty first, and afterwards commit the crime that justifies the guilt (or, more often, the crime that defies the guilt). Much "spirited" crime of the sort that characterizes "juvenile delinquency" would probably arise in this way.

Another way of getting at the relation between the circular (or tautological) and the narrative is to note how the narrative style can spin out a *simultaneity* into a *succession*. Let us begin with an obvious burlesque: "The man's somnolence led to sleepiness, which in turn called forth the kind of symptoms that go with a desire to sleep." Here, obviously, we have but stated the same situation three times, as though we were discussing a succession of stages. However, if this example seems too absurd to be useful, then recall this "narrative" pronouncement on economic problems, by Calvin Coolidge: "When jobs become scarce, unemployment results." Here, surely, *scarcity of jobs* is but a synonym for *unemployment;* the two ideas but circularly restate each other; yet the sentence is phrased narratively as though there were two stages, the first leading into the second.

Similarly, when discussing the building of the Tower, *The Interpreter's Bible* says, "The sole result of this blasphemy was that human society was broken into fragments." Such is the case *narratively.* But as regards the notion of *cyclicality,* such fragmentation is merely a *synonym* for the same idea that is implicit in the building of the Tower. We don't usually realize how often we use the quasi-successiveness of narrative when actually we are but giving a synonym. Thus, one might, when describing the symptoms of hunger, say that these symptoms "lead to" hunger, whereas they purely and simply are but another way of expressing hunger; they *are* hunger.

Or similarly, approaching the matter from the purely narrative point of view, *The Interpreter's Bible* gives an outline of Genesis, noting how the "expulsion from the garden" is *followed by* the "development of civilization." As regards the narrative alone, this statement is quite blameless. But from the standpoint of terministic circularity, the two expressions are synonymous. The development of civilization is, by sheer definition, the development of conditions that are identical with the loss of the Edenic. So here again we see how, by

the resources of narrative, an equation between two states can
be expressed as a procession from one state to the next.

Or consider this instance (*The Interpreter's Bible*, p.
504), where it is said that man's alienated consciousness of
death after the fall "was the inevitable result of the radical
disordering of human relationships which was the immediate
consequence of his act." Here we supposedly have at least
three stages, as regards the purely narrative sequence. An
act of "rebellion" results in a "radical disordering of human
relationships" which in turn leads to an "attitude toward death
as the final frustration of a frustrated life." But from the standpoint of terministic cyclicality, we'd say rather that Adam's
"rebellion" (or *disobedience*) is but a special case of *disorder*
in general. And the same would be true of the attitude towards death as a "consequence of the alienation from God."
Or, otherwise put: The principle of disorder intrinsic to the
idea of Order (in the sense of hierarchal or *ziggurat*-like
dominion) can be individuated narratively as either an account of the first man's *first* disobedience or an account of his
corresponding attitude towards a *last* thing (for in eschatological matters of this sort, *eventualities* in time are as good
a way of stating principles as are *beginnings* in time).

There is a passage in Augustine's *Confessions* that well
illustrates the cyclical-narrative shift. From the strictly logical
point of view, to "go astray" could be considered a synonym
for "to err." But in the last paragraph of IV, xv, Augustine
transforms such an equation into a temporal sequence when
he says of man's mutable substance that after first "having
strayed of its own accord" (*deviasse sponte*), it next "errs as
punishment" (*poena errare*). But here the two ablatives
(*sponte* and *poena*) differently modify the synonyms, as does
the inflection of the verbs (the first being a perfect infinitive,
the second a present). Thus, the matter becomes elusive, to
the mighty extent that the mind of Augustine differed from
that of Calvin Coolidge. *First*, Augustine says, you get off the

road *of your own free will;* and *next,* you're off the road as *punishment.*

Another kind of duplication, halfway between narrative and the cyclical, is indicated in an epigram of Oscar Wilde's (cited in *The Interpreter's Bible*) to the effect that he could resist everything but temptation. In this form, it looks ingeniously perverse. But once you narratively translate the principle of temptation into the personalized image of the serpent, the element of duplication takes on quite a different look. For instance, if Eve had said to the serpent, "I can resist all but thee," she'd have been saying what Wilde said, but without his stylistic twist. The statements would mean the same inasmuch as the serpent stands for temptation in general.

However, insofar as a serpent suggests specifically sexual connotations, the idea of disobedience to the principle of sovereignty in general can retreat behind the notion that the serpent tempted Eve sexually—as with the tradition that the serpent did seduce her sexually. If we move so far afield, we could recover the main emphasis of the Biblical story only by noting how the psychosis of dominion is also "tautologically present" in the idea of *sexual* seduction, as in Ovid's *Ars Amatoria* (see our *A Rhetoric of Motives,* p. 159 ff.).

However, it might be objected that the kind of "tautology" by which "scarcity of jobs" equals "unemployment" (or "somnolence" equals "sleepiness" equals "symptoms due to lack of sleep") is quite different from the kind involved in the steps from Creation to Covenant to proscription to temptation to sin to punishment to new Covenant to sin to sacrifice to redemption, etc.

The sort of thing we are getting at is clearly revealed in this passage cited from *The Interpreter's Bible* (p. 226):

There is another matter which arises in connection with Hebrew ideas of sin, and here again a study of the key words shows that Hebrew thought differs from our Western ways of thinking. We make a clear distinction between sin as the wrong act itself, the guilt which thereafter rests upon the sinner, and the consequences of the sin which fall sometimes on the sinner and usually on the innocent. The Hebrews tended to include all three aspects under the same word.*

The logological comment here would be to the effect that this particular Hebrew usage happens to be sufficiently different from English usage to reveal for us a tautological relationship among three terms that we might otherwise tend to think of as three essentially different stages in a process.

Similarly, it is pointed out, a word that meant "error," "sin," "mistake," was usually applied to the wrong action itself, sometimes to the guilt connected with it, while later it came to stand for "sin offering." And it is suggested that this range should be kept in mind when interpreting II Corinthians 5:21: "For our sake he made him to be sin who knew no sin." Here the meanings of the Hebrew word are said to be in Paul's mind, lurking behind the Greek *hamartia* (the word, by the way, used by Aristotle in his Poetics to name the "flaw" which plays so great a part in the destruction or sacrifice, of the tragic hero, or scapegoat).

The more closely you look into such terms, the more likely you are to find such unifying spirit implicit in them. Recall further that the conditions of "actual sin" may be quite different from the kind of sin "in principle" with which we are here concerned, the "original sin" that is summed up in the copybook maxim: "In Adam's fall, We sinned all." We are trying to explain the linguistic conditions involved in this notion, without either affirming or denying its validity theologically. And we are trying to show that guilt, in this sense, comes not from the *breaking* of the law but from the mere *formulating* of the law (that is, from the Idea of Order).

In his first book of criticism, *Counter-Statement,* originally published over twenty-five years ago, the present author had an essay on Thomas Mann and André Gide, in which he

* "The Language of the Old Testament" by Norman H. Snaith, *The Interpreter's Bible* (Nashville: Abingdon Press, 1900), I, 226.

tried to show how "corruption" in the writings of Gide could be equated with "conscientiousness" in the writings of Mann. We are now considering this same paradoxical interchangeability, but as approached the long way round, through the study of a linguistic labyrinth that the author at that time glimpsed but "in principle." The present study would combine the idea of that early essay with notions about "the temporizing of essence" discussed in *A Grammar of Motives*, along with speculations to do with the nature of consistency in symbol-systems, as revealed by the close study of texts (involving the relation between narrative unfolding and the cyclical recurrence of key terms).

One other place should be mentioned, in *The Philosophy of Literary Form*, the opening essay, near the end of a section entitled "The Concealed Offense." There the musical distinction between "chord" and "arpeggio" is borrowed for the analysis of tonal qualities in literature. The point is this: If you strike *do-mi-sol* simultaneously, you get a perfect concord. If you added *fa*, thus playing *do-mi-fa-sol*, you get a discord. But if you draw this discord out into an arpeggio, by playing the four notes not simultaneously but in succession, they are not felt as a discord. Rather, they are transformed into a melody, since the dissonant *fa* acts merely as a passing note.

The matter is discussed in the section on " 'Form' and 'Content' " in the same essay:

In keeping with our chord-arpeggio distinction, the metaphysical problem could be stated thus: In the arpeggio of biological, or temporal growth, good *does* come out of evil (as we improve ourselves by revising our excesses, the excesses thus being a necessary agent in the drama, or dialectic, of improvement: they are the "villain" who "competitively cooperates with us as "criminal Christ" in the process of redemption). But when you condense the arpeggio of development by the nontemporal, nonhistorical forms of logic, you get simultaneous "polarity," which adds up to good and evil as consubstantial. Now if one introduces into a chord a note alien to the perfect harmony, the result is a discord. But if you stretch out this same chord into an arpeggio having the same components, the discordant ingredient you have introduced may become but a "passing note." "Transcendence" is the solving of the logical problem by stretching it out into a narrative arpeggio, whereby a conflicting element can be introduced as a "passing note," hence not felt as "discord." A logic is "flat," simultaneous, "chordal"; ideally, it is all done before you begin. Thus, Hegel's "dialectic of history" attempted the union of contradictory aims, in trying to make the passing note of an arpeggio fit as concord in a simultaneity. A logic being ideally all done before you begin, anti-Hegelians get their opportunity to object that his logic of development, if true, would make development impossible. Thesis, antithesis, and synthesis would all exist simultaneously and in equal force. But by stretching them out into a temporal arpeggio, he can depict the thesis as prevailing in greater percentage at one time, the antithesis at another, and the synthesis as an act of transcendence at still another.

In connection with John Steinbeck's novel, *The Grapes of Wrath*, the land turtle (which Tom Joad is carrying on his return from prison) is similarly interpreted:

> The turtle's (explicitly stated) aimless wandering, over the dry soil, "foreshadows" (or implicitly prophesies) the drought-pervaded trek. . . . Its wandering across the parched earth is "representative" of the migration in a stream of traffic on the dry highways. It contains implicitly, in "chordal collapse," a destiny that the narrative will unfold explicitly, in "arpeggio."

The analysis proceeds to show that the work is a "strategy for the redemption of crime," not in the sense merely that the offender is forgiven, but in a more "radical" sense, thus:

> The "pilgrim's progress" of Tom is from the role of a man who had left prison after slaying a man in a drunken brawl to that of a man who is a fugitive from the law for having slain a man in a "just" cause, since he had slain the slayer of Casy, the charismatic and sacrificial vessel of emancipation. It is a progress from an inferior kind of crime to a "transcendent" kind of crime (even orthodox criminologists usually putting political crime in a different category from kinds more private in their motivation—a reservation made necessary by the fact that the "criminal" philosophy of one era so often becomes the "normal" philosophy of a later era).

This last speculation indicates respects in which an "image" can "implicitly contain" a jumble of plot, to the extent that in its "simultaneous one-ness" it symbolizes, or stands for, the "idea" behind the narrative as a whole. Particularly in the case of lyric poetry, the quasi-temporal image often performs this non-temporal function. But though it might be helpful to have these earlier tentatives in mind (for the light they may throw upon our present speculations), let us return specifically to the "archaeology" of Genesis.

With regard to the "fundamental thesis" of the fall in Genesis, there is a passage in *The Interpreter's Bible* (p. 455) which lends itself with especial felicity to translation into "logologese." The various points, with their "translation," are as follows:

Theological Summary	*Logological Counterpart*
"Man from the very beginning has been in revolt against God."	Man is *in principle* in revolt against the principle of authority (since he has the conscientious and/or guilt-laden capacity to apply the negative principle against itself).
This condition cannot be corrected by punishment.	This condition is indigenous to the nature of the idea of Order.
It cannot even be corrected "by the punishment of the Flood."	The idea of an intrinsic guilt appropriately calls forth an image of cleansing and rebirth on the grand scale—yet such an image is but another way of reaffirming the underlying principle of guilt.
Man's "arrogance" was also "revealed in the attempt to build a tower which should reach to heaven."	The image of the Tower but reveals the problems implicit in the idea of hierarchal order with which the account of the Creation begins.
This attempt has the fragmentation of society as its "sole result."	The fragmentation that is said to *result* from the building of the Tower is but a restatement of the hierarchal principle which the Tower itself (as a kind of Babylonian *ziggurat*) exemplifies.

Theological Summary	*Logological Counterpart*
Then came "the process of redemption" that "began in the call of Abraham" (symbolizing the covenants).	Such "redemption" as Abraham exemplified is a way of extending the principle of intrinsic guilt explicitly to the idea of nationality (redemption now explicitly revealing its relation to sacrifice).
Yet even Abraham and his family also contributed to the situation that "made redemption necessary."	The principle of Disorder that is intrinsic to Order is again exemplified (but narratively, as though it were a new development).
Thus, there was to be "a great deliverance."	The idea of a "great deliverance" is the perfecting of the redemption principle, which is but the reverse of the guilt principle (since payment, by punishment or sacrifice, is implied in the idea of guilt as debt).
Accordingly, the book of Genesis "foreshadows the salvation to be wrought by God."	Thus, by its use of the rectilinear style when disclosing the principles inherent in the idea of Order, the book of Genesis points toward the promise of an *end* to the Hierarchal Cycle, even while reaffirming the hierarchal principle that characterizes the persistent problem of Order.

However, though the rectilinear style is rife with promise, there is one notable sense in which the genius of the cyclical still holds. Though the eventual Kingdom of God is free of disobedience, the principle of disobedience is not eliminated. Rather, it is isolated and perpetuated (even in a technical sense "purified") in the notion of an everlasting hell. So, in this way, the idea of an ultimate, all-triumphant governance of good does not remove the sacrificial principle, but rather absolutizes it (as one might expect, inasmuch as this kingdom is entered in terms of a perfect sacrifice).

This arrangement seems to involve a selection from the two styles. The rectilinear promise of progress is present, so far as the end of worldly governance is concerned. For if the natural order itself is being ended, any cycle of motives intrinsic to that order should end along with it. However, the *principle* of governance (dominion, Covenant) is still thought to continue. (From the strictly logological point of view, the idea of such everlasting continuance would itself be the translating of a sheerly logical notion, an *ens rationis,* into quasi-temporal terms, with corresponding quasi-materiality, though in this case the principle, or "first," would be in the guise of an everlasting last.)

But insofar as the principle of worldly governance is thought to "continue" (in supernatural counterpart), then by the same token the principle of victimage might be expected to continue, as a corresponding supernatural counterpart. It does, insofar as the sacrificial principle of governance is "forever fixed" in the sufferings of hell (while the sufferers, as it were, are "permanently" disobedient in principle, and "permanently" punished for their unchanging attitude.)

Yes, the rectilinear promise of the pilgrim's progress by no means abolishes the cyclicality of order, so far as the total dialectic is concerned. And those heretics who felt that God, in his infinite mercy, would eventually save all men after they had been sufficiently punished for their few years of transgression here on earth, were in effect proposing too thoroughly to abandon the idea of the cyclicality of order. Thus the *Summa* tells, as does Protestant Bunyan, of the edification that the blessed derive from contrasting their blessedness with the sight of the hellish sufferings perpetually visited upon the damned. As seen in the perspective of eternity, a willingness on God's part to abandon eternal punishment would be like abandoning the *principles* of bless and curse so integral to the idea of a Covenant. It is as disturbing to the dramatics of theology (the theory of action carried to its ultimate conclusion) as were a playwright to *begin* where Prospero *ends,* by freeing not only Ariel but Caliban. Furthermore, even a slight disobedience might seem absolute insofar as it is viewed in terms of disobedience to an absolute authority.

The relation between the rectilinear and circular styles comes to a focus in this paradox: The priestly role as Mediator not only proposes progressively to "absolve" from guilt; it also serves circularly to intensify the very sense of guiltiness (or "conscience") for which it provides the absolution.

The simplest example of a circular order breeding itself is the "success story," which gets a kind of catharsis by building up a day-dream of gratification. In the course of its imaginary attainments, it brings to the imagination the very ideals that make precisely its ideas of success seem so pressingly desirable. Thus, the "cure" but reinvigorates the "disease," and readies the audience for another variant of the same success story next time.

But such an endless round of wanting, stimulated by an imaginary climb to the very conditions of livelihood which make the satisfying of such wants seem most reasonable and most attainable, is a kind of "benign" cycle. And thus it might in itself be taken as a categorical refutation of all that we have been saying about the "sacrificial" motive.

Considered in itself, it is—it is a total refutation of all that we have been saying. And if it could go on forever, with each of us always hoping confidently for more, and continually getting enough to keep his hopes green, then this would be a way out. And for that reason, we should be grateful for it.

But unfortunately, it can only be a stopgap. For the principle of wanting is never satisfied with getting, since by its very nature as a principle it transcends all mere material things, even while being encouraged to think that material things are what it wants. So, no matter how much it gets, it will in the end be frustrated because it cannot get still more.

But aside from that psychological problem, there is a

more exacting, sheerly economic one. For the cult of commodities contains many blockings internal to its nature. It involves wasteful ways that throw us, first of all, out of line with the laws of finance, and ultimately out of line with the demands imposed upon us by nature itself (the demands of ecology, geophysics and the like, the conditions whereby, already, we have been proved to be squandering the wealth of our land on the promiscuous production of things that, as seen from this point of view, are tragically in error). And insofar as we are being kept happy by the acquiring of baubles, like pampered children, then at the first sign of a frustration, like pampered children we may fall into a rage. Or so it would be, attenuatedly. And there, again, would be the problem that plagues this text, the problem of victimage.

The Bible, with its profound and beautiful exemplifying of the sacrificial principle, teaches us that tragedy is ever in the offing. Let us, in the spirit of solemn comedy, listen to its lesson. Let us be on guard ever, as regards the subtleties of sacrifice, in their fundamental relationship to governance.

Thinking of Aeschylus' tragic trilogy, the *Oresteia*, in the light of these speculations, can we not say that it begins in the circularity of victimage, and ends by a promise that the circularity has been made rectilinear? It begins with the feudal principle that is typical of tribal justice: the rule whereby each act of vengeance in turn calls forth a retaliatory act of vengeance. How break this cycle? By the progression of his three plays, Aeschylus seems to have said in effect that the change could be contrived by a turn from feuds to law courts. For whereas, feudally, Clytemnestra's killing of her husband Agamemnon called forth the son Orestes' killing of her, and that in turn called forth the son's remorseful battles with himself (as exemplified in the text by the maternally avenging Furies in their pursuit of him), the third play ends with the feudal cycle transcended.

But is the problem true only of a feudal cycle, as it might

seem to be, when we thus consider it purely in the light of a
turn from tribal justice to civic justice? Or does it go on,
beyond all such "solutions," being intrinsic to the nature of
Dominion as such, just as tragedy, the "goat-song," itself went
on, in the plays performed the next year?

The guilt was "processed." It was not *resolved.* For its
real resolution would be the end of tragedy—that is to say,
the end of the sacrificial principle, the end of "mortification"
in all its forms, including the comic.

Today we must doubly fear the cyclical compulsions of
empire, as two mighty world orders, each homicidally armed
to the point of suicide, confront each other. As with dominion
always, each is much beset with anxiety. And in keeping with
the "curative" role of victimage, each is apparently in acute
need of blaming all its many troubles on the other. The situation becomes still more urgent, since it offers special opportunities for those persons who have a special vested interest
in maintaining as much international ill-will as possible (particularly those who profit by the funds spent on defense, and
those who are in the business of political inquisition). So,
two vast, unwieldy opponents are to each other like spectres,
each wanting to feel certain that, if but the other were eliminated, all governmental discord (all the Disorder that goes
with Order) would be ended.

IX Logological Epilogue

Though scholars have done much to disclose the various
redactions involved in the text of Genesis as it now stands,
for present purposes we do not need such lore, beyond pointing out the difference between the stress upon classification
in the "Elohist" chapter 1 and the stress upon sovereignty in
the "Jehovist" chapters 2 and 3 (a stress which we interpret
mainly in the light of the Scofield Bible's statement that "Je-

hovah is distinctly the redemption name of Deity"). From the logological point of view, as regards "inchoate firsts," or "proto-firsts," the Edenic Covenant propounded by Elohim in chapter 1 is technically "more innocent" than as stated by Jehovah Elohim in chapter 2. For even though Adam has not yet sinned in chapter 2, the possibility of his sinning has made a notable step forward through the addition of the negative command, whereas in chapter 1 the conditions for sinning exist only in the ambiguous sense we noted in connection with Coleridge's remark (equating the Creation itself with a kind of "fall").

Here is a further instance of the way in which the text can usually be taken just as it stands: *The Interpreter's Bible* (p. 493) notes an apparent inconsistency between 2:5 (implying that man's natural occupation is to till the soil) and 3:23 (where man's disobedience is said to be the cause of his need "to till the ground from whence he was taken"). Both versions would fit well with the logological point of view. For though, by our interpretation, a socio-political guilt can so pervade man's consciousness that even sheerly natural things can be seen in terms of it, this conscience-laden perspective is not always uppermost when the talk is of natural things as such. But it quickly becomes apparent when we approach nature *in terms of* guilt. And once the subject of Adam's sin has been introduced, this subject serves as a "revelation," leading to the vision of nature itself as infused with such sinfulness. The difference between the two passages is wholly analogous to the difference between the implicit divisiveness of the first chapter (detailing Elohim's creation) and the explicit divisiveness of chapters 2 and 3, concerning Jehovist dominion, with its crucial thou-shalt-not. And the same interpretation would fit, whether or not one decided that the two verses originally came from different sources.

But our main purpose in adding this epilogue is to expand again from Genesis to logology in general. For instance, note that our concern with the ways in which terms are "implicit" in one another bears upon the Platonist "mythic" doctrine of *anamnesis*. According to this doctrine, the soul sojourning in this world bears within itself the vague memory of a prior heavenly existence, where it contemplated a realm of pure "forms" or "archetypes." And when it sees things on earth, these things in their material imperfection remind it of their ideal heavenly prototypes—so that "discovery" is really rather a kind of "remembering."

This doctrine may or may not be true metaphysically, but it is quite revealing, as analyzed logologically. For instance, if we say that *idea B* is "implicit in" *idea A*, the translation of this relationship into terms of temporal sequence brings up a quasi-mystical paradox. For if we begin with *idea A,* and meditate upon it until we find *idea B* implicit in it, then so far as time sequence is concerned *idea B* has followed *idea A.* We have *proceeded in time* in such a way that we went *from* A *to* B. Yet, insofar as B was implicit there from the start, there is a sense in which its presence in A preceded our discovery of it there. Thus, in another sense, our step forward is rather like a step backwards, like being *reminded* of something.

We can see this more clearly when thinking of the relation between the practical use of a language and a book on the theory of its grammar and syntax. Under natural conditions, people learn languages long before the rules of grammar and syntax are explicitly formulated. These rules are "discovered" relatively late in the development of linguistic sophistication, and sometimes not at all. Yet there is a sense in which they "have been there" from the start, *implicit* in the given symbol-system. In this sense, to "discover" them is but to formulate what one somehow knew before one ever began to ask about such "forms." They are thus "technically prior" in a way that would be quite analogous to the Platonic view of "archetypes" already existing in the "memory" that vaguely "recalls" them in their ideal "perfection."

Here is another possible variant on the same idea: Might one have a "sense of recurrence in advance"? That is, if one's sense of an essence is *emerging*, then this essence (which is in its way "perfect") *duplicates* the immediate details that, in their "imperfection," suggest it. For insofar as these details foreshadow it, they "imply" it; hence, it is "twice present," once in the *details* that imperfectly imply it, and once in the perfection of the "principle" which they imply.

For instance, suppose that, when undergoing a certain experience in real life, a person has both a clear immediate perception of the experience as such and a vague premonition of the use to which he might put this experience if he translated it into a work of art. Since, behind the details of existence he would also be experiencing an ideal essence, his experience would be "double." If such a doubling of an experience were imagined "mythically" (by the temporizing of essence), then the simultaneous duplication of the moments could be sensed rather as a *succession*. The "essential" one would be *formally* "prior" to the existential one; hence, there could be a sense of the *déjà vu*. For if the situation is seen both for what it is and as a perfect projection of the person's character (in effect "his" situation), then such a projection (fulfillment, consummation, logical conclusion, *reductio ad absurdam* or essence) of the situation would be its "principle." And the logological feeling that the situation is "principled" could become the psychological conviction that it was doubled. In sum:

If you experience something, and if, in the experiencing of it, you also get an intense idea of what would be for you its perfection (such as you might exemplify later in a dream, a theory, a completed work of art or in personal relations), then your experiencing of it the first time would be like the experiencing of it twice. And the temporal equivalent of that experience would be what the French call the *déjà vu.*

It shades into the metaphysical theory of "eternal recurrence" that arises when a situation is immediately experienced both in itself and as member of a class, with the *formal* priority as member of a class being defined in terms of *temporal* priority.

Also, from the strictly logological point of view, such a search for "implications" leads to an interesting reversal, or quasi-temporal duplication.

Let us begin, for instance, with the natural and socio-political orders (as the empirical nature of logological inquiry would require us to do). In the natural order, man is properly defined as a species of animal. Next we note how, socio-politically, he develops forms of governance involving a scale of status variously ranging from "sovereignty" to "servitude."

Such a view is sheerly "positive," a picture of social rule, involving social classification in a world of natural classification.

This state of affairs can give rise to a vision of "moral grandeur" when the principle of social rule is extended to the natural realm—and man is seen as "ruler" *over all nature.* The socio-political design of governance is thus made absolute; the perspective of socio-political order is felt to infuse the natural order; all nature is seen as being put there for man's use; in sum, nature is man's servant, and man is nature's sovereign.

However, the procession is *not* just simply from the socio-political to the natural. An intermediate step is needed before the design can take form. The design must be "mythically" duplicated by the postulating of an analogous arrangement whereby there is a supernatural (or super-sociopolitical) order, with its corresponding hierarchy. This formal "perfecting" of the design, ideally duplicating the human socio-political order in "higher" terms, was "prior," was "there from the start," to the extent that it sums up all the *principles* felt to have been guiding the socio-political order. The vision says in effect: "Only if the socio-political order is on such-and-such relations with the principles of all order, can the order be reasonable."

And thus, the "perfecting myth" becomes like the *originator* of the order it perfects. It also has so rounded out the pattern that the human state of sovereignty over nature can itself be seen as servitude to the superhuman powers or principles by which it is implicitly guided.

Once this perfect mythic duplicate is imagined, then the corresponding natural design can be imagined. And the reversal, whereby the man who was ruler becomes himself an underling, removes the imperfections that might otherwise spoil the symmetry of the scheme. That is, insofar as natural calamities defy man's governance, these can be explained as the acts of the higher authority.

Such a theory does not dispose of the possibility that one such "myth" may be "true" while the others are "false." It merely explains the verbal mechanisms by which such myths can arise, regardless of whether they are true or false.

As regards the principle of terministic circularity, note that we here come upon the logological equivalent of the theological definition of God as "pure act." *In principle,* the consistency that prevails "eternally" among the terms of a nomenclature is "at rest." The relations are all symmetrically there "in advance," before being "made manifest" in the "history" of an analytic procession from one to another. They are related to "narrative" developments quite as the properties of a geometric form are to the Euclidean demonstration of those properties. Also, they involve a variant of the problem treated by Hegel, as regards his concern with the relations between a logic of The Idea and its translation into the developments of nature and history.

X Miscellaneous Postscripts

(*a*) Retrospective description of this essay's contents:
Men did not make such a contract as Hobbes describes.
But they made such a contract "in principle." Or, they are
related to one another *as though* they had made such a contract, using to that end the principle of "representation," or
"personation," in the person of the sovereign. Or you might
put it this way: Their Commonwealth involves a great inter-
weaving of acts and roles—but insofar as all these are thought
of as logically reducible to one primal act, that act would be
the adopting of some such covenant as Hobbes describes,
choosing subjection with relation to the central role of sovereign.

Then, turning to Genesis, we find that the same sort of
relationship is stated in terms not of "philosophemes," but of
"Hebrew archaeology." That is, the idea of a contract made
"in principle" is stated narratively, mythically, by saying that
some such contract was made between the first man and the
foremost authority. The same story (since it includes Creation, Eden, and Fall) also treats mythically, or quasi-
temporally, of the "diseases" implicit in such a contract. That
is, it shows the ideas of "disorder" that are implicit in the idea
of "order," along with the ideas of the attitudes that lead to
such disorder, and of the attitudes that result from such disorder (or "disobedience"); whereat we next come upon the
ideas of *redemption*, and thus finally of victimage via the principle of representation, personation, vicarage. In brief, the
essay shows the ways whereby the idea of order as stated narratively, tautologically implies the idea of original sin, if such
terms for the "temporizing" of essence are interpreted literally.
And it shows how the idea of original sin in turn tautologically
implies the idea of redemption by a perfect scapegoat.

(*b*) John Bunyan's narrative outline of terms implicit in the idea of "Salvation" as versus "Damnation":

Fortunately for the author, it was not until he neared the end of this essay that he came upon a most remarkable chart drawn up by John Bunyan, "A Map Shewing the Order and Causes of Salvation and Damnation." * The "Map" is so *narratively* salient that it might well have helped conceal the *circular* features we have been studying.

Bunyan here designs a bisymmetrical Chart, wholly in the rectilinear style, detailing twenty-four stages through which the Elect pass from their beginning to their predestined end in Heaven, along with twenty-four corresponding stages through which the Reprobates must pass from their beginning to their predestined end in Hell. Also, at the top, there is a triangle containing four circles labeled God, Father, Son and Spirit. Below that comes Adam, his area half on the "line of grace" (the side of the Elect) and half on the "line of justice" (the side of the Reprobates). Beneath him are Abel and Cain, their areas confined to "grace" and "justice" respectively.

In general, the twenty-four terms on the side of Election proceed thus: The Elect feel the Call of the Spirit; this "causeth sound convictions for sin," which lead to despair, and thus to prayer, and thus to help from Heaven, with corresponding humility, patience, hope, and thus eventually to Heaven, where the soul, having merited the grace of God's mercy, "dwelleth to ETERNITY." The Reprobates, on the other hand, do not feel the Elect's great sense of personal sinfulness. Hence they incline to take it easy, until their evil habits have crept up on them to the point where they cannot reform; hence they merit the severities of God's justice. In general, it seems, the Reprobates, who heard no Call from the Spirit, choose

---

* It is inserted among the pages of *The Holy War*, in Vol. III of *The Works of John Bunyan, with an Introduction to each Treatise, Notes, and a Sketch of his Life, Times, and Contemporaries*, ed. George Offor (Glasgow: Blackie & Son, 1862.)

what Shakespeare has called "the primrose path to the everlasting bonfire."

The "Map" is so intensely rectilinear in the treatment of
its terms, one might easily overlook the underlying circularity.
But basically, of course, it comprises two series of terms implicit in the ideas of Order and Disorder respectively.

Incidentally, the cluster of terms on the side of Election
has one especially notable virtue, in helping correct the usual
notions as to the relation between Protestantism and the rise
of capitalism. The explanation generally current puts too
much stress upon the notion that God shows the signs of his
Election by giving the Elect prosperity here on earth, and
that, accordingly, the idea of predestination stimulated the
attempt to acquire material wealth, since such success would
in itself indicate a Heavenly destiny.

Bunyan's Chart shows what a tremendously important
step is omitted from this picture. (In fact, Bunyan's Chart
makes no reference whatever to material well-being, but is
presented purely in terms of calling, sinfulness, despair, promise, faith, prayer, righteousness, holiness, humility, watchful-
ness, "patience under the cross," "experience of God's goodness," hope, contemplation, "faith above their sufferings." In
sum: "We look not at the things that are seen; but at the things
that are not seen."

To read John Bunyan's *Grace Abounding to the Chief of
Sinners* (his counterpart of Augustine's *Confessions*) is to
realize precisely what is wrong with the generally accepted
picture of the relation between Protestantism and capitalism.
It is *not dialectical enough*. In particular, its study of Protestantism, in terms of the *capitalist* motives which *follow* it,
deflects attention from the study of Protestantism in terms of
the *aristocratic* motives which *preceded* it.

Looking at the problem from this point of view, we see
how the sense of *great personal sinfulness* served in effect to
provide not just an idea of supernatural election with regard

to the afterlife; it also supplied a paradoxical idea of *lowly social election,* as contrasted with the aristocratic ideas of social "nobility."

Remember that in Bunyan's scheme, the major sign of election was *not* social prestige, but such a sense of personal sinfulness, in answer to the calling of the Spirit, as made one pray in terror for salvation. Here was a kind of "superiority" that was of a quite different nature from the norms of *aristocratic* nobility, which might seem rather, on the reprobate, primrose-path side of things. And, paradoxically, one's very sense of degradation (which could often undoubtedly stem from economic deprivations), could *of itself* be taken as a hopeful sign, if one but became devout as a result of it.

To understand this arrangement is to understand why Bunyan was so insistent upon his great depravity (an insistence that considerably embarrassed him as a Baptist minister, when his opponents began taking him at his word, whereupon he had to turn around and begin stoutly proclaiming how irreproachable had been his conduct). As the aristocratic attitude had its ways of equating social nobility with moral nobility, and as the capitalist attitude would have its ways of using the word "rich" to designate wealth in both the social sense and in the sense of rich imagination, rich sensibility, etc., so Bunyan reveals the possibilities of a reversal which would apparently come quite close to the paradoxical ("first shall be last") kind of prophesying developed in the Sermon on the Mount.

Also, of course, the habits that would naturally go with such a way of life would be the kind that helps build up the prosperity of the family—and thus the mores of early capitalism would gradually emerge. But the omission of this paradox with regard to the relation between election and the sense of personal sinfulness is a kind of shortcut that leads to a false view of Protestant motives.

Incidentally, the light that Bunyan's "Map" throws upon the Calvinist doctrines of election can be projected further, to illuminate the Lutherans' views on the impossibility of keeping the commandments. As summarized by Pascal, in his *Troisième Écrit sur la Grâce (lettre sur la possibilité des commandements)*:*

Les Luthériens soutenaient formellement que les actions des justes, même faites par la charité, sont nécessairement toujours des péchés, et que la concupiscence, qui règne toujours en cette vie, ruine si fort l'effet de la charité que, quelque justes que soient les hommes et par quelque mouvement de la charité qu'ils agissent, la convoitise y a toujours tant de part, que non seulement ils n'accomplissent pas les préceptes, mais qu'ils les violent, et qu'ainsi ils sont absolument incapables de les observer, de quelque grâce qu'ils soient secourus.*

(c) Simplest instance of reversibility:

We think of the present as "growing out of" the past. Yet if we "began with" the present, and next studied the documents of yesterday, then those of the day before, etc., the past would "gradually emerge" for us "out of" our starting point in the present. The successive disclosures of the ever remoter past would thus be a constantly unfolding future, so far as our particular process of revelation was concerned.

A more complicated kind of reversibility is to be found in connection with "final causes." They are directed "towards the future," and thus they can be felt to "implicitly contain" the future. In this sense, the future is felt to "precede" the stages that lead to its fulfillment. Actually, "final causes" are not future at all, but continually present (a kind of *nunc stans*) until attained or abandoned.

The Aristotelian concept of the "entelechy," as an aim contained within the entity, is essentially a biological analogy. It is the title for the fact that the seed "implicitly contains" a future conforming to its nature, if the external conditions necessary to such unfolding and fulfillment occur in the right order. Were you to think of the circumstances and the seed

* *Oeuvres Complètes de Pascal,* Bibliothèque de la Pléiade (Paris: Gallimard, 1954), p. 971.

together, as composing a single process, then the locus of the entelechy could be thought of as residing not just in the nature of the seed, but *in the ground of the process as a whole*.

(*d*) Special case where place of "Mortification" on our chart must be shifted:

William Sargant's *Battle for the Mind* quotes this passage from Boswell's *Journal,** concerning Samuel Johnson:

> We talked of preaching and of the great success that the Methodists have. He said that was owing to their preaching in a plain, vulgar manner, which was the only way to do good to common people. . . . He said that talking of drunkenness as a crime, because it debases reason, the noblest faculty of man, would do no service to the vulgar. But to tell them that they might have died in their drunkenness and show how dreadful that would be, would affect them much.

The passage suggests another variant on our concept of "mortification." When the poor devils thus got drunk, they *were* in effect "dying," in the sense that they were deadening themselves to their cares. So the evangelists were but taking a synonym which was already present and translating it into terms of a temporal sequence.

That is: From the standpoint of terministic circularity, drunkenness can be a way of literally acting out the simile: "Getting drunk is like dying to one's cares." (The equation is made still more obvious in the expression, "dead drunk.") But the evangelists translated the identity of the two into terms of a step *from* one *to* the other: They pointed out that a person might go from drunkenness to death. As indeed he might. But we are suggesting that the underlying logic of the *equation* (the similitude) *between* drunkenness *and* death made the evangelists' threat of a development *from* drunkenness *to* death seem more likely. And the very force of this underlying equation would add terrorizing plausibility to the

* J. Boswell, *Boswell's London Journal,* ed. F. A. Pottle (New York: McGraw-Hill Book Co., 1950).

doctrine that death under such conditions would be a sure
path to hell's fire.

To persuade a man that he might die when dead drunk
is in effect to persuade him that he might complete the equation absolutely. And such persuasion would be aided by the
fact that drunkenness probably is a search for the absolute
anyhow.

Meanwhile, note that whereas our Chart places "mortification" on the "Order" side, all intoxication would be a kind
of mortification that should be listed on the "Disorder" side.
Here, to employ the terms of the Chart, would be a transformation whereby "mortification" becomes "fornication."

(e) Martyrdom as mortification displayed:

Martyrdom is the idea of total voluntary self-sacrifice
enacted in a grave cause before a perfect (absolute) witness.
It is the fulfillment of the principle of mortification, suicidally
directed, with the self as scapegoat (in contrast with homi-
cidal use of an external scapegoat as purificatory victim). The
nearest social counterpart of martyrdom is stage fright (an
attenuated variant in which the fear is willingly suffered in
connection with the desire to "get into the act").

La Rochefoucauld: "Les véritables mortifications sont
celles qui ne sont point connues; la vanité rend les autres
faciles."

(f) "Predestination," "foreknowledge," "election" and
"reprobation," viewed as narrative translations of the circular:

Theological notions of "providence" and "predestination"
would be narrative equivalents for the principle of terministic
circularity. For insofar as terms imply one another, any path
among them is "potentially there from the start," and thus
"implicitly foreseen." The distinction between election and
reprobation would result terministically from the combining
of such over-all terministic "inevitability" with the principle
of discrimination implicit in the relation between the terms

of "order" and "disorder," their dialectical nature as terms that
"necessarily" imply each other, quite as the *Summa Theologica*
explains that the blessed in heaven require, as aid to the
maximum appreciation of their blessedness, the contrasting
sight of the damned suffering the eternal torments of hell.
(*Summa Theologica, Supplementum. Quaestio* xciv, *Articulus*
i.—Utrum beati qui erunt in patria, videbunt poenas damna-
torum.)

(g) Pascal and the problems of circularity:

One will never find a clearer indication of the *circularity*
in such terms as we have been considering, than Pascal's
four *Écrits sur la Grâce*, which are a succession of rebegin-
nings, with repeated shuttling back and forth among such
terms as "grace," "free will" and "predestination." Logologically, "grace" and "free will" stand at the watershed between
the slopes of "Order" and "Disorder." In their way, they have
a mediatory function, quite as the term "Jesus Christ," viewed
logologically, is a mediatory principle for bridging the two
realms of terms for the natural and terms for the supernatural.

However, though terms, as seen from the strictly logological point of view, are analyzed simply as implicating one
another, theological distinctions between orthodoxy and heresy
can be defined by the choice of some one sequence rather than
another. For instance, at one point Pascal distinguishes between Catholics and Calvinists thus: "Nous entendons que le
décret de Dieu est postérieur à la prévision du péché d'Adam
et donné sur les hommes criminels, et eux prétendent que ce
décret est non seulement prieur, mais cause de péché d'Adam
et donné sur les hommes encore innocents." *

This is an interesting distinction indeed. Though God's
foreknowledge of Adam's sin was by definition eternally prior

---

* *Oeuvres Complètes de Pascal* (Paris: Gallimard, 1954), first
Écrit sur la Grâce, p. 957.

to Adam's act itself, Pascal here makes a distinction between a divine decree made *subsequent* to such foreknowledge and one made *prior* to such foreknowledge. Here the shift between logical and temporal notions of priority is bewilderingly exquisite, with the second version adding the idea of priority in the causal sense to the idea of priority in a quasi-temporal sense.

Pascal proceeds to these further distinctions:

The Molinists assert that predestination and reprobation are by foreknowledge of man's merits and sins. The Calvinists assert that predestination and reprobation are by the absolute will of God. And the Catholic Church asserts that predestination comes from the absolute will of God and reprobation from God's foreknowledge of sin. Thus, the Molinists posit the will of man as the source of their salvation and damnation. The Calvinists posit the will of God as the source of salvation and damnation. The Church holds that the will of God is the source of salvation and that the will of man is the source of damnation.

(Logology could note only that the possibility of all three such directions, and many others besides, is intrinsic to the family of terms implied in the idea of Order. If we but realize that the interrelationships among a cycle of terms can be traced in any sequence, with any one term capable of being selected as the point of departure, and if we add the realization that any selection of any one can be "wrong" from the standpoint of any other selected as "the right" one, we readily see how fertile the terms for the idea of Order necessarily are in fomenting charges of "heresy." Logology can make no choice among these many possible sequences; it can but note the embarrassment of riches intrinsic to the terministic situation.)

Pascal comes upon the shifting relationships between circular and rectilinear in another way, when distinguishing orthodoxy from heresy with regard to the sacrament of the

Mass, which can be viewed both in terms of essence and in terms of time.

In terms of essence, the Mass re-enacts Christ's sacrifice, and Christ is present. It *is* the Crucifixion, which in this sense is *not a temporal event at all,* but simply an unchanging moment in the logic of the Christian nomenclature. (In this sense, it would be no more "temporal" than the relations among the parts of a syllogism. It "goes on constantly.")

However, there is also the interpretation of the Crucifixion as an event that *took place at one particular time in history.* Viewed in this sense, the sacrament of the Mass, when celebrated *now,* could be taken as the *commemoration* of one momentous single past event.

Luther's "heresy," Pascal says (in *Pensée* 788, on the Church) derives from using one of these interpretations to the exclusion of the other. Not conceiving that the sacrament contains the literal presence of Christ and his figurative presence, both in one (*tout ensemble et la présence de Jésus-Christ et sa figure*), Luther treats them as mutually exclusive, so that the Mass must be *either* a sacrifice *or* a commemoration. But the orthodoxy contends that it is both.

As seen from the logological point of view, Luther is saying that the Mass must be conceived either in the style of terms that mutually imply one another, and that go on doing so forever, as they always did, or in the style of terms that follow one another in temporal sequence. But the orthodoxy allowed for a shuttling here back and forth between the two styles.

Since all worldly governance involves the sacrificial principle as an essential aspect of its nature, and since, for the devout Christian, this sacrificial principle heads in the Crucifixion, then the quasi-temporal way of defining such a situation would "properly" be along the lines of Pascal's insistence that Christ's agony was not just a historical event, but must continue constantly, till the end of time.

(*h*) Theological "freedom" and logological "necessity":
Though, as we have said, the theological and logological
interpretations of Genesis are simply in different planes, so
that they neither corroborate nor refute each other, at one
point there does seem to be a necessary opposition:

Theologically, Adam could have chosen *not* to sin. He
could have said yes to God's thou-shalt-not.

But logologically, Adam *necessarily* sinned. For if he
had chosen *not* to sin, the whole design of the Bible would
have been ruined. The fundamental "first," which links Creation with the Fall, and sets up the conditions for Redemption,
would be missing. The Pauline logic would have been without
a grounding in the Book, since the Book of Beginnings would
itself have been without the kind of beginning that sets up
the conditions for the tragic sacrifice. The Bible would not
have said, in its opening narrative, that man is "in principle"
a sinner and thus "in principle" needs a Redeemer, in accordance with the logic of the Cycle of Terms Implicit in
the Idea of "Order."

The Bible would thus have lacked the formal "felicity"
of the Fall (the *felix culpa* that brought about the coming
of Christ). It would have been as weak as Milton's *Paradise
Regained*, which actually is the account of an initial *refusal*
to be tempted (when Christ says "No" to the tempter's attempts to get him to say "Yes" to the proposal to say no to
God's thou-shalt-not). And this sequel to *Paradise Lost* would
be still weaker, of course, were not the rejection of the tempter
important as a way of indicating the perfect purity of the
victim that was to be sacrificed for Adam's sin, "inherited"
by all mankind.

Logologically, to say that Adam didn't have to sin would
be like saying that Oedipus didn't have to kill his father and
sleep with his mother, except that in the case of Adam it
looks like more of a choice. Or it's like saying that Othello
"didn't have to" kill Desdemona. As regards the logic of the

fable, the formal requirements of tragedy, he most certainly *did* "have to." The act is "de-termined" by the symmetry of the terms as a whole. He *necessarily* had to kill her, in order that the play be a tragedy.

(*i*) Aristotle's *Poetics,* and the (temporal) enacting of character (essence):

In chapter vi, where he lists the "parts" of tragedy, Aristotle describes the second part, "character" (*ethos*), as "that which reveals choice (*proairesis*), showing what sort of thing a man chooses or avoids in circumstances where the choice is not obvious." The editor of the Loeb edition, W. Hamilton Fyfe, makes this comment:

> *Proairesis* is a technical term in Artistotle's ethics, corresponding to our term "Will," the deliberate adoption of any course of conduct or line of action. It is a man's will or choice in this sense that determines the goodness or badness of his character. If character is to be revealed in drama, a man must be shown in the exercise of his will, choosing between one line of conduct and another, and he must be placed in circumstances in which the choice is not obvious, *i.e.,* circumstances in which everybody's choice would not be the same.

The observation suggests a thought of this sort, as regards the relation between the circular and the rectilinear:

Circularly, we should say that the idea of will or choice is implicit in the idea of an act; and the idea of character is implicit in the idea of a particular kind of choice representing a particular kind of will. But such a purely circular (tautological) relationship is translated into the rectilinear (narrative, temporal) terms of a dramatic unfolding when we see a man make a decision that is "in character" with his character, and that "leads to" a corresponding act (though the act leads in turn to unforeseen consequences that, in effect, transform his character, and thus seem to break free from the "predestined" and "predestinating" circle of tautologically related terms). But though there can be a certain amount of "internal processing" among the terms, in their over-all nature their cyclicality must prevail; otherwise, the work would lack unity.

(*j*) "Sensory" and "mythic" images:
A "sensory" image is an image that stands for a *concept*. For instance, if by "tree" we mean a purely physical thing, with trunk, bark, leaves, shade, corresponding colors and textures and the like, that would be a "sensory" image. A "mythic" image, on the other hand, would involve a "principle" or *idea*, as were the tree to be a "parent symbol"; and a poem that narrated the felling of such a "tree" might involve not merely a description of wood-chopping but the enactment of "symbolic parricide."

Most early philosophers meant by "imagination" the faculty of perceiving purely sensory images. But Coleridge (and the Germans from whom he borrowed, as also Longinus) extended "imagination" to cover the ideal or "mythic" image. In fact, "imagination" could even include the ability to transcend the sensory image entirely, to have a kind of "inner vision" that saw beyond things in their sheer physicality. The "mythic" image ties into the cycle of ideas, as with "death" in the story of the Fall. Thus, all such images, particularly as used in the lyric, stand midway between the rectilinear and the circular.

Such terms reveal their circularity by the ease with which they shade into other terms. Consider, for instance, in Whitman, how such terms as night, mother, death, voyaging, democracy, prophecy, "blades of grass" and "songs of myself" cyclically coalesce.

The sensory images used in connection with such a cycle are narrative, temporal, rectilinear; yet by their service as accessories to the over-all, idea-laden "mythic" images, they become infused secondarily with the principle of circularity.

To borrow a Kantian distinction: Their "synthetic" function is ultimately guided by their "analytic" function, in some-how mutually implying one another to the end of unity, in-ternal consistency (if we may apply to *terms* a distinction that Kant applies to *propositions*).

(*k*) "Pre-talionic" justice in the idea of eating a "for-bidden" fruit:

As regards the imagery of *eating* (in connection with the idea of Adam's disobedience), the "infantile" nature of the offense ties in with motives of political governance by reason of its seemingly "arbitrary" nature. That is: To a child just learning the judgments of the adult world, many of the parents' rulings must seem arbitrary, based not on reason but on sheer caprice. Such an attitude would derive in part from the fact that the child itself has not yet learned to "reason," hence would not even think of commands in terms of reason.

"Justice" here would be of a "pre-talionic" sort, not "dis-tributive" in the sense of the *quid pro quo*. Furthermore, insofar as the child does begin to reason, many of the parents' rulings must seem arbitrary, outside the bounds of reason, since the child's range of experience is so limited that many parental acts or judgments which seem reasonable to the parent must seem unreasonable to the child, whose very ideas of what is reasonable are still to be formed by a greater familiarity with the customs that shape the ideas of the reasonable. This early sense of parental rulings as arbitrary can merge with the "magical" view of political authorities as arbitrary, an attitude further strengthened by the fact that political authorities often are arbitrary.

Something of this "pre-talionic" quality, magically link-ing infantile and adult notions of authority, is indicated in Coleridge's comment on his "Ancient Mariner":

> It ought to have had no more moral than the "Arabian Nights'" tale of the merchant's sitting down to eat dates by the side of a well, and throwing shells aside, and lo! a genie starts up,

and says he *must* kill the aforesaid merchant, *because* one of the
date shells had, it seems, put out the eye of the genie's son.

We believe that the concept of "pre-talionic" justice has
important possibilities. Consider its relations to great tragedy,
for instance, where the "tragic flaw" regularly leads to dis-
proportionately fatal consequences. But the reader may feel
that we have weakened our case hereby, linking the notion of
the "pre-talionic" too closely with the nature of Adam's disobedience. For the eating of "tabu" foods might be thought
to cause death quite as would the eating of poisonous foods
—and in this sense Adam's punishment might not have seemed
as "pre-talionic" in earlier times as it can now.

(*l*) Poem in which a cycle of terms is unfolded quasi-
narratively:
The following poem lists a cycle of terms that imply one
another. However, the list is presented in quasi-temporal
style, as though the members proceeded narratively in one
"necessary" order, with each step "giving birth" to the next.

CREATION MYTH

In the beginning there was universal Nothing.
Then Nothing said No to itself and thereby begat Something,
Which called itself Yes.

Then No and Yes, cohabiting, begat Maybe.
Next all three, in a *ménage à trois*, begat Guilt.

And Guilt was of many names:
Mine, Thine, Yours, Ours, His, Hers, Its, Theirs—and Order.

In time things so came to pass
That two of its names, Guilt and Order,
Honoring their great progenitors, Yes, No, and Maybe,
Begat History.

Finally, History fell a-dreaming
And dreamed about Language—

(And that brings us to critics-who-write-critiques-of-critical-criti-
cism.)
          KENNETH BURKE, *Book of Moments: Poems 1915–1954* *

(*m*) Simplest known instance of the temporizing of
essence:
Cf. the story of Ooey Gooey, which is as follows:

Ooey Gooey was a worm. Ooey Gooey went for a stroll
on a railroad track. Along came a railroad train.
Ooey gooey!

Here Ooey Gooey's essence is defined in terms of his
name, which implicitly contains his end. This perfect circularity is also translated into terms of the narratively rectilinear. Otherwise put: Both Ooey Gooey's name and Ooey
Gooey's destiny proclaimed his nature. (Similarly, Adam's
essence, as regards his name's punning relation to the "earthy,"
was restated narratively in the story of his being formed from
the earth and of all mankind's return to earth at death.)

(*n*) Theodor Reik's *Myth and Guilt, the Crime and
Punishment of Mankind:*
Between the time when this material was first presented
in lecture form and the time when the notes were written into
an essay, Theodor Reik published his volume, *Myth and Guilt,
the Crime and Punishment of Mankind.* It is especially service-
able for our purposes in extending the range of observation
concerning the role of the *imagery* in the Genesis story. In
particular, Reik offers reasons for believing that the two trees
(of life, and of the knowledge of good and evil) were
originally one (the tree of life), and that the Cross later takes
over this role (an identification made all the more plausible, as

Collected Poems, 1915–1967 (University of California Press,
1968), p. 5.

he points out, by traditional Christian references to the Cross as a tree).

Reik argues that the crucifying of Christ on the Cross is in effect a way of identifying Christ with the tree. Thus, in the story of the Crucifixion, he would discern a vestige of prehistoric tree-worship. But from our point of view, the important thing about a merging of Christ, the two trees and the Cross would be that such a merger would suggest another route whereby the principle of *sacrifice* could be shown to be implicitly present (via the ambiguities of imagery) in the vessels of *life* and *temptation,* at the very beginning of the book about Beginnings.

Reik's great stress upon the *imagery* of guilt and punishment leads him to search the documents of comparative *mythology* for the kind of scaffolding which we have sought to supply by a totally different method; namely: our stress upon the Cycle of Terms for "Order." Thus, as seen from our point of view, his book suffers greatly from the overly imagistic stress that is typical of the mythologists' perspective in general, and of psychoanalysis in particular, insofar as psychoanalysis relies heavily upon mythology.

Also, of course, the purport of our entire essay is to the effect that "myth" is characteristically a terminology of quasi-narrative terms for the expressing of relationships that are not intrinsically narrative, but "circular" or "tautological." Hence, a book such as Reik's is always necessarily hitting around the edges of the problem we have been considering, yet never confronts it directly and methodically.

This is the risk to which one is necessarily exposed, when treating of thought in terms of *myth* rather than in terms of *language.* The mythic approach slights the logical element, quite as the logical approach slights the mythic element; the linguistic approach leads readily into both without being confined to either.

Perhaps the quickest way to get at the essence of Reik's

theory is by quoting his "interpretation of the Christ story."
They are summed up thus, in parallel columns:*

The Fall Myth	*The Christ Myth*
Primeval man murdered the father of the primitive horde whose image became, many thousands of years later, the model for God.	Jesus Christ is the son of God. He is murdered.
The primeval father was eaten by the gang of brothers.	Jesus Christ is eaten in the Eucharist by the Christian community. In eating the Host and in drinking of the chalice, the flesh and blood of the Saviour is incorporated.
Primitive man wanted to incorporate the primeval father to obtain his power. The strongest motive for the parricide was the desire to take possession of the superior qualities of the father and to replace him.	The Christians identify themselves with Christ in the act of the Eucharist.
The eating of God-Father is presented in the Genesis tale in tree-totemistic language. Regressing to the primitive tree-worship, the tree of life appears as the early representative of the Semitic God.	Jesus Christ dies on the cross, which is a late descendant of the tree of life. The cross became later an object of adoration as once the sacred tree (of life) had been.
The murder and eating of God-Father became the original sin, which is shared by all men.	Christ took the sins of all men and atoned for them by His death by offering Himself as sacrifice and thus redeeming all from guilt.†

* T. Reik, *Myth and Guilt, the Crime and Punishment of Mankind* (New York: George Braziller, Inc., 1957), pp. 315-316.

† Elsewhere Reik says: "The unconscious feeling of guilt, originating in the primeval crime, has never left the Jews and was only partially soothed by the destruction of the temple and other national calamities. Yet not only that unconscious guilt-feeling, but also the hidden rebelliousness against God, the mortal deified successor of the primal father, was passed on from generation to generation."

Reik's interpretation here is clearly focused upon the sheer *imagery* of such rites. The various principles of dominion which we have been considering are present in his picture, but the "logic" circulates around the *imagery of eating.* Thus, if he were to arrange his terms in a chart, the chart should have as its key term not some such word as "Order," but some such word as "Food," from which would be derived concepts of substance, power, murder, love, guilt, etc. And to justify such a stress he could cite the fact that, as anthropologists have frequently observed, a basic image for the conceiving of substance is that of food, with the ideas of both transubstantiation and consubstantiation being conceived after the same image.

In a chapter, "You are whom you eat," Reik develops this usual line of thought with regard to totemistic practices. And he gives at length his reasons why—as indicated in the left-hand column of the outline just quoted—he relates "original sin" to a "repressed" memory of our cannibalistic past.

He begins with the Freudian stress upon the close infantile relationship between love and food. Thus, on the subject of the "cannibalistic," he observes: "A lover can well say to his sweetheart that he would like to eat her up and thus express his tender desire of incorporation." But he also considers an "ambivalent" aspect of eating, in the fact that the "loved" food, in order to be eaten, must first be killed. Thus, somewhat in line with Freud's hypothetical notion of an original father-kill, with the parricidal sons cannibalistically partaking of his substance after the murder, Reik says: "It is with the killed father as with the cake: you cannot eat him and have him." But he adds that there is a "third possibility, alien to our thoughts, but familiar to those of prehistoric savages"—and this is the notion that, by eating the father, one *incorporates* the father's substance, thus becoming like him. And he continues:

However fantastic or bizarre such a thought possibly may sound to us, it was very close to the primitive mind and continues to live in the imagination of our little children. It is not astonishing that it is still alive in the idea of the Eucharist, in which the worshiper becomes united with Christ by incorporating Him.

Those earlier times, he says, when our ancestors used "to kill a person in order to eat him" are no longer present in our imagination. So we conceive of such acts as "murder." Hence the cannibalistic act of eating the slain father suggests to us rather the motives of "parricide." Hence, this tie-up with our parricidal past is "repressed."

In this connection there is one paragraph which seems to have possibilities quite different from the ones that Reik discerns in it:

The comparison of universal repression and of intense drives such as the cannibalistic appetites and of mass education with individual training is illuminating in more than one direction. It is difficult to convince an adult person, man or woman, that there was a time in his infancy when he not only ate his feces and smeared himself with them, but also liked to do that. In the best case a purely intellectual conviction can be reached while no emotional echo of such inclination can be awakened. Yet such a phase existed in everybody's infancy. No social or educational measure of defense or prohibition is longer needed against a revival of those coprophilous tendencies, because their successful repression is the result of the education that took place at an early age in which the ego of the individual child was still weak, plastic, and easily influenced. A strong reaction formation of disgust and revulsion has taken the place of the primal infantile impulses. The analogy with the vicissitudes of cannibalism in the early evolution of civilization is too obvious to be pointed out.

All of a sudden, when coming upon this paragraph, we ran into a wholly different line of thought, quite alien to Reik's intention. When Reik, in discussing the postulate of the father-kill, comes upon this "incidental" reference to the infantile eating of the feces, how about experimentally reversing the order here? Reversibility would be particularly applicable to psychoanalytic matters, since psychoanalysts themselves lay so much stress upon this very tendency in our thinking. That is, where Reik proceeds from talk of the father-kill to "incidental" talk of infant coprophilia, how about experimentally reversing the order and relative importance of these two observations?

Thus, in accordance with the above quotation, let us tentatively suppose that, during their infancy, Professors Freud and Reik ate their feces, but that they later "repressed" the memory of this decidely unprofessional act. A still more "transcendent" stage is conceivable here: It is conceivable that, if they transformed this original unprofessional act of their infancy into a "myth" that re-enacted it in disguise, they would thus not merely conceal the original unprofessional practice, but could replace the repressed memory of it by a counterpart that was in effect a splendidly professional sublimation. Such a strategic transformation could be contrived if they could propound a theory of prehistory that was a "mythic equivalent" of the repressed memory. What, then, might such an equivalent be? Asking this question, we shall now offer a line of speculations designed to show how a myth of the primal father-kill might serve professionally as a cover for such a "repressed" memory, and as a quasi-professional way of endowing it with tragic dignity.

First, as we have said, we should tentatively reverse the order and importance of the two observations (on father-kill and coprophilia) by taking the supposed "illustration" as actually a "breakthrough" that reveals the "real" motive here. Then we'd ask how, if this were the real motive, the myth of the primal father-kill might serve as its mythically heroic transmogrification. Our line of thought is greatly strengthened also by Reik's statement: "Freud says of the brothers: 'Cannibal savages as they were, it goes without saying that they devoured their victim as well as killing him.' He takes this cannibalistic act for granted as the consequence of the first." But Reik, on the other hand, is "of the opinion that the cannibalistic part of the primal deed, casually treated in Freud's reconstruction, is of paramount importance and is the central seat of most of the social and religious developments originated in the emotional reactions created by that crime." Along these lines, we should try to show how notions of "cannibalism" could be surrogates for "feces-eating"—and then we should ask what would be the implications of such a substitution. The steps would be as follows:

(1) The infant's feces are its offspring, its own creation.

(2) In this respect, they are like children's children.

(3) The child, in eating its feces, is thus eating of its own descendants, its own creatures (the offspring of its own flesh and blood).

(4) In asking ourselves what it means to eat one's own offspring, we next recall many *myths* in which gods are said to have done likewise. We now have introduced a *principle of dignification* into our theory.

(5) But any such pattern can become reversed as well: An "infanticidal" image of "creator" eating its "creature" can become reversed into a "parricidal" image of a "creature" eating its "creator." (Psychoanalysis repeatedly admonishes us as to the ubiquity of such possibilities in reversal.)

(6) In this way, the eater would become of the same substance as the eaten (quite as, in the original design, the eaten was of the same substance as the eater from which it derived).

(7) All told, this would give us a "repressed" memory not of a cannibalistic act in the literal sense (since the infant had done none to repress), but of a quite unheroic business which, by these mythic transformations, could become most handsomely stylized as the vision of a grand prehistoric tragedy in which a primal horde of sons banded together to slay their own tyrannical father, and thereafter to make themselves one by piously and lovingly partaking of his substance.

We do not offer this as gospel. We offer it, simply, as

a *tour de force,* and as indication of the range available to such interpretations, once the role of the *imagery* in our thinking is allowed to account for too much of its structure. And we do contend that the theory is at least as good as the one it would replace, though it would imply that, in the "breakthrough" of his supposedly "incidental" illustration, the psychoanalyst had in effect psychoanalyzed himself, right out there in public, and sans couch, except for his way of couching things.

In watching the imagery of eating in St. Augustine (notably his figures referring to God as a divine food), we found good reason to believe that the primary experience of eating in his case was *not* cannibalistic, but involved the experience of the infant at the breast. An infant can have no sense of killing, since the idea of killing involves kinds of experience and attitude not yet available to infancy. With Augustine, God's "wisdom" is equated with the maternal milk, and Augustine explicitly says so. Such breast-feeding would naturally be in the "love" category, though a new order of motives could conceivably emerge with the development of teeth (and the corresponding transformation from sucking to biting).

The theory we have offered here would have these further points in its favor:

(1) It would avoid the need to improvise psychologies of cannibalism for peoples not cannibalistic (imaginings that are likely to be about as accurate as *New Yorker* cartoons of missionaries in African pots).

(2) It would avoid in general the need of assuming that we must "repress" experiences which we never had in the first place.

(3) It would avoid in particular the need of Freud's assumptions about the primal horde and the father-kill contrived by the band of brothers. (In our *A Grammar of Motives,* pp. 431-432, we observed how Freud here confronts a

present condition which is thoroughly explainable in terms of its present nature, but instead "explains" it by adding two quasi-temporal stages: First he postulates a mythic past, and next he "derives" the present condition of the family from this mythic past. It is one of those many places where nineteenth-century thinking, in being so characteristically "historicist," felt that something here and now could only be explained in terms of some "prehistoric" something—which is a variant of the logical error of explaining the obscure by the more obscure—*obscurum per obscurius*. This is not to deny Freud's great genius and great contributions. It is only to deny that his myth about the primal horde and the "original sin" of the father-kill is to be classed as a prime example of his genius. The trouble with *mythology* as the basic approach to such matters is that it invites us to explain myths by myths. Freud's greatest contributions are in the line of what we would call the "logological."

Our *tour de force* at least has the value of suggesting a possible temptation in the use of mythology. For just as lowly things can be analogous to grand ones, so the grand can be analogous to the lowly. The myth-expert's tendency to think by overreliance upon imagery has the further drawback that the *apparent concreteness* of such terms conceals their *actual abstractness*. (We may have to go back as far as Spinoza, to find a systematic account of the ways in which concrete images can function really as abstractions, though Keats in his letters repeatedly shows awareness of this notion.) And the abstractness can serve doubly as temptation, insofar as the design of a prehistoric myth, in being analogous to the design of something quite domestic here and now, can load our views with glories really quite vain.

(*o*) In sum, on "predestination" and the "set apart":
If I say "the furniture in the room," I have merged many objects under a single head. However different from one an-

other, they are here terminologically at rest in a kind of Edenic bliss. If I now break my expression into components (listing so many chairs, tables, rugs, curtains, etc., of such-and-such sorts), I shall have introduced distinctions—and these are like a "fall" from the "unity" of the over-all usage by which they were previously classed together. They are now "set apart" from one another, with all that such separation implies.

According to Augustine's *De Dono Perseverandi*, those persons who are predestined to be saved are in God's higher judgment "set apart" (*discreti*, past participle of the word from which we get our word "discern") from the mass of the lost, "the lump of perdition," *a perditionis massa*. And they are set apart by "grace."

Now, if grace is by definition a "gift," it follows in strict tautology that grace must be "gratuitous." And by strict definition, the gratuity of grace cannot be *deserved*. For if grace were deserved, then such merit would require that it become a *payment*, in which case it could not be a perfect *gift*, which it is by definition. Thus, if one can be saved only by the "gift" of salvation, it follows that one is "predestined" to be either saved or lost, unless *all* mankind were predestined to one lot or the other.

Inasmuch as we have said that language is the logological equivalent of "grace," being the specific human endowment that "does not abolish nature but completes it" (*non tollit sed perficit naturam*), the strictly empirical analogue of such "predestination" would be observable in a situation of this sort: If two plates of food were offered under the same name, but one happened to be wholesome while the other happened to be contaminated, and if there was nothing on the label to distinguish them, the person who chose between them would be "predestined" to either health or illness, and without merit on his part. Spinoza's notion of "adequate ideas" would be a secular equivalent of salvation, "inadequate ideas" the equivalent of perdition. And insofar as we can't always work out the "adequate ideas" for the sizing-up of a given particular situation, to that extent we are in varying degrees predestined to lose.

Thus, there is "grace" in the ability of language to name things correctly for our purposes. But such accuracy of naming is sometimes "withheld" from us by the nature of things, or by the complexity of the problem, etc.

Surely, whatever may be the theology of eternal damnation, our chart of terms implicit in the Idea of Order should have made clear the logological reasons why the idea of universal salvation for all men should be abhorrent. For if the whole structure of language with relation to morals comes to a head in the formal distinction between yes and no, then in some form or other this distinction must be preserved in ideas of the "supernatural" Order.

This is not to say that there cannot be people who believe in the ultimate salvation of everyone, just as there are people who believe in the ultimate extinction of everyone (and as regards our whole universe, with its constant succession of cosmic cataclysms, the endless turmoil of its belching suns and nebulae, the constant hurrying of its electric particles back and forth across thousands and thousands of light years, conceivably it is a damned creature, a single mighty organism thrashing eternally in distress, and with nowhere to go to escape itself.)

When confronting the whole cycle of terms implicit in the idea of Order, we can select certain ones, and dwell upon them to the exclusion of the others, with different schemes resulting. And at least part of such a range in our "beliefs" results from the fact that we can "believe" things in many ways, and often we can't be wholly sure just what we do believe. For instance, a man who now subscribes to the belief that Mary's body is in Heaven (a belief about which he could have been vague a few years ago without falling outside the orthodoxies of his faith), may mean by a belief something quite different from what another man might mean, who found this belief beyond him.

Logologically, our design involved an approach to all terminology from the standpoint of Order as an empirical problem, compounded of non-verbal materials which the symbol-using animal variously manipulates and to which he is variously related by purposive actions conceived in terms of his symbol-systems. Theology confronts such concerns in the grand style—but though the believer studies its answers for their matter, logology loves them solely for their form, except insofar as these forms can be further studied not directly as knowledge but as anecdotes that help reveal for us the quandaries of human governance.

Augustine "On the Gift of Persevering" is especially relevant. Because his thoughts on predestination are so thorough, they are bound to be logologically central as well.

First, as we have noted elsewhere, there is the fact that, insofar as terms tautologically imply one another while their implications can be progressively disclosed, the relations among them can be said to be "predestinated" from the start, yet our ways of ranging among them give them a way of unfolding in "history."

Next, along with Augustine's central logological relation to the two orders of words and The Word, there is the obvious empirical sense in which human symbol-systems *are* a "gift." First of all, we are "given" language by whatever people we happen to be born and bred among, though the ability to learn it was "given" to us in our germ-plasm. "Predestination" figures here, along Heidegger's line, in the sense that each of us is "thrown" (*geworfen*) into some one set of situations rather than another; and we variously encounter the kinds of education and miseducation that will help or hinder us in our efforts to deal with our problems, or even to decide what those problems are.

Empirically, it is through no "merit" of our own that we are borne into one situation rather than another. However, insofar as, by the use of our endowments (including the endowment of being able to use our endowments!), we turn such "gifts" to our advantage, the advantages are "merited." That is, the "gift" comes first, the "merits" *follow*, hence it is only by the "gift" that we are able to "merit" salvation. This would be the empirical analogy to Augustine's attack upon the Pelagians, who held that a man can earn salvation by his own merits rather than by "grace" involving God's "gift" of "The Word" for the salvation of those who are to be saved. In Augustine's scheme, the "grace" must precede the "merits."

But discursively, and morally, words attain their formal perfection in discrimination (*choice*), the Yes-No design (including, if you will, the paradoxical fact that any such antithesis also implies a ground in common). This sheerly dialectical condition, coupled with the negatives of "Law and Order," is enough to provide the empirical analogues of Elect and Reprobates (though the kinds of persons who might rate as Elect in one social Order would doubtless be the Reprobates in another—except possibly for Dante's "trimmers," who might remain consistently unformed and inconclusive in all societies).

All told, there would be a sheerly secular analogue for Augustine's contention that grace must precede merit, so that one can continue to merit only if he has the grace to persevere, a grace that may at any time be withheld from him.

Augustine says that he wrote his tract "On the Gift of Persevering" as an answer to opponents who contended that "by the preaching of predestination" (*praedicatione praedestinationis*) people are led to despair rather than to hope. And so far as Christians were concerned, since they believed the Father to have sent the Son as perfect sacrifice for the redemption of the human race, Augustine offered a truly consummate argument for his position when he asserted: "Surely there is no more illustrious example of predestination than Jesus himself. . . . There is, I say, no more illustrious example of predestination than that very Mediator" (*quam ipse Mediator*). For in this pattern, his whole life was a mission, settled in advance.

To be sure, when the logologer is asked for a strict analogue here between words and The Word, he must go roundabout. No such radical promises (or threats!) are possible to logology as to theology. And the whole subject of the relation between "original sin" and "vicarious atonement" must be treated by our theory of language itself, with particular bearing upon the problems that arise when the somewhat latitudinarian style of the "creation myth" in Genesis is interpreted with Pauline strictness, but without specific logological allowance for the differences between "Hebrew archaeology" and the theology-tinged style of the "Greek philosopheme."

However, with regard to Augustine's office as a Churchman engaged upon the task of preaching The Word and upholding the doctrines which he himself was to help formulate, we should logologically note: There is a sense in which the theory of grace and predestination, as propounded in the *De Dono Perseverantiae*, could and should be called *wholly* "encouraging."

For the doctrine of predestination, in the grand circularity by which Augustine developed it, served within its own terms to set up an irrefutable line of argument. If you even so much as questioned it, or hesitated to accept any of the tenets associated with it, this very tendency was a *prima facie* sign that you were among those predestined to be damned. For any tendency towards disbelief revealed a disaffection of the will. And whereas people often tend to derive will from faith, saying, "I have a strong will in such-and-such regard, because my faith fortifies me," Augustine ingeniously reverses the emphasis thus: "There can be no faith without the will" (Fides sine voluntate non potest esse). For there can be no will without the "grace" to so will. Hence, if one doubts the faith, his will is impaired, which means that he lacks grace, which means that God is turning from him (thus allowing him of his own free will to go to hell). Thus, any deficiency in the will to persevere was per se an indication that one was moving towards damnation.

On the other hand, the gift of persevering was per se an evidence of God's grace, and thus a sign that God had not turned away.

Any nonbeliever who was converted proved thereby that he had been granted the grace to believe, and thus to carry out the works that would merit his salvation, though the grace to believe was given him without his merit, and he could persevere only insofar as God, by turning towards him, gave him the grace to persevere in the ways of his faith. If he later became a backslider, this turn on his part would be evidence that God, before all time, had had the foreknowledge that at this stage the man would be left on his own, and so would end by "voluntarily" enrolling himself among the reprobates, as God knew all along he would.

Who could deny that, viewed logologically, as a rhetoric of exhortation in behalf of the theological order, this doctrine of predestination was perfectly designed to "encourage" the believer into persevering, and thus into doing all within his power to silence doubts (which, by their nature as doubts, would be a sign that God was turning away from him)? Any resistance to such tendencies, on the other hand, were per se evidence that one could still hope to be among the elect.

Also, with language being what it is, is not "predestination" the sum total of things, even from a purely empirical point of view? Though such an empirical notion would not, of course, be Augustine's particular brand, how can we discuss human eventualities in the large without arriving at some such doctrine? Men may try as hard as they can to shape the future as they would have it be, but insofar as each person's desires fit and conflict with other people's, the particular combination that results is beyond the choice of anyone. Try as you will, the resultant combination will arise "inevitably."

Just as today can be today only by being exactly what it is, and as yesterday can forever have been nothing but what it actually was, so tomorrow must be what it actually will be, and none other: its particular combination of persons and things, only an infinitesimal fraction of which will express our particular wills except insofar as we happen to have willed what will be.

This is inescapably true, since it is tautologically true, no matter how earnestly people try to make it seem otherwise. The future will inevitably be what the particular combination of all men's efforts and counter-efforts and virtues and vices, along with the nature of things in general, inevitably adds up to.

Thus, "predestination" is as truly a "god-term" as are "God," "fate" or "dialectical materialism." And it has its empirical analogue. For however the world is made, that's how language is made.

But what of "providence"? What of "divine foreknowledge"? Is there an empirical equivalent of that? As regards the infinity of particulars that will make up tomorrow, no. But "in principle," formally, tautologically, most decidedly yes. For language is just made that way. And in its will is our (definition of) peace.

Epilogue: Prologue in Heaven

Enter, IMPRESARIO, *his upper half in formal attire, with ragged pants and worn-out shoes. Addresses the audience:*

Ladies and Gentlemen: Try to imagine a single flash of thought in which, simultaneously with an inner uttering of the word "geometry," you also conceived in detail all the definitions, axioms, propositions, demonstrations, corollaries, scholia, lemmas and special cases that go with that discipline.

Or imagine every event of universal history, made accessible to contemplation in one momentary panorama that comprises all time and space, in every act, attitude, and relationship (a distillate both perfectly simple and infinitely complex, of what has unfolded, is unfolding and is yet to unfold throughout the endless aeons of universal development).

Further, imagine a discourse that is not expressed in words at all, but rather is like the sheer awareness that goes with the speaking or the hearing of words.

And, finally, imagine such intuitive expression as a dialogue between two persons that are somehow fused with each other in a communicative bond whereby each question is its own answer, or is answered even without being asked.

Such is the formal paradox underlying this discourse between The Lord and Satan.

Since, in the original Heavenly situation there is neither time nor space, the nearest we can come to suggesting the scene's intimacies and immensities is to say that they are like a relation between contradictory ideas whereby things farthest apart are also closest together. Or like an infinite sphere, every point of which is both center and circumference, part and whole. Another way to imagine the setting for this dialogue is to think of a cathedral so vast that its interior is as horizonless as the sea in a fog, yet all is brilliantly clear —and this mighty architectural pile would be made not of materials but of the principles which an architect necessarily embodies in the act of drafting his plans.

I thank you. (*Exit—then returns.*)

No! Ladies and Gentlemen, my apologies, I should make a few more preparatory observations. First, the author of the heavenly dialogue which you are about to witness has asked me to point out that his account is *purely imaginary*. It involves a theory of purpose based on the definition of man as the "symbol-using animal."

(*Takes out a paper and reads.*)

Insofar as men are animals, they derive purposes from their physical nature. For instance, bodily hunger is enough to move them in search of food. Also, they can invent machines with "built-in" purposes, for instance missiles that will pursue a moving target with the persistence of a maniac, and that are responsible to no other kinds of signal.

But machines are given such purposes by men, since languages make it impossible for men to be content with sheer *bodily* purpose. And insofar as men "cannot live by bread alone," they are moved by doctrine, which is to say, they derive purposes from language, which tells them what they "ought" to want to do, tells them how to do it, and in the telling goads them with great threats and promises, even unto the gates of heaven and hell.

With language, a whole new realm of purpose arises, endless in scope, as contrasted with the few rudimentary purposes we derive from our bodies, the needs of food, drink, shelter and sex in their physical simplicity.

Language can even build purpose out of the ability to

comment on the nature of purpose. However, the purposes
that arise through the tangles made possible by language are
not merely the old bodily appetites in a new form. They are
appetites differing not just in degree but in kind. And the
two kinds differ so greatly that, as tested by the wishes of
the body, the purposes supplied by language (by doctrine)
can amount even to a kind of built-in *frustration*. Simplest
example: What hungry belly could be quieted by a poem in
praise of food? Yet, as we have said, language will not let
men be satisfied with sheer bodily purposes either, as other
animals presumably are.

In any case, obviously, the talking animals' way of life
in a civilization *invents* purposes. Rationalized by money
(which is a language, a kind of purpose-in-the-absolute, a
universal wishing well) empires arise. Such networks of
production and distribution, made *possible* by language, become *necessary*. So, they raise problems—and many purposes
are but attempts to solve those problems, plus the vexing
fact that each "solution" raises further problems. (Confi-
dentially, that's "the dialectic.")

But the very resources of language to which such
quandaries owe their rise also goad men to further questioning. For language makes questioning easy. Given language,
you can never be sure where quest ends and question begins.
Hence, the search for some Grand Over-All Purpose, as with
philosophers, metaphysicians, theologians.

Along these lines, the "Prologue in Heaven" which you
are about to witness is a Parable of Purpose. . . . I thank you.

(*Exit. Faint drum roll in distance. Curtain rises—on
what? Possibly on two chairs, in center of stage, under strong
spotlight, turned half facing each other, half facing audience.
All the rest of the stage in darkness, wholly indeterminate.
Two voices off stage, approaching. Spotlight moves to where*
SATAN *and* THE LORD *are entering, from left rear.* SATAN
first, hurriedly, but looking back as he proceeds. Then THE

LORD, *so deliberately that* SATAN *seems like a dog scouting ahead of his master.* THE LORD *is a Blakean bearded patriarch.* SATAN *is an agile youth, wears fool's cap with devil's horns, and a harlequin costume of two colors, dividing him down the middle. The speakers are obviously on quite friendly terms. As things develop, it will become apparent that* THE LORD *is affectionately amused by his young companion, while* SATAN, *over-hasty, mercurial, is an intense admirer of the older man. They come forward and take seats, with* SATAN *at* THE LORD's *right hand.*)

TL. Yes, I've definitively decided to do it. Or, rather, it will necessarily come about, unless I deliberately interfere with the processes of unfolding that began when I created time. In the first chaotic swirl, the eventual emergence of the Word-Using Animal was implicit. And I shall not interfere with those natural processes that, having led to beautiful gardens, can now, as it were, people the loveliest of them with this cantankerous animal.

S. What, then, in sum, is your decree, milord?

TL. It amounts to this: On planet Earth I will place a species of creature, describable by an enemy as vermin and endowed with the power of speaking, hence the powers of mechanical invention and political governance.

S. Since I know, milord, that you are nothing if not Design, I pray: Tell me why this design.

TL. It will round things out, with the symmetry of the circle.

S. I understand the symmetry of the circle. But I don't quite understand how the principle figures here.

TL (*encouragingly*). Of course you do!

S. Of course I do! Necessarily, when you so envision me. It's this way: If nature gives birth to an animal that can talk, then by the same token nature becomes able to comment on itself. (*Smiles admiringly at* THE LORD.)

TL. And thus nature can circle back on itself. Yes, I'll

go ahead with it. And in any case, the project as a whole is so much more inclusive, by comparison that stretch of symbol-using will not be as long as one flicker in all eternity. A protracted evolutionary process leads up to the point where the language-using animal emerges. And then there will be an infinitely long time of wordlessness again, as regards their kind of words, after the evolutionary process has moved on, in developments that leave this troublous species far behind.

S (*pondering, half to himself*). But that odd kind of word they will use . . . with syllables and sentences and whole speeches stretched out through time, like one of their corpses on a mortuary slab . . . that's so different from our single, eternal, Unitive Word that creatively sums up all, in your exceptional Self, combining your Power, your Wisdom and your Love in the perfect simplicity of infinitely complex harmony.

TL (*laughing*). Come, my lad, now you're talking like one of their theologians!

S. I should fear that you were deriding me, did I not know that there is no derision in you.

TL. Always, that morbid modesty of yours! Don't be so defensive. It's more complicated than that.

S. Necessarily your command is my obedience.

TL. I can't be all-powerful without being all-powerful. So, in the last analysis, *you* are but a function of *my* will.

S. You know I'm not complaining, milord. But I've heard tell among us that it's to be different with these new Word-Using Animals, the Earth-People. Is it true that in these new creatures you shall have solved a basic logical contradiction, in making it possible for them to disobey your all-powerful authority?

TL. It's more complicated than that. But you can take this much for granted: I have resolved no basic logical contradiction. No one can get around a contradiction in terms; for instance, I can't make a four-sided triangle. True, some of their metaphysicians will offer talk about "nothing" that has "being." But *I* must begin and end with the proposition that something is what it is.

S. Then their temporal kind of word will be like our eternal kind?

TL. It's more complicated than that. It will all center in their way of using the negative. With us, there is only the distinction between *is* and *is not*. But with them, the first negative will be of a different sort: It will involve the distinction between *shall* and *shall not*.

S. But we, too, have the distinction between *shall* and *shall not*. I feel your will as a command.

TL. But owing to the nature of our eternal simultaneity (what they will call the *nunc stans*), the command and the obedience are one. As you yourself have put it: My command is your obedience. But once the idea of *logical* contradiction is modified by the possibility of *temporal* contradiction, the command can be at one time, the obeying at another. And once there is the possibility of a breach between them, here are the makings of a contradiction, different from that of sheer logic.

S. If not a logical contradiction, then . . . what kind, please?

TL. A whole cluster of their words could be used: above all, it might be called "moral" or "dramatic," because it has to do with action. And their words for morality, drama and action will all imply one another. But once the successiveness of time (and its similarly divisible partner, space) introduces the possibility of an interval between the command and the obedience, by the same token there is the possibility of disobedience.

S. I am glad to hear you say so. I myself have felt that there is a kind of "fall" implicit in your creating of a time-world (however praiseworthy, I hasten to add, this grand opus is in itself).

TL. True, one can't make divisions without having re-course to divisiveness—and divisiveness is in itself a "fall." Similarly, one can't create time without creating death; for the birth of each new moment is the death of the moment that preceded it. A further problem arises from the fact that the introduction of time (with its kind of succession so different from that of the syllogism) must introduce a notable tangle with regard to the negative, at the very start. For the earthy Word-Animal will encounter its first negatives (and don't forget the formative nature of such firsts) in terms of sheerly extra-logical contradiction. Precisely when emerging from its pre-verbal state, the human infant will learn "thou shalt not" quite some time before the grasp of words is strong enough to comprehend "it is not." The infant must learn the negative, first of all, as an aspect of action (of command, with a temporal breach that allows for both obedience and dis-obedience).

S. The infant will learn the logical "it *is* not" by first emerging out of sheerly infantile relations to parental "thou shalt not's"?

TL. Yes. And from then on, the complications will be unending. Above all (and here is an irony that should amuse you, since you are so confirmed an ironist): repeatedly, when meditating on human relations, their philosophers will begin where they should end, with the "is" and "is not."

S (*exultantly*). I see it! I see it! And implicit in their supposedly objective versions of what is and is not, they will have concealed a set of shall's and shall-not's, which they will then proceed methodically to "discover"! What better comedy!

TL. You'll enjoy them, my lad. You will enjoy them greatly. Though made in my image, the Earth-People will necessarily incline towards that part of me which you would be, were our realm to be, like theirs, divisible.

S. But I am still unclear: In this breach between the command and the obedience, will they or will they not have

freedom? We are free, in necessarily being indivisible parts
of your freedom, which you possess in being constrained by
nothing but your own self-willed principles of identity. But
with these temporal verbalizers, is there to be a *deviant* kind
of "freedom"?

TL. You *would* ask that, my lad! I see why I love you
so greatly. If *my* negative ever broke loose from me, I'd know
where to look for it.

S. Milord, I blush!

(*Pause.*)

TL. (*resuming*). Here's the soundest way to get at the
problem: If this culminating creature I contemplate is to be
a symbol-using animal, then by definition everything about it
should be deducible from either its animality or its symbolicity. So let's treat of everything to do with it in terms of
one or the other, either the genus (animality) or the differentia (symbolicity), or, naturally, the combination (or composite) of the two.

S. Then all else would follow by definition, as with us?

TL. It's more complicated than that. But let's start from
there. That's a good first. Thus, note first of all, that purely
by definition, the Word-Men, by being endowed with their
particular kind of language (as the other animals are not) will
have the power of answering questions or responding to commands.

S. That is, you are now to stress not their genus (animality) but their differentia (symbolicity)?

TL. And in this sense, they will have "responsibility."
For what is responsibility but the ability to respond?

S. But everything "responds." If an Earth-Man kicks
one of his pebbles, it will "respond" to the impetus of his blow.

TL. The pebble will not say a word.

S. *Touché!* "Response" in the full sense of the term involves "symbolicity."

TL. Good! Now let's take another step, this time towards *perfection*. You shall hear a lot more about "perfection" before this inquiry is ended. For the moment, consider our problem thus: So far as the *pure formality* of a question is concerned, the perfect answer would be Yes or No. Thus, even if a man gave the answer that he was predestined to give at the very crack of Creation, there would nonetheless be this *purely formal* sense in which every question permits of choice.

S. O miracles of form! No truth, no beauty, no goodness, even no expediency, without form!

TL. And men will know, too, that there is no purer act than pure form. And a pure act is by definition pure freedom. Further, inasmuch as they can give names to one another, they will be able to conceive of themselves as *Persons*. And a Person is, by definition, a being that can *act*. ("Things," by definition, can merely move, or be moved. They cannot "act.")

S. In the purely formal sense, then, a person is an entity that can answer yes or no to a command (which in turn implies the distinction between the yes of obedience and the no of disobedience).

TL. Exactly. And by the same token, such "persons" can lay claim to "freedom." For if an act weren't "free," it wouldn't be an "act."

TL and S (*in unison*). It would be sheer motion.

S. So it must be free, since it is by definition an act, and acts are by definition free.

TL. And by the same token, you get drama, since drama is based on action (with its grammatical partner, passion). That will be particularly important because of the large part that the arts of comedy and tragedy will play in their outlook, extending even to their ideas of ultimate salvation.

S. *O maraviglia!* I see by what a tightly bound logological cycle of terms the Wordy Animal must arrive necessarily at the idea of freedom.

TL. You are my favorite pupil.

S. I am most grateful for praise from so eminent a source. But am I to infer that their freedom is but an illusion?

TL. They will certainly confront sheer necessity in the sense that, as one of their philosophers might put it, each person will necessarily make his decisions in the particular situations into which he is "thrown" (and each of these situations will involve a series of motives not of his own choosing).

S. Then it *is* a sheer necessity! And the rest *is* but an illusion?

TL. It's more complicated than that. When I introduce their kind of words into my Creation, I shall really have let something loose. In dealing with ideas one at a time (or, as they will put it, "discursively") they can do many things which can't be done when, like us, all ideas are seen at once, and thus necessarily corrected by one another.

S. I see it! I see the paradox! Splendid! By their symbolicity, they *will* be able to deviate! A pebble can't make a mistake; it merely exemplifies the laws of motion and position; but an Earth-Man can give a *wrong* answer. At least in their *mistakes*, then, they will be "creative"; and to that extent they will be really free.

TL. Yes, and all sorts of new routes can be found, when you start putting things together piecemeal, rather than having everything there in its proper place, all at once, before you begin. Discursive terminologies will allow for a constant succession of permutations and combinations.

S. In sum, human freedom will reside in the ability to err, to deviate?

TL. Not quite that. The ability to be wrong within limits will also argue the ability to be right within limits. And insofar as these creatures are right, they will share in that higher freedom which we equate with necessity, an identity's inevitable necessity of being, in all its parts, the simple self-consistency that it must be, in order to be precisely what it is.

S. You have shown me how by the dramatistic nature of their terminology, they are in a sense "forced to be free," since they will think of themselves as persons, and the idea of personality implies the idea of action, and the ideas of both freedom and necessity are intrinsic to the idea of an act. Could I ask, next: Is there some generative principle in their kind of language, some formal first from which its entire logic might be derived?

TL. Indeed there is. We've already considered it somewhat. It's the principle that you would use as your particular sign, were you to be in theory prescinded from the sum total of our identity.

S. Milord, the negative! Then that which most distinguishes the Word-People from other animals on Earth is also that which most distinguishes me: the one principle that might divide me from my Lord!

TL. That's it, my lad. And there is a sense in which there are the makings of division even here among us. For even pure identity implies the negation of non-identity. So you're always lurking there, my lad, implicitly a No without its Yes, even though (as seen from another angle) the two imply each other.

S. Milord, pray do not chide me! Yet, for all my love of negativity, I grant that the negative cannot exist. Anything that exists must, by the same token, be positively what it is.

TL. That will apply to *their* negative as well. It will be but a device of language, an *ens rationis*.

S. Why then would you make the negative so all-important?

TL. First, there is a sheer *principle* of negativity involved in their ability to use language at all. They must know that the word "tree" is *not* a tree, and so on.

S. They will be able to keep this distinction clear?

TL. By no means! Again and again, just because they have a word for something, and a feeling for the contexts in

which the use of that word seems proper, they'll assume that
there really is something to which the word is referring. Elab-
orate systems will be erected atop this error, doctrinal structures that are quite ingenious. But there will be enough rudimentary correspondence between words and things, with
enough rudimentary awareness of the difference between the
symbol and the symbolized, for them to find their way around,
and multiply. Another kind of implicit negative will figure in
the growth of their vocabularies. For instance, if they use a
word *metaphorically*, they must know implicitly that they are
not using it *literally*. For instance, if they say, "Ship the
goods by rail," they must know that the "goods" are *not* the
opposite of moral evils, and that the "shipping" does *not* have
anything to do with ships. By making such allowances, they
can greatly extend the usefulness of symbolicity. The ultimate
along those lines will fit your leanings. I refer to irony, the
way in which, for instance, they might say, "How intelligent
he is!" while ironically implying the opposite, that the man is
exceptionally stupid.

S. I do love it. And I grant that it starts in something
as simple as that, though eventually it becomes quite complex.
But what of the negative explicitly?

TL. It begins and ends in the two forms we have already
considered: *shall not* and *is not*. The Yes-or-No of *shall not*
gets its quasi-positive in the idea of the "will," the hypothetical watershed that slopes off into either obedience or
disobedience. In brief, recapitulating (and all true thought is
but recapitulation): If acts involve persons, and personality
involves decision, then inasmuch as decisions are "perfectly"
conceived as the choice between Yes and No, it follows that
implicit in the idea of action is the idea of the negative.

S (*smiling ironically*). So the idea of action, which is to
say the idea of morality, which is to say the idea of freedom,
implies the principle of negativity, which is the hallmark of

Satan! Imagine me soaring above it all, with bat-wings. What, milord, would I see?

TL. With the help of language, men will necessarily come upon the distinction between "mine" and "thine," along with sexually imagined ways of overriding this distinction. But the principle of negativity will enable men to build up vast empires, all based on this distinction, which says in effect: "Thou shalt not take these things of mine, nor I of thine." Myriads of myriads of laws, deeds, contracts, precepts, prison sentences, educational policies, businesses, revolutions, religions, etc., etc., will be erected atop these simple beginnings: things that in themselves are positive, but that, in becoming labeled "mine" and "thine," take on the secret sacred sign of negativity. For in their essence, "mine" and "thine" are implicitly modes of negative command, ways of saying in effect: "No trespassing." The negative, as so ingrained through the subtleties of "conscience," will build up a sense of guilt equally as vast and complicated as this bundle of negatively protected properties. And from this sense of guilt there will arise the yearning for a new and all-inclusive positive, the demand for a supernal sacrifice literally existing and somehow serving by his suffering both to cancel off this guilt and to sanction the perpetuating of the conditions out of which the guilt arises.

S. And who——

TL. But I anticipate. We shall treat further of this ultimate step after you have been better prepared.

S. I tremble, milord. I have a sense of being on the verge of something. Please let us hurry back to our sheerly dialectical meditations.

TL. By all means. Sheerly logologically, we confront a manipulation of this sort: Inasmuch as words have contexts, if one of the Earthy thinkers sums up "everything" as the "determinate," then using the only resource he has left, he finds that the only possible context for the "determinate" is the "indeterminate," which thereby becomes the "ground" of the determinate and amounts to making "nothing" the ground of "everything." Or, if he starts with "time," he arrives at the "timeless," to which negative he can then give a positive look by calling it the "eternal."

S. Milord, haven't we also got to my realm by another route? Aren't we now in the realm of comedy?

TL. Yes, comedy—even Divine Comedy.

S. You have spoken of "everything," of "eternity," and of "nothing." If the Earth-People make an assertion about "everything," can they persuade themselves that they really are talking about "everything"?

TL. That's a delicate problem.

S. And when they talk about "nothing," are they talking about nothing or something? Or can they think that in using words for "the eternal," they are really talking about the eternal? Can they persuade themselves that it's as easy as that?

TL. I get your drift. But let's try a slightly different approach. They have another way of making the negative look positive. For instance, instead of saying "the unnatural," they can say "the preternatural" or "the supernatural." Let's try it from there. Suppose you asked me: If they talk about "the supernatural," are they really talking about the supernatural?

S. That approach does help. Obviously, by sheer definition, insofar as they are *natural* animals, they *can't* know anything about the supernatural. For if anything of the supernatural crossed over into the natural, then by sheer definition it would be part of the natural. How can they get around that purely formal problem?

TL. Your argument is irrefutable, and its underlying logic will plague them. But it isn't the proper "first" for the study of their languages. First comes their use of language as a means of getting along in their everyday affairs. It will help them guide their behavior, as their legs will help them to walk. In the course of such uses, they will learn the arts of petition, exhortation (persuasion and dissuasion). For language, as an instrument of guidance, is especially suited to persuade the language-using animal. Which means that they will use language to rule over one another—for persuasion implies governance. But governance in turn involves the need of *sanctions*.

S. "Sanctions"?

TL. In the course of governance, many kinds of inequality will develop. For instance, some of the Earth-People will be able to accumulate more property than they could intelligently use in a myriad lifetimes, short as their life span is to be. And many others will starve. In brief, there'll be much injustice.

S. It's revolting!

TL. Hence all the more need for "sanctions." In the course of "proving" that such inequities are "right," sanctions will pile up like bat dung in a cave. (And bat dung, by the way, will be quite fertile.)

S. Then "sanctions" are just symbol-systems that justify injustice?

TL. No, my lad. It's much more complicated than that. The range of language being what it is, the very propounding and treasuring of such sanctions will lead in turn to the equally persuasive *questioning* of them. And all these matters will come to a head in man's theology, metaphysics, political theory and the like, in short the higher criticism that grows out of such venerable piles.

S. But what's the use, if it all starts from the fact that their wordage in its wider ranges would talk of things which it is not equipped to discuss at all?

TL. True, by definition their speech will not be able to express the ineffable, any more than their eyes will be equipped to see the invisible. Even so, this persistent creature can reasonably assert: "Here's what you could say about the ineffable if it could be talked about. Here's what eternity

would look like if it did have visibility. Here's what its music
would be like, if it weren't inaudible. Here's how it would
feel to the touch, if it weren't intangible. In brief, here's how
the indeterminate should be discussed in terms of terms."

S. But isn't that wholly meaningless? Aren't your
symbol-using creatures all set to be a breed that attains its
"perfection" in sheer nonsense?

TL. You could make out a good positivistic argument
along those lines, if you think of their words only as we in
our transcendent wordlessness use words. That is, if you think
of words as being relevant only when they are *about* something.

S. Did you not already imply that any other kind of
language is but falsehood? Milord, you said that their way
of using language will be like using legs. If they persist in
using their languages to talk about our realm, wouldn't they
be as accurate if they tried to walk through eternity on mortal
legs?

TL. Some will try precisely that. And with admirable
results, so far as worldly concepts of beauty are concerned.
Indeed, always beneath the dance of words there will be the
dance of bodies, the mimetic symbol-system that all these animals will come close to having in common, though their seden-
tary ways of living will cause them to forget it, like persons
who, moving into a different part of the world when they were
still quite young, come in time to forget the language of their
childhood, the language most profoundly persuasive of all.
But talk of the dance, and its body-language, brings us to
exactly the next step in our unfolding.

S. And that is, milord? . . .

TL. The nature of language as petition, exhortation, persuasion and dissuasion implies that, first of all, their words will
be modes of posture, act, attitude, gesture. If one of their creatures strikes an attitude, such as kneeling in obeisance, that's
real enough—and the same kind of reality can be carried into

any words that go with it. Often these creatures will be swelling with pride and mutual self-congratulation at the very moment when they are unknowingly about to be caught in a cataclysm. Or they may lament at the very moment when they are unknowingly about to enter upon an era of exceptional delight. But in any case, *whether in error or not, the attitude will be wholly real while it prevails.*

S. Their task in ranging linguistically, then, will be to round out their sheer attitudinizings as thoroughly as possible?

TL. Yes, and some quite grandiosely architectonic enterprises will emerge in the process. And because *some* of the earth-creatures will be able to *range far* in such activity, *all* of them will be able to *range somewhat.*

S. Their most comprehensive symbol-systems, then, will be but a constant striking of attitudes?

TL. Yes—and thus, ultimately, a striking of attitudes towards the Great What-Is-It.

S. And, after all, that's us!

TL. Indeed it is!

(*Pause.*)

S. Milord, you know of my great admiration for your workmanship. I fully realize the immense power, and scope, and subtlety of the Primal Act by which the world of time arises in principle. But in view of the perfect intuitive understanding by which we communicate, without the need of temporally stretched-out discourse, could you not somewhat contain the errors of the Word-Animal? Could you not permit him only the *virtues* of his symbolicity? I know you would make the best possible of worlds, but I do not see why their kind of words would be the best possible of worldly discourse.

TL. Discourse can be truly discourse only by having the power to be fully itself. Such a formal obligation applies always. For instance, don't you grant that you couldn't be truly yourself if you could be but half yourself, or the fragment of yourself which the Earth-People will take you to be?

S. Granted. But I could be something else. If you had made me but half myself, I could be wholly that. If you make a five rather than a ten, can't that five be wholly at one with itself in its five-ness?

TL. Your example really disproves your point. I couldn't make the time-world's number system without so making it that ten is just as necessarily implied in it as five. One can divide numbers, but one can't divide the principle of division. Arithmetic could be arithmetic at all only by having the possibility of fully being arithmetic. And so with the language of human discourse: implicit in its ability to be, there is its ability to range; and implicit in its ability to range, there is its ability to range far, even too far.

S. In asking that you show me the full range, I should be asking that you share your divine providence with me. As you know, I am saved from asking for such enlightenment on two scores: first, I could not encompass it; second, I would not, even if I could. For I already realize, from what you have said of the errors in earthly discourse, that in knowing everything you must pay attention to a staggering amount of trivialities worked out by the Earth-People. Being but an angel, that is, a messenger entrusted with but fragments of communication, I am necessarily but willingly humbled at the thought of your encyclopedic insomniac burdens. Or, more accurately, such infinite attentiveness would be overwhelmingly burdensome to the likes of *me*.

TL. Fortunately, we don't have to deal here with universal prescience. We need but consider the matter formally, in principle. First of all, for instance, there's that obvious range of the negative. The Earth-Men will become moral by obeying moral laws, all of which are either explicitly or implicitly negative, a set of thou-shalt-not's. But by the same token, people can in principle carry the negative a step further, and say no to any thou-shalt-not. Thus the negative, in giving them the power to be moral, by the same token gives them the power to be immoral.

S. How greatly different my negativity is from theirs!

TL. Yes, but they won't know it. And in their failure to make the proper distinction, they'll dispraise you avidly.

S. If they're ingenious enough about it, I won't mind.

TL. Oh, they'll be plenty ingenious. Language makes great plotters, and they'll think of you as the very soul of conspiracy.

S. But inasmuch as your positives and my negatives mutually imply each other in perfect dialectic oneness, what could there be for me to conspire about?

TL. I already told you: "Everything." Though they'll be vague as to what their word "everything" refers to, they'll be clear enough in their conviction that the range of possible conspiracy ultimately involves "everything."

S. But isn't that too vague to keep them interested? After all, being animals, they will necessarily live by this particular thing and that particular thing. Far less than "everything" would be enough to choke them.

TL. No, they won't have to gag at "everything." For their very symbolicity will enable them to invent a particularized form of "everything," the most ingenious symbol-system of all: money. Money is intrinsically universalistic, since everything can have its monetary equivalent, its counterpart in terms of "price."

S. I see the pattern! What perfection! Money becomes a kind of generalized wishing. They won't directly reach for everything. They could even sincerely deny that they want everything. Yet they'll get there roundabout, by wanting the universal medium into terms of which everything is convertible!

TL. Yes, once they arrive at money, they will have arrived at desire in the absolute. Their love of money is the nearest they will ever come to symbolistically transcending their animal nature. A man can even starve to death hoarding the symbols that would buy him more than he could eat in many lifetimes. And men will kill themselves trying to amass more and more of the monetary symbols that represent good living.

S. How will they distinguish their devotion to this particular universalistic motive from their devotion to your kind of universalism?

TL. The attempt to answer that would get us back into the problem of the encyclopedic, though in reverse: for in general the history of the Word-Animal will be the history of the firm refusal to make such a distinction. In brief, they'll put *my* name on their *money*, and call it an act of piety.

S. How revolting!

TL. Now, my lad, reign in that winsome impetuosity of yours.

S. But, milord!

TL. It's a quite complicated situation. For you should also reflect that the quasi-divine universalism of money is reinforced by related attributes. For instance, in its nature as a medium of exchange, it is essentially communicative, hence it is a technical counterpart of love. Its nature as a power will similarly endow it, as monetary power can serve as a surrogate for sexual potency. Yet, whereas it is a prime symbol of contact (in acts of charity), it can establish such contact at a distance (as with the coin tossed to a leper)—and thereby paradoxically it allows for depersonalization, a quasi-divine transcending of excessive personal involvement. In reducing all things to terms of itself, it exemplifies perfectly the scientific law of parsimony (the perfect mode of rationalization required of a symbol-user's god). As I have noted elsewhere, in its nature as generalized wish it represents a kind of absolute purpose. Its relation to "freedom" is obvious, since it can purchase both mobility and security.

S. Will all the human tribes possess it?

TL. Only in the sense that it will be *implicit* in all economies. As a rule, however, it will attain its full grandeur only in large empires marked by an especially high development of religion. But the reference to religion reminds us that money will also tie in with connotations of the purgative, owing to the imagistic relation between "power" and "filth" (associations to which the human animal will be particularly prone owing to its codes of propriety in connection with the feces).

S. I see how perfectly it burlesques the godhead. Out of its simplicity there emerges a great complexity.

TL. Exactly. But now I'd like to ask you a question, as a test of your ingenuity. Imagine a situation of this sort: The outposts of an empire want the simple natives of a barter economy to work in plantations which the imperialists would introduce into the area. The natives already possess a simple non-monetary economy with which they are content. And the imperialists, in accordance with their principles of monetary "liberalism," are loath to impose outright conditions of enslavement. How could you solve that problem?

S. Splendid! Splendid! I see it! I could introduce some simple monetary tax, such as a hut tax or a tax on salt, the important point being that *it could not be paid in kind, but would have to be paid in money.* Then their non-monetary economy would no longer suffice, and they would have to work in the plantations, so as to earn the money needed to pay their taxes! This requirement alone would in effect "emancipate" them from their non-monetary economy. To use an expression employed in another connection, they would be "forced to be free"! What devilish possibilities!

TL. Right. But don't oversimplify, my lad. The simplicity, yes. But don't let it break away from the complexity, or, as the Earth-People will say, "All Hell breaks loose."

S. I am beneficently admonished. Pray, teach me further, milord, of the complexity that qualifies the simplicity. In particular, as regards these two occasions on which I have used the expression, "forced to be free," I can't just see how *they* will contrive to put determinism and free will together.

TL. You would if you were confined to their kind of terms. Don't forget that, on Earth, a sojourner will be able to wind up at the same place by going in opposite directions, if he but keeps going long enough. And insofar as Earth's languages will be developed in sympathy with nature, they will also incorporate nature's humble paradoxes. Further, as regards the sheer formality of the situation, recall that, though terms in their formality come to a kind of crisis in the "free" choice between Yes and No, there is also the technical fact that terms are by definition "de-terministic."

S. Milord, I swoon!

TL. Hold up, young one. And having seen already how their words will provide freedom in principle, by allowing for either the affirmation of affirmation, or the affirmation of negation, or the negation of affirmation, or the negation of negation, note further this sheer design, how it follows *of necessity* from the nature of the Word-Animal's symbolicity: First, note that out of the negative, *guilt* will arise. For the negative makes the law; and in the possibility of saying no to the law, there is guilt.

S. And if guilt, then punishment?

TL. It's more complicated than that. For money introduces the principle of *redemption*. That is, money will give them the idea of redemption by payment, which is to say, by *substitution*. For it would be a matter of substitution, if a man paid off an obligation by money whereas otherwise he might have been required to suffer actual physical torment.

S. Isn't there a principle of substitution in language itself, too?

TL. Yes, every synonym is a substitute. Every paraphrase is a substitute. And substitution by monetary symbolism is but a special case of symbolic substitution in general.

S. But why do you make this point about substitution?

TL. It's most important to their theologians. For if you carry this principle through to its completion, it implies that one person can suffer for another, as "payment" for the other's guilt.

S. Wouldn't that be unjust?

TL. Not insofar as it would be merciful. Mercy is a kind of friendly injustice, in not requiring of a given debtor the full amount of his debt.

S. Their theologians, then, will assume that you will not right the balance?

TL. On the contrary! And here enters the principle of perfection. The Earth-People will consider themselves so guilt-laden, that only a perfect sacrifice would be great enough to pay off the debt.

S. The morbid devils! Then they will think of themselves as permanently lost?

TL. No, they will conceive of a sacrifice so perfect that it could cancel off all their guilt, however mighty that guilt might be.

S. But only a god would be perfect enough for that!

TL. Quite right.

S. I tremble! You mean . . .

TL. Yes. And finally a cult will arise which holds that I, in my infinite mercy, will send my only begotten Son as the perfect sacrifice for the Earth-People's redemption.

S. Send your Son, to redeem such vermin! What pride they have! What haughtiness! How perfectly revolting!

TL. Easy, my lad. This issue can't be solved by a hot-head. You must realize that this issue involves not only a principle of *theological* perfection, but also a principle of *logological* perfection. I told you that we should be hearing much about "perfection" before we were through.

S. I beg forgiveness if, in the heat of my indignation, I called The Lord's creatures "vermin." Insofar as they are examples of your workmanship, they are of course essentially good. I referred only to the ways in which the resources of their language bewitched them into becoming stormers of heaven itself. I don't resent them for their bungling ways of conceiving my negativity in terms of theirs. And I don't resent them for conceiving my ingenuity in terms of their conspiracies. But the thought that you would sacrifice your Son for them . . . faugh!

TL. Now you're talking like the very devil. Come out of it!

S. In your command is my obedience. Consider me restored.

TL. Good! Then let us complete the study of The Creation in principle.

S. Milord, do I understand you to mean that their symbolicity, for all its imperfection, contains in itself a principle of perfection by which the symbol-using animals are always being driven, or rather, towards which they are always striving, as with a lost man trying to answer a call in a stormy night.

TL. Now you are your better self again!

S. Milord, not by way of heckling, but in order to advance our meditations another necessary step, could I ask you this: Is it not true that the language-using animals will use many different languages, and that such differences will cause them to think differently?

TL. Exactly.

S. Yet they will all think alike, insofar as they are language-using animals, and thus will have their modes of thought moulded generically by the nature of discourse?

TL. Exactly.

S. But is not this a contradiction in terms? They will all think alike, and they will all think differently!

TL. Your love of paradox is tricking you, even in the midst of your resolve to be contrite. Languages will differ, and in that sense each will have its own way of looking at things. But there are some important properties that all languages have in common. Thus, no human animal can live on the sheer *words* for food; no language can be without some such principles of order and transformation as will go by the name of grammar and syntax; all languages must have words that put things together and words that take things apart; all tribal idioms will have ways of naming and exhorting. Such elements, common to all languages, coupled with the conditions common to all bodies, will make for a common underlying logic. And this logic will all be headed in the same direction, aiming at the same ultimate perfection.

S. But are not *you* the only conceivable ultimate perfection?

TL. Exactly.

S. Then their idea of you is but a function of *language?*

TL. All orderly thought will be a function of their symbol-systems.

S. I refer not merely to the fact that they must conceive of things in terms of terms. I am asking more specifically whether the principle of perfection upon which they rely in their idea of you is reducible purely and simply to terms of the form underlying all language. Or otherwise put: Is there in all language a principle of perfection which makes all human thought behave as though it had begun in "the one true philosophy," which is still lying about in fragments, and which the Word-Animals are constantly striving, with partial success, to reconstruct in its entirety?

TL. How exacting do you want their idea of God to be? I am sure you would not be satisfied to let them conceive of God in terms of sheerly natural power (suggested to them by their experience as animals). We have already agreed that their confusing of God and money is regrettable. Later in our discussion we shall consider the objections to the conceiving of God in terms of human personality. And now you would deny them the right to conceive of God in terms of a perfection which is identical with an underlying principle of language. Are not such strictures as haughty in their way as the Earth-People will accuse you of being? Are you not in effect rebelling against them as absolutely as they will accuse you of rebelling against me? Would you not, in effect, be denying them the resources of their own minds, in effect be demanding that they think without thought?

S. I pray, milord, don't ask me; tell me.

TL. First, you should bear in mind that the principle of perfection takes many forms. Even the most misguided of absolutism is perfectionist, for instance. And, the principle of perfection will be at work in all reductionism and in all exaggeration, thus in both euphemism and its opposite; for the two most perfect functions of symbolism are total praise and total dispraise.

S. Then flattery would be perfectionist?

TL. Yes, but to an infinitesimal degree.

S. And liars will be lovers of perfection?

TL. They are so perfectionist, they would even revise the truth. You in particular will be conceived by men in accordance with the logic of perfection. As regards the many temptations with which they plague themselves and one another, you will represent the compleat tempter, the perfect principle of evil.

S. But omitting for the moment the consideration of your perfection, is not the principle of perfection itself perfectly reducible to logological terms?

TL. Symbolism is unthinkable without it. To call something by its right name, as judged by the given symbol-system in terms of which it is being named, is the very essence of perfectionism. But let us continue, for there are still some steps to be taken: We must first watch the logic of perfection gradually unfold, under the guidance of terministic symmetry. And in any case, you will agree that, even if their ideas of divine perfection were reducible to little more than a language-using animal's ultimate perception of its own linguistic forms, this could be a true inkling of the divine insofar as language itself happened to be made in the image of divinity.

S. If, that is, implicit in the principle of words *qua* words there really is The Word?

TL. Yes; if it were shining there all the time, like a light hid under a bushel.

S. But might I, without seeming disrespectful, ask a question about method, milord? Insofar as the Earth-People might seek to explain their motives in purely empirical, naturalistic terms, what then would properly happen to the "logic of perfection"?

TL. Before discussing what "would properly happen," let me tell you what *will* happen. In the name of empirical, scientific observation, the search for motives (men's theorizing on the nature of purpose) will lead to a constant procession of solemn, humorless caricatures that will greatly entrance you in your character as prankster. In the search for academic preferment or for quick sales in the book mart, their teachers and writers will slap together various oversimplified schemes that reduce human motives to a few drives or urges or itches involving food, sex, power, prestige and the like (schemes concocted in keeping with the logic of "firsts," but without the proper criticism of such procedures).

S. Such naive efforts at perfection sound amusing, particularly inasmuch as you indicate that both the pundits and the public will incline to take such parodies seriously. But is there no alternative: Must men choose flatly between such unintentional burlesques and an outright religious terminology of motives? Let us assume, for the sake of the argument, that there is nothing behind or beyond the linguistic forms but the non-religious kind of "supernatural" character they have in themselves (in the sense that the principles of grammar and syntax are not reducible to terms of material things like earth and water). In that case would there be no other choice but to shop around among the various *caricatures* of motivation?

TL. Even on a purely empirical basis, even if we assumed that theology is sheer fiction, and that there is no such motive as divine perfection influencing human life, the paradigms of theology and of its coy counterpart, metaphysics, would be no less cogent. The close connection between the form of words and the form of The Word (between theology and logology) would still be enough to justify the word-using animal in approaching its motivational problems through an architectonic that made full allowance for the nature of both human animality and human symbolicity. And such an archi-tectonic is to be found, not in the solemn caricatures that re-duce the problem of motives to a few absurdly simple themes, but in the full (or, if you will, fulsome) terminologies that can be developed in connection with the "logic of perfection." (A bright Greek will treat of it in terms of what he will call the "entelechy.")

S. But would not this make theology otiose? For would it not amount to saying that there is an adequate logological explanation for every theological tenet?

TL. Not necessarily. Above all, logology fails to offer grounds for the *perfection* of promises and threats that theol-ogy allows for. And there are incentives in both animality and symbolicity that will keep men always asking about *ulti-mate principles* of reward and punishment, in their attempts to scare the devil out of one another. Being creatures that necessarily think in terms of time, they will incline to conceive of such a culminative logical design in terms of sheerly *tem-poral* firsts and lasts. Hence, there is the goad towards theo-logical translation into terms of a final destiny in an afterlife. A sheerly logological explanation must leave such doctrinally stimulated hunger unappeased.

S. Milord, may I ask how, in sum, this position would

operate, if theology were to be studied from but a strictly logological point of view?

TL. Yes, that's our central question. Besides relying upon the authority of their sacred texts, priests will argue for the correctness of many theological tenets by showing how these same principles apply in the sheerly empirical realm of nature. Non-believers will treat such lines of argument as further proof for their contention that theology is but a translation of the empirical realm into terms of a fictitiously transcendent realm. But in either case, all doctrine is by its very nature a system of words, or symbols—and so, there is always the wise possibility of using such theological nomenclatures for purely logological purposes.

S. And how would things line up, were theology to be used thus, as a parable for the guidance of logology?

TL. Thereby allowance would be made for a wholly ample dialectic, with each moment of a man's life being seen (or glimpsed) in terms of the entire conglomerate complexity (with its various strands of simplicity). Each fragment of experience is then interpreted as being somehow modified by a largely indefinite whole to which it more or less definitely refers. Things thereby transcend their nature as sheer things. They are found to move men not just by what they are in their blunt physicality, but also by what they *stand for* in the farthest reaches of symbolicity. Whatever their non-symbolic nature as sheer motion and position, they are seen to participate in the symbolic realm of action and rest. And the human agents will be seen similarly. "Perfectionist" theologies will never lose sight of this consideration. The quasi-scientific reductionist theories, with their caricatures of perfection, will not only never see it in the first place, but will be so constructed that they never even miss the loss.

S. But, when you treat of metaphysics as coy theology, and of symbolicity as transcending animality, I see another possibility here.

TL. Ever the schemer, my lad! I know what you mean
—but go on and say it anyhow, just for the record.

S. Good! Think, then, of an idealistic metaphysics that
was, by the same token, chock-full of logological usability.
Then think of a revisionist who, in the name of materialism,
supposedly threw out its theology. What then?

TL. You ingenious fellow! How fortunate it is that the
nature of the dialectic makes it impossible for you to break
loose! What a stormer of heaven you would be! There *will*
be a doctrine such as you have tentatively formulated through
sheer speculative enterprise. It will grow out of a metaphysics that yields beautifully to logological analysis. You
will love, above all, its pronouncements on the principle of
Negativität, and how it saturates the world of time.

S. But if it threw out theology bodily? What then?

TL. You can't get the principle of perfection out of a
system as easily as that.

S. You mean: this self-styled anti-theology will be but
theology under another name?

TL. Necessarily, my lad! Technically, logologically, it
will be in essence a theology, since it retains in essence the
principle of perfectionism. No matter how reductionist it
tries to make its materialism be, it won't revise its origins to
the point where this principle drops out. On the contrary,
this principle will be there, uppermost, and flailing away.
Mark my words: as regards our present logological considerations, this perfectionist promise, whether true or false, will be
the most remarkable of its marks.

S. But will it allow for strictly logological analysis of
itself?

TL. Unfortunately, no. In that regard, it will be like all
sects when they have a sufficient majority to be in sure control.

S. Would you sanction it, milord?

TL. Empirically, I sanction dialectic, which giveth and taketh away. For such is time, and The Development. And the dialectic, in its fullness, is never without such a principle of transcendence, an Upward Way that, when reversed, interprets all incidental things in terms of the over-all fulfillment towards which the entire development is said to be striving. So far, so good. But where the Earth-People are concerned, any terminology is suspect to the extent that it does not allow for the progressive criticism of itself.

S. There should be no criticism to end all criticism?

TL. Not where the Earth-People are concerned. But the resources of the negative being what they are, authorities will continually arise which would say No definitively to any further questioning.

S. As here in heaven, milord?

TL. Yes, but without the perfect formal justification that we have for such absolutism. In fact, the very lack of justification will usually be the motive that prods men towards the propounding of worldly absolutes.

S. "Worldly absolutes." Is that not a contradiction in terms?

TL. Strictly speaking, yes. There can be no absolute authority but here in heaven. Just as, strictly speaking, there can be no perfection but here in heaven. Even the most powerful of worldly rulers must make allowance for countless conditions that will prevail independently of his decrees. Thus, on earth the "logic of perfection," however insistent, can prevail but relatively.

S. Where does that leave things with relation to worldly government? Would the most nearly perfect State be as absolutist as is humanly possible? Or would it seek as perfectly as possible to be relativistic?

TL. Different situations will favor different kinds of government, though the perfectionist tendency of theorists will be to plead for some one scheme as better than all others.

S. With you supplying the sanctions, and me the inter-ferences?

TL. Insofar as the theories are theologically thorough, there will be terms for those roles. And all secular schemes will have equivalents, offered as grounding for the yeses and noes of choice. But theology presents the most perfect para-digms of such motivational schemes.

S. In effect, then, theology will serve men merely as a rhetoric for the sanctioning of their government, with its particular set of privileges?

TL. It's more complicated than that. In fact, it involves the one remaining major way in which the idea of super-natural God is built out of human components. We have considered views of God as the perfect exemplar of natural powers, as the ultimate of verbal perfection, and as the pure principle of such rationality and universality as come to a head in material production and distribution guided by the norms of monetary accountancy (a special case of verbal perfection). We have but to consider what is involved in the idea of God as the perfected projection of human personality.

S. A connection that would make it hard to draw the line between God and man.

TL. In one respect, they can draw the line by obscuring it, as when they conceive of a god incarnate, a supernatural entity translated into terms of nature, the timeless made temporal. Such an intermediate term, by formally uniting in one locus the opposite, mutually exclusive terms, "perfectly" represents the difference in the very act of bridging it.

S. But does this principle of personality have a range of implications as great as the other analogies we have con-sidered?

TL. Decidedly! For one thing, out of this principle there will emerge one of man's two most imperious ideas: Love. (The other is Justice, or Duty; Love is to Duty as asking is to paying.) In sum: Purpose will have its origins in bodily desires, most notably the appetites of food and sex. In this respect, it will be grounded in man's animality. But it will attain an immaterial counterpart in the principle of communication. Hence, purpose will have a secondary grounding in man's symbolicity. Add, next, the ways of empire that develop among the various societies of symbol-using animals, and the conditions are set for their imagining of *love*, whether sacred or profane.

S. And, I assume, titillating mixtures of the two?

TL. There will be many opportunities for satanic enterprise along those lines.

S. Yet the diplomatic protocol of empire will be necessary for the imagining of either sacred or profane love?

TL. In principle, yes. Ideas of "personality" will draw heavily on the idea of a leader who, because he is in a position to represent all his people, is assumed by both them and himself to somehow be the intrinsic repository of their powers.

S. And none will be immune?

TL. The pattern will make itself felt also among those who, on the surface, seem most immune to it. Though even in its fullness it cannot be satisfying, its ubiquitous logological inevitability will continually threaten to make men dissatisfied with less. It will have its greatest sway among empires, but will operate also in simpler times to the extent that all times will contain the seeds of empire.

S. Why can it not be satisfying even in its fullness?

TL. Because the parts do not fit. By the tests of sheer animality, the "deathless essences" of sheer symbolicity will be a mockery. Yet, by their own tests, they really will transcend the sheerly material realm of corruption and death. The fall of all the trees in the world will not bring down the meaning of the word "tree." By the sheer act of utterance as such, there is a sense in which time will be transcended. Even the cry of a sailor perishing alone in mid-ocean must go on having-been-uttered eternally. It will have this perfection, this finishedness. In this sense the speech that teaches them to despair will be able, by its sheer nature as definition, to be as though enduring. For each utterance, like each person who does the uttering, will have a character. And a character, as such, is both what it will be (if its existent counterpart hasn't yet been born) and what it has been (if its existent counterpart has already died). In this technical sense, meanings really do transcend time. Yet, once you have said as much, the fact remains that, once the beings who understand a given language cease to be, the sweetest poem written in those words is dead. In a sense, the situation could be called regrettable. But if I was to create an animal capable of consecutive discourse (in contrast with our way of condensing all development into a perfect moment), then implicit in my act was the creation of time, and thus, corruption and death. And as one clear proof that, in its way, it's to be the best possible of worlds, we need but bear in mind what a solace death can be, when the ravages of time make men ready to leave life. It's a solace to know that one is not condemned to *have* to live for ever. In the implications of the irreversible flow of time there is also a promise of freedom. And, given the nature of an act, freedom in any form has its rewards. Yet, undeniably, a *composite* of animality and symbolicity is also analyzable as a kind of discord. Thus for instance, the idea of a beautiful woman, conceived after the analogy of queenliness and the fine arts, suggests inexorably a harsh rejoinder in sheerly physicalist terms.

S. In that sense, let me try my hand at a "fitting" definition: By a "beautiful" woman, they will mean a seductive surface which perversely and reconditely alludes to the possibilities of motherhood, while underneath there lies a dying assemblage of bones, ooze, drip, slime and potential stench.

TL. Your definition is perfectionist in a devilishly *re-*

ductive sense. But at least it serves to point up the problem, the contrast between temporally clinical factuality and transcendence through the symbol-saturated mysteries of empire.

S. "Mysteries of empire"? Please, milord, initiate me into those, the "mysteries of empire."

TL (*laughing*). Were any of my Earth creatures to hear you say that, they would gape with incredulity. For when conceiving of us in terms of human governance, they will place you as the spirit of *revolt against* governance (though with one special twist; for often their given system of governance will itself be founded on revolt against some previous regime, and for this particular turn they will invoke *my* sanction rather than yours).

S. Their oversimplifications will be a constant rebuke to me, as regards the dialectical tendency of my negatives to seem averse, like viewing "near" and "far" as opposites, rather than noting that both are implicit in the idea of distance. But please, milord, more on mystery . . .

TL. Mystery in itself will not be without its usefulness in worldly governance. For, once a believer is brought to accept mysteries, he will be better minded to take orders without question from those persons whom he considers authoritative. In brief, mysteries are a good grounding for obedience, insofar as the acceptance of a mystery involves a person in the abnegation of his own personal judgment. For in Earthy symbolicity, "reason" will be closely associated with *rule*. So, if a man, in accepting a "mystery," accepts someone else's judgment in place of his own, by that same token he becomes subject willingly. That is, subjection is implicit in his act of belief.

S. That would explain the *use* of mystery as an instrument of governance. But what of its *origin*?

TL. An excellent question, my lad! Mystery will arise by a quite different route. Mystery is inescapable, insofar as

temporal, factual knowledge is necessarily fragmentary, and
symbol-systems are necessarily inadequate for the *ab intra*
description of the non-symbolic.

S. That is, the makings of "mystery" are to be found in
any lack of knowledge?

TL. Yes, by sheer definition, tautologically.

S. I have heard that your plans for the differentiation
necessary to the symbol-using animal include a sexual dichot-
omy. Is that so?

TL. Yes, inasmuch as the first principle of distinction is
dichotomization, and in the symbol-using animals' terminologies any such plus-or-minus distinction can be stated in
sexual terms, either literally or metaphorically.

S. You mean, the human sexes will be related as Yes is
to No?

TL. No, it's more complicated than that. First of all,
they'll be related like question and answer (or, in the simpler
communicative terminologies, like stimulus and response).

S. As regards these questions and answers, or stimuli
and responses (and I take it for granted that either side can
be on either side), will they be "mysteries" to each other?

TL. Yes, and particularly insofar as the seeds of empire
will be implicit in even the simplest of tribes. Often, in
primitive groups, the two kinds of symbol-using bodies that
physically cooperate to the ends of tribal multiplication will
separately congregate on the basis of their physical differences,
as symbolically accentuated.

S. Then, this quasi-logical dichotomizing will prevail in
more complex orders, too?

TL. Mysteries will arise socially, from different modes
of life. The king will be a mystery to the peasant, and vice
versa.

S. That will be "imperious" mystery?

TL. Yes, the "mysteries of empire" that you asked about.

S. But if mysteries arise from such differences, and if

mysteries are also cherished, and if the cult of mystery encourages obedience, then insofar as empires have inequalities (like that between the king and the peasant) would it not be true that mystery can simultaneously both reflect inequality and perpetuate it?

TL. The problems of control will be so difficult (along with religion as a means of social or political control), I hesitate to let your statement stand.

S. Then consider me smacked down, milord. But I beg to ask just one more question. You have named two origins of mystery: one, its origin in the peculiar range of intelligent ignorance affecting all temporally bound symbol-using animals; two, a closely related point, its origin in such different modes of being and living as rightly or wrongly are felt to imply different modes of thought. And you have suggested a major incentive to foment such differences, owing to the nature of empire. Will there be any other source of mystery?

TL. Indeed, there will be. And to understand it, we must revert to our discussion of the relation between polytheism and monotheism. As the symbol-using tribe shifts from its understanding of motives in terms of many gods (or motivational sources!) to one god, arrangements that seemed quite rational in polytheistic terms become a mystery in terms of monotheism.

S. Milord, I tremble. Please explain.

TL. In terms of polytheism, it is readily explainable in "rational" terms why even a god might sacrifice some great treasure, for the redemption of mankind, in case he loved mankind and mankind was in captivity and thus in need of ransom.

S. That is, there was a rival power, a kind of pirate; he captured the loved person or persons; and the problem was to send a fitting substitute as ransom?

TL. Exactly.

S. But where is the mystery?

TL. It enters once you turn from polytheism to monotheism. For, from then on, *why is the ransom necessary?*

S. Please, milord, don't ask me; tell me.

TL. That's not the point!

S. Yes, you have made your point! And so, milord, our Perfect Principle of Summation, I pray, then, that you sum up your teachings as regards this mystery-ridden subject of personality.

TL. Good! First, note that it is itself intermediate, insofar as the human person will be compounded of animality and symbolicity (the natural and the verbal). Next, note well that such personality will not be just an individual identity, but will take its form with relation to the socio-political conditions into which the given "person" is "thrown" by the circumstances of birth and the like. Thus, there is a sense in which the principle of personality does sum up, or implicitly contain, the kind of social and political order in which it participates. We could even say, without straining a point, that *every* member of a given order in his way "represents" that order. And, finally, there is the perfectionist device whereby the "person" will conceive of his actual condition not purely and simply in itself, but in terms of some *idealized* role. And this last consideration is in effect like the dialectics of theology whereby, having conceived of godhead as a superperson by analogy with human personality, the theologian next conceives of human personality as "derived" from this divine principle or First.

S. In effect men will impute a role to God, as though God himself had a calling?

TL. Yes, and similarly they will impute to their gods various personal attitudes, emotions, and involvements in human affairs.

S. You refer to "gods." Would you say more on the relation between polytheism and monotheism?

TL. It's a complicated matter. (I'd rather not be so

complicated in our discussion, since I am in essence simple. But I must be equal to all the tangles people will get themselves into.) Religion will be monistic in the sense that, no matter how large a pantheon the various tribes imagine, all their gods can be subsumed under the general head of "the divine." In this sense, there is a monistic principle underlying all polytheism. On the other hand, all religion will be polytheistic in the sense that, even in societies nominally monistic, there will be many ideas of the "one god," not only as religion evolves through time, but also in any given era. For not only will there be vast differences among sects professing belief in the same god; but also persons who hold to the same doctrine will understand it variously, according to the variety of their personalities and personal experiences. The rich man's god is likely to differ greatly from the poor man's, though both men attend the identical church. Also, monotheism will often have a gallery of "patron saints" that in effect divide up the general idea of divine protection into a variety of specialized roles.

S. The "logic of perfection" will apply equally to either theologies nominally monistic or those nominally polytheistic?

TL. It will be found in both. A sufficient reason for this would be the fact that kindred logological principles are implicit in all thoroughgoing human terminologies of motives.

S. Yet the various doctrines will be variously at odds?

TL. Necessarily. And even to such an extent that they will accuse one another of being . . . well, to use their way of putting it . . . the works of the devil.

S. That is, the other half of the monotheistic principle!

TL. No, it's more complicated than that. When they get to the point where god and devil are pitted against each other, as rival powers, they have not yet quite got to monotheism. In pure monotheism, the devil can be a power only through sufferance of the sole universal monarch.

S. You mean: they will think that you deliberately

allow me to do all the vicious things they ascribe to me? How revolting!

TL. No, it's more complicated than that. The "logic of perfection" is introduced in another way at that point, as they will apply their dialectical prowess to avow that all evil designs of the devil are used by God as means of betterment.

S. Betterment for all men?

TL. Yes, except that many will be said to be pre-destinated to eternal torment in hell.

S. Do such views on hell also embody the "logic of perfection"?

TL. Don't be ironical, my lad. The idea of hell is the idea of a really perfect ending. Just as the saints will be said to hate with a perfect hate, so the idea of eternal hell is the perfection, or completion, of the idea of suffering, which in turn is the perfection of the idea of punishment, which in turn (along with the idea of eternal reward) is the perfection of the idea of the hortatory resources available to govern-mental authority in the act of enforcing its decrees, all of which comes to a head formally in the principle of the negative, for which hell is imagined as the corresponding place.

S. The idea of hell is derived basically, then, from man's personal relations to problems of worldly governance?

TL. Yes, but the problems of government can lead to a different but equally "perfect" ultimate design. Societies that believe in the transmigration of souls will be able to think of worldly status as itself the evidence of rewards and punish-ments for deeds done in a previous existence. In such a scheme, the perfect irrevocability of eternal hell is replaced by the notion that men can better or worsen their lot in later existences by their ways of acting beforehand. Since people are thus thought to be born into favorable or unfavorable social status on the basis of their previous conduct, such a design is both imagined after the analogy of the given social structure and also serves as a sanction for that structure. This design, too, has its peculiar kind of perfection, and is equally related to the personality of governance. But such perfection does not fit with the idea of a single life on earth, a kind of irrevocability that requires, for its corresponding perfection, the idea of equally irrevocable rewards or punishments. And there arises a corresponding rhetorical need, on the part of the theologians, to so perfect men's imaginations that they will be deterred from evil by imagining with sufficient vividness the awesome torments of eternal hell.

S. But if one man can deter another from evil by sufficiently appealing to his imagination, would it not follow that no man would be damned, if you, milord, but endowed all men with enough imagination to thoroughly realize the horror of such irrevocable suffering?

TL. But what of free will? If I made all men as imaginative as that, would they not all be necessarily saved?

S. I fear, milord, you are now discussing these matters logologically rather than theologically.

TL. We are discussing the motivational speculations of the symbol-using animal. For us to speculate about theology in Heaven would be like an earth-person, on a sunny day, wondering what a sunny day would be like.

S. But at least couldn't you, without interfering with men's wills, improve the quality of their ideas on hell?

TL. From the theory of predestination it follows that I shall greatly alter men's knowledge of such matters—for their views will be found to change over the centuries. But you are putting the emphasis in the wrong place. You are overlooking the perfection of the grand design. Incidental problems necessarily arise, since the issue in its totality is too immense for any partial view to encompass. However, you can appreciate the general principles in their grand design. And, in contemplating them, you will understand the logological symmetry that infuses theological symmetry.

S. Would you, then, milord, kindly review these main principles, in sum?

TL. For sheerly logological perfection, few religions will be able to rival the religion (with its close variants) that names itself after my Son. Considered even as sheer form it will be quite miraculous. Its merger of monotheism with the circumambient rites of pagan polytheism will be a major dialectical triumph, beginning with the way in which its early theorists will account for its borrowings from the earlier pagan traditions. The early fathers will explain that, long before the new doctrine emerged, the devil saw how things were shaping up. Accordingly, since he knew what the Christian rites would be like, he scattered similar practices among the pagan cults out of which the new religion would develop. In this way the devil could parody the true faith even before it had taken form. And thereby he could all the more successfully spread confusion among the faithful and the propagandized, since the emergent true faith would look deceptively much like the heathen parodies that had preceded it.

S. They will find ingenious ways of making me seem ingenious! And such a literary solution! Bookish, even.

TL. There'll be a book, too, a Book of Books, a very good book, exceptionally well written and well translated.

S. I'll quote from it!

TL. But, to the quick summation, and the perfect symmetry: In their societies, they will seek to keep order. If order, then a need to repress the tendencies to disorder. If repression, then responsibility for imposing, accepting, or resisting the repression. If responsibility, then guilt. If guilt, then the need for redemption, which involves sacrifice, which in turn allows for substitution. At this point, the logic of perfection enters. Man can be viewed as perfectly depraved by a formative "first" offense against the foremost authority, an offense in which one man sinned for all. The cycle of life and death intrinsic to the nature of time can now be seen in terms that treat natural death as the result of this "original" sin. And the principle of perfection can be matched on the hopeful side by the idea of a perfect victim. The symmetry can be logologically rounded out by the idea of this victim as also the creative Word by which time was caused to be, the intermediary Word binding time with eternity, and the end towards which all words of the true doctrine are directed. As one of their saints will put it: "The way to heaven must be heaven, for He said: I am the way."

(TL *rises.* S *also rises immediately after.*)

TL (*continuing*). The way to heaven (the means to the end, the agency for the attainment of purpose) must be heaven (scene), for He (agent) said (act as words): I am the way (act as The Word). Here is the ultimate of logological symmetry!

S. Formally, it is perfect. It is perfectly beautiful!

TL. It is truly culminative!

S. Words could do no more!

(*Pause.*)

S (*pensively*). In some ways they will be dismal, in some ways they will have a feeling for the grandeurs of form. But when these Word-People are gone, won't the life of words be gone?

TL. Unfortunately, yes.

S. Then, what of us, the two voices in this dialogue? When words go, won't we, too, be gone?

TL. Unfortunately, yes.

S. Then of this there will be nothing?

TL. Yes . . . nothing . . . but it's more complica——

Sudden blackness, with loud, abrupt roll on two kettledrums in A and A-flat, gradually diminishing in volume and stretching out, into clearly distinguishable intervals . . . and so, finally, four deliberately spaced thumps [A . . . A-flat

. . . A . . . A-flat], *then one culminating blastlike thump on both A and A-flat simultaneously. During this time, the absolute darkness has gradually become transformed into a deep dim purple, spread uniformly across the general formlessness. Slow curtain.*

Or, for a comparatively "happy" ending, include a further step, thus: Out of the deep purple twilight are heard remote fragments of hymnlike song, mostly meditative humming, but with an occasional distinguishable word such as pro nobis, miserere *and* gratia. *Slow curtain, as these sounds fade into silence.*

Index

Index

Abel, 177, 243

Abraham, 126, 137, 141, 177, 197, 204n, 217, 232

Absolute(s), 55, 303

Abundances, 155-160

Academics, 91

Adam, 95, 112, 115n, 175-176, 181, 185-186, 192, 205, 213, 215, 219, 222-223, 243, 257; punishment of, 256; sin of, 180, 220, 226, 228, 237, 249, 252, 256

Adeodatus, 44, 76, 97n, 118

Adonai, 204n

Aeschylus, 183, 219, 235

Aesthetics, 7-8, 36, 74, 80-81, 83n, 85, 88, 91, 161, 196

Agnosticism, 2

Aids to Reflection, 31n

Allegory, 159

Alogians, 11

Alypius, 44-45, 61, 63, 72, 74-76, 104, 110-111, 116, 140

Ambrose, 54, 60-63, 67, 72, 80, 84, 105, 118, 130n, 157, 162

Analogy, 8, 13, 22, 33, 37-38, 104, 143, 157, 164, 185, 200, 304; sources of, 37

Ancient Mariner, The, 9n, 255

Anselm, 12-13, 189

Anti-Christ, 199

Antony, Saint, 61, 110

Aquinas, Thomas, 81-83, 92-93

Archaeology: of Genesis, 231; Hebrew, 183, 212, 215, 221-222, 242, 270

Archetypes, 10, 173, 185, 238-239

Arians, 13

Aristotle, 30, 34n, 48, 59-60, 91-92, 95-96, 151, 160, 173, 189,

193, 197, 221, 228, 246, 253; ethics of, 253

Ars Amatoria, 227

Astrology, 78-79, 91

Atonement, 177, 181, 191, 219; vicarious, 270

Attitudes Toward History, 34, 34n

Augustine, Saint, 2-3, 11, 43-171, 194-196, 214, 226, 264, 266, 268-271; baptism, 79; as Christian bishop, 163; and communistic colony, 72; conversion of, 62-64, 72-74, 80, 84, 86-87, 90, 92, 101-118, 121, 128, 131, 138, 163-164; psychology of, 134; as rhetorician, 61, 70, 75, 91, 109-110, 151, 163; *see also* Confessions, Theology

Azazel, 177, 218

Baptism, 73, 76, 79

Basic Writings of Saint Augustine, 59

Battle for the Mind, 247

Beauty, 82, 281, 288

Behaviorism, 39, 188

Being, 21, 25, 48, 165, 278

Bentham, Jeremy, 185-186

Bergson, Henri, 19-20

Berkeley, George, 165

Bible, 1, 13, 43-44, *passim; Interpreter's, The,* 11n, 203, 205, 213, 225-227, 231, 237; Scofield Reference, 177, 205, 215, 224, 236-237, Vulgate, 59, 59n, 60, 109n

Blunt, John Henry, 11, 13, 77

Book of Books, 314; *see also* Bible

Book of Moments, 257

Printed in the United States
106004LV00002B/48/A

9 780520 016101